Information Security Policies and Procedures

Second Edition

Information Security Policies and Procedures

A Practitioner's Reference

Second Edition

Thomas R. Peltier

AUERBACH PUBLICATIONS

A CRC Press Company

Boca Raton   London   New York   Washington, D.C.

Library of Congress Cataloging-in-Publication Data

Peltier, Thomas R.
    Information security policies and procedures : a practitioner's reference / Thomas R.
Peltier.--2nd ed.
        p. cm.
    Includes bibliographical references and index.
    ISBN 0-8493-1958-7 (alk paper)
    1. Computer security. 2. Data protection. I. Title.

QA76.9.A25P428 2004
005.8—dc22   2004041113

Visit the Auerbach Publications Web site at www.auerbach-publications.com

Dedication

To my mother, who taught me that dignity and honor are expressed in what you do and not in what you have.

Contents

Acknowledgments

As a child I knew that I wanted to make my life's work one of writing policies and doing risk analysis. Actually, I wanted to be a cowboy; but being a kid from Detroit, I had to settle for other things. As I was completing my undergraduate work at the University of Detroit, my boss Larry Degg came and asked me if I could help. Our organization was in the midst of a massive audit and we had few polices and procedures. For the next nine years, Larry helped me refine the skills needed to understand how policies and procedures worked in the business environment.

My second number-one is my wife Lisa Bryson. We are both information security professionals and it is her ability to take my big-picture ideas and help me flesh out the concepts. We have worked as a team for the past nine years and have developed some truly remarkable concepts.

Next on my list of acknowledgments is my mentor and friend, John O'Leary, the Director of the Computer Security Institute's Education Resource Center. John and his wonderful wife Jane have sat with me through many a dinner, listened to my problems, and then offered the wisdom that comes from people who care.

My working buddies must also be acknowledged. My son Justin is the greatest asset any father — and more importantly, any information security team — could ever hope for. Over the past two years, we have logged nearly 150,000 air miles together, and each day we learn something new from each other.

The other working buddy is John Blackley. The strange Scotsman who makes our life more fun and interesting.

Who can leave out their publisher? Certainly not me! Rich O'Hanley has taken the time to discuss security issues with numerous organizations to understand what their needs are and then presented these findings to use. A great deal of our work here is a direct result of what Rich discovered that the industry wanted. Rich O'Hanley, not only the world's best editor and task master, but a good friend and source of knowledge. Thanks, Rich!

And finally, I extend a thank you to our editors, Claire Miller and Andrea Demby. They take the time to take the raw manuscript and put it into a logically flowing work. Sometimes they have to ask me the same question more than once, but finally I get what needs to be done.

About the Author

Thomas R. Peltier (CISM, CISSP) is in his fifth decade of computer technology. During this time he has shared his experiences with fellow professionals and, because of this work, has been awarded the 1993 Computer Security Institute's (CSI) Lifetime Achievement Award. In 1999, the Information Systems Security Association (ISSA) bestowed its Individual Contribution to the Profession Award; and in 2001, Tom was inducted into the ISSA Hall of Fame. He was also awarded the CSI Lifetime Emeritus Membership Award. Currently, he is the President of Peltier and Associates, an information security training and consulting firm. Prior to this he was Director of Policies and Administration for the Netigy Corporation's Global Security Practice. Tom was the National Director for Consulting Services for Cyber-Safe Corporation, and the Corporate Information Protection Coordinator for Detroit Edison. The security program at Detroit Edison was recognized for excellence in the field of computer and information security by winning the Computer Security Institute's Information Security Program of the Year for 1996. Tom previously was the Information Security Specialist for the General Motors Corporation, where he was responsible for implementing an information security program for GM's worldwide activities.

Over the past decade, Tom has averaged four published articles a year on various computer and information security issues, including developing policies and procedures, disaster recovery planning, copyright compliance, virus management, and security controls. He has had four books published: *Policies, Standards, Guidelines and Procedures: Information Security Risk Analysis; Information System Security Policies and Procedures: A Practitioners' Reference; The Complete Manual of Policies and Procedures for Data Security;* and *How to Manage a Network Vulnerability Assessment,* and is the co-editor and contributing author for the *CISSP Prep for Success Handbook;* and a contributing author for the *Computer Security Handbook, Third and Fifth Edition* and *Data Security Management.* Tom, along with his son Justin and partner John Blackley, is currently co-authoring the book *Information Security Fundamentals.*

He has been the technical advisor on a number of security films from Commonwealth Films. Tom is the past chairman of the Computer Security

Institute (CSI) Advisory Council, the chairman of the 18th Annual CSI Conference, founder and past-president of the Southeast Michigan Computer Security Special Interest Group, and a former member of the board of directors for (ISC)^2, the security professional certification organization. Tom conducts numerous seminars and workshops on various security topics and has led seminars for CSI, Crisis Management, the American Institute of Banking, the American Institute of Certified Public Accountants, the Institute of Internal Auditors, ISACA, and Sungard Planning Solutions. He was also an instructor at the graduate level for Eastern Michigan University.

Introduction

Policies, standards, and procedures are a key element in the business process. The implementation of these documents should never be undertaken to satisfy some perceived audit or security requirement. These requirements do not exist. There are only business objectives or mission requirements. This book is dedicated to the concept that policies, standards, and procedures support the efficient running of an organization. We examine how policies support management's directions. Standards and procedures are the elements that implement the management policies.

It is easy now to run out to the Internet and pull down some organizations' policies and the like. However, this book cautions against this approach. We examine how best to use available examples of policies, standards, and procedures. We also put into perspective the influx of national and international standards and how best to use them to meet your organization's needs.

Keeping the process simple is the objective of clear and concise writing. We approach writing policies and such as a project with a clearly defined objective, deadlines, and a communications plan.

Perhaps the most important element of this book is how information security is integrated into all aspects of the business process. Every organization needs to address at least 12 enterprisewide (Tier 1) policies. We examine each of these policies and then map information security requirements into each one. We also discuss the need for topic-specific (Tier 2) policies and application-specific (Tier 3) policies and how they map with standards and procedures.

Although this text is identified as information security policies, standards, and procedures, the skill set discussed can be used throughout the enterprise. We concentrate on information security needs, but we always keep the organization objectives at the forefront.

Part 1
Information Security Policies and Procedures

Years ago, I saw a cartoon in magazine that showed a huge construction project in downtown Manhattan. There was this massive hole and the crews were busy excavating even deeper, there was a great deal of activity, and in the foreground two men were reviewing the blueprints when one began to yell, "The prints are upside down!" I had that cartoon up in my office for a number of years as a way to remind me that the goal of writing policies and procedures is to provide a clear "blueprint" on how tasks are to be done.

The following material is a blueprint on how to begin to develop policies and procedures. My goal is to provide readers with enough information and examples so that they can be successful. The old adage, "Give a person a fish and they can eat today; teach a person to fish and they can eat for a lifetime" is the direction this document takes. While it is important to provide examples, it is more important to explain why and how things are done. This book was written with the goal of transferring knowledge to the reader. No two organizations are exactly alike, so no two sets of policies and procedures are going to be exactly alike. Knowing what to do and how to present the material is the best method for success.

Being charged with developing policies and procedures might seem to be an overwhelming task. So take the material and examine the examples and modify them to meet the needs and culture of your organization. Use the discussion material provided in this information security reference guide to help sell the concepts. Above all, have fun. You are going to learn more about your organization than just about anyone. Once you have completed a policy or two, you will have the courage to take on even more tasks. The skills needed to write policies and procedures will assist you in all other areas of your professional and private life.

You will be able to express an idea in a clear and concise manner. You will be organized and will be able to work to a deadline. You will be able to create a project plan and manage the work of others. Above all, you will have the satisfaction of knowing that you have created something that will still be in effect after you have moved on.

Chapter 1
Introduction

As security professionals, we often take the view that the overall objective of an information security program is to protect the integrity, confidentiality, and availability of that information. Although this is true from a security perspective, it is not the organization objective. Information is an asset and is the property of the organization. As it is an asset, management is expected to ensure that appropriate levels of control are in place to protect this resource.

An information protection program should be part of any organization's overall asset protection program. This program is not established to meet security needs or audit requirements; it is a business process that provides management with the processes needed to perform the fiduciary responsibility. Management is charged with a trust to ensure that adequate controls are in place to protect the assets of the enterprise. An information security program that includes policies, standards, and procedures will allow management to demonstrate a standard of care.

As information security professionals, it is our responsibility to implement policies that reflect the business and mission needs of the enterprise. This chapter examines the reasons why information security policies are needed and how they fit into all elements of the organization. The development of information security policies is neither an information technology or audit responsibility, nor do these policies remain solely in these areas. The concept of information security must permeate through all of the organization's policies.

In this chapter, we discuss 11 organizationwide policies and, at a minimum, what each should have with reference to information security. The policies that we initially discuss are high-level (Tier 1) organization-wide policies and include the following:

- Employment Practices
- Employee Standards of Conduct
- Conflict of Interest
- Performance Management
- Employee Discipline
- Information Security
- Corporate Communications

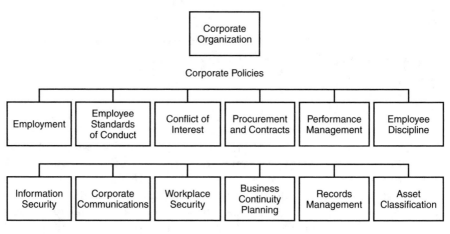

Figure 1. Corporate Policies

- Procurement and Contracts
- Records Management
- Asset Classification
- Workplace Security
- Business Continuity Planning

We discuss the different levels of policies — Tier 2 policies (topic specific) and Tier 3 policies (application specific) — throughout the remainder of the book.

1   CORPORATE POLICIES

Most organizations have a standard set of policies that govern the way they perform their business (see Figure 1). There are at least 11 Tier 1 policies; this means that a policy is implemented to support the entire business or mission of the enterprise. There are also Tier 2 policies; these are topic-specific policies and address issues related to specific subject matter. Tier 3 policies address the requirements for using and supporting specific applications. Later in the book we present examples of a number of each of these policies; for now, we present the Tier 1 policy title and a brief description of what each policy encompasses.

2   ORGANIZATIONWIDE (TIER 1) POLICIES[1]

Employment Practices. This is the policy that describes the processes required to ensure that all candidates get an equal opportunity when seeking a position with the organization. This policy discusses the organization's hiring practices and new employee orientation. It is during the orientation phase that new employees should receive their first introduction to the information security requirements. Included in this process is a Non-Disclosure Agreement or Confidentiality Agreement. These agreements require the signatory to keep confidential information secret and generally remain in effect even after the employee leaves the organization.

The employment policies should also include condition-of-employment requirements such as background checks for key management levels or certain jobs. A side part to the Employment policy and the Performance policy is the publication of job descriptions for every job level. These descriptions should include what is expected of employees regarding information security requirements.

Standards of Conduct. This policy addresses what is expected of employees and how they are to conduct themselves when on company property or when representing the organization. This policy normally discusses examples of unacceptable behavior (dishonesty, sleeping on the job, substance abuse, introduction of unauthorized software into company systems) and the penalties for infractions. Also included in this policy is a statement that "Company management has the responsibility to manage enterprise information, personnel, and physical properties relevant to their business operations, as well as the right to monitor the actual utilization of these enterprise assets."

Information security should also address confidential information: "Employees shall also maintain the confidentiality of corporate information. (See Asset Classification policy)." A discussion on unacceptable conduct is generally included in an employee code of conduct policy; this should include a discussion on unauthorized code and copyright compliance.

Conflict of Interest. Company employees are expected to adhere to the highest standards of conduct. To assure adherence to these standards, employees must have a special sensitivity to conflict-of-interest situations or relationships, as well as the inappropriateness of personal involvement in them. Although not always covered by law, these situations can harm the company or its reputation if improperly handled. This is where discussions about due diligence will be addressed. Many organizations restrict conflict-of-interest policy requirements to management levels, but all employees should be required to annually review and sign a responsibility statement.

Performance Management. This policy discusses how employee job performance is to be used in determining an employee's appraisal. Information security requirements should be included as an element that affects the level of employee performance. As discussed above, having job descriptions for each job assignment will ensure that employees are reviewed fairly and completely at least annually on how they do their job, and part of that includes information security.

Employee Discipline. When things go wrong, this policy outlines the steps that are to be taken. As with all policies, it discusses who is responsible for what and leads those individuals to more extensive procedures. This policy is very important for an effective information security program. When an investigation begins, it may eventually lead to a need to implement sanctions on an employee or group of employees. Having a policy that establishes who is responsible for administering these sanctions will ensure that all involved in the investigation are properly protected.

Information Security. The bulk of the remainder of this book will address writing an effective information security policy. This is the cornerstone of the information security program and works in close harmony with the enterprisewide Asset Classification Policy and the Records Management Policy. This policy established the concept that information is an asset and the property of the organization and that all employees are required to protect this asset.

Corporate Communications. Instead of individual, topic-specific policies on such items as voice-mail, e-mail, inter-office memos, or outside correspondence, a single policy on what is and is not allowed in organization correspondence can be implemented. This policy will support the concepts established in the Employee Standards of Conduct, which address employee conduct and include harassment, whether sexual, racial, religious, or ethnic. The policy also discusses libelous and slanderous content and the organization's position on such behavior.

The policy will also address requests from outside organizations for information. This will include media requests for information as well as representing the organization by speaking at or submitting white papers for various business-related conferences or societies.

Workplace Security. This policy addresses the need to provide a safe and secure work environment for the employees. The need to implement sound security practices to protect employees, organization property, and information assets is established here. Included in this policy are the basic security tenets of authorized access to the facility, visitor requirements, property removal, and emergency response plans, which include evacuation procedures.

Business Continuity Plans (BCPs). For years this process was relegated to the information technology (IT) department and consisted mainly of the IT disaster recovery plan for the processing environment. The proper focus for this policy is the establishment of business unit procedures to support the restoration of critical business processes, applications, and systems in the event of an outage.

Included in the Business Continuity Plan Policy are the needs for business units to:

- Establish effective continuity plans
- Conduct a business impact analysis for all applications, systems, and business processes
- Identify preventive controls
- Coordinate the business unit BCP with the IT disaster recovery plan
- Test the plan and train its employees on the plan
- Maintain the plan in a current state of readiness

Procurement and Contracts. This policy establishes the way in which the organization conducts its business with outside firms. This policy addresses those items that must be included in any contract, and this includes language that discusses the need for third parties to comply with organizational policies, procedures, and standards.

This policy is probably one of the most important for information security and other organization policies and standards. We can only write policies and establish standards and procedures for employees; all other third parties must be handled contractually. It is very important that the contract language reference any policies, standards, and procedures that are deemed appropriate.

All too often I have reviewed policies that contained language that was something like "the policy applies to all employees, contractors, consultants, per diem, and other third parties." Just because this language appears in a policy does not make it effective. Third parties must be handled contractually. Work with the procurement group and legal staff to ensure that purchase orders and contracts have the necessary language. It would be wise to include a confidentiality or nondisclosure agreement. An example of a confidentiality agreement is included in the Sample Policy and Standards section of this book.

Records Management. This policy was previously referred to as *Records Retention* but the concept has been refined. Most organizations know that there will be a time when it will be necessary to destroy records. The Records Management Policy will establish the standards for ensuring information is there as required by regulations and when it is time to properly dispose of the information. This policy normally establishes:

- The record name
- A brief description of the record
- The owning department
- The required length of time to keep the record

Asset Classification. This policy establishes the need to classify information, the classification categories, and who is responsible for doing so. It normally includes the concepts of employee responsibilities, such as the *Owner, Custodian, and User.* It is a companion policy to the Records Management policy in that it adds the last two elements in information records identification. In addition to the four items identified in the Records Management policy, the Asset Classification Policy adds:

- The classification level
- The owner's job title

3   ORGANIZATIONWIDE POLICY DOCUMENT

Throughout the enterprisewide policy document, references to information security and the information security program should be incorporated. These concepts should begin with a review of the enterprise's shared beliefs that usually discuss such important concepts as teamwork, accountability, communication, continuous improvement, and benchmarking. Because of the increased emphasis on proper conduct, a formal discussion of the enterprise's support of due diligence concepts should be established.

The use of the term "accountability" when establishing organization goals and beliefs allows the enterprise to commit to the concept that it is willing to accept accountability for the results of decisions made to support the business process or mission of the enterprise. To ensure that appropriate, informed business decisions are made in an open climate of discussion and research, a formal risk analysis process should be implemented to document all management decisions.

By establishing this level of accountability, the enterprise is creating a climate of due diligence throughout the organization. A formal business-related risk analysis process will ensure that all decisions are made quickly and efficiently, and that the process is recorded. This will allow third parties to examine the process and verify that due diligence was performed.

As a security professional, it is very important that you establish due diligence as an enterprise objective and guiding principle. Risk analysis will ensure that all decisions are based on the best needs of the enterprise and how those prudent and reasonable controls and safeguards are implemented. With the implementation of more stringent reporting mechanisms and laws (*Sarbanes–Oxley*) or international standards such as *British Standards 7799 (BS 7799)* or *ISO 17799*, the formal adoption of a risk analysis process will assist in proving that the enterprise is being managed in a proper manner.

Another important element found in most enterprisewide policy documents is a section on Organizational Responsibilities (see Figure 2). This

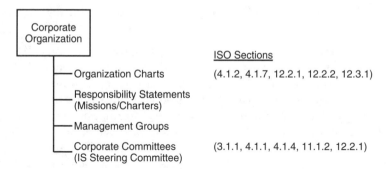

Figure 2. Corporate Policy Document

section is where the various mission statements of the enterprise organizations are resident, along with any associated responsibilities. For example:

- *Auditing.* Auditing assesses the adequacy of and compliance with management, operating, and financial controls, as well as the administrative and operational effectiveness of organizational units.

Information Security. Information Security (IS) is to direct and support the company and affiliated organizations in the protection of their information assets from intentional or unintentional disclosure, modification, destruction, or denial through the implementation of appropriate information security and business resumption planning policies, procedures, and guidelines.

Other organizations that should be included in the Organization Responsibilities section include:

- Corporate and Public Affairs
- Finance and Administration
- General Counsel
- Information Security Organization
- Human Resources

Later in this book we discuss in detail what makes up a mission statement or charter. For now it is important to know that to be effective, the Information Security organization must have an established charter and it must be published where all of the other enterprise charters are recorded. While this may seem trivial, it will lend significant credence to the overall information security program.

Included in the opening section of an enterprisewide policy document is a discussion on enterprise committees. Standing committees are established to develop, to present for executive decision, and, where empowered, to implement recommendations on matters of significant, ongoing concern to the enterprise. Certain committees administer enterprise programs for which two or more organizations share responsibility.

The Information Security Steering Committee was identified in ISO 17799 (4.1.1) and discussed as a requirement in the Gramm–Leach–Bliley Act (GLBA) to involve the board of directors in the implementation of an enterprisewide information program. The first key responsibility of this committee is the approval and implementation of the Information Security Charter, the Information Security Policy, and the Asset Classification Policy. In addition to these two enterprisewide policies, the committee is responsible for ensuring that adequate supporting policies, standards, and procedures are implemented to support the information security program.

The Information Security Steering Committee (ISSC) consists of representatives from each of the major business units and is chaired by the Chief Information Security Officer (CISO).

The ISSC is also the group responsible for reviewing and approving the results of the enterprisewide business impact analysis that establishes the relative criticality of each business process, application, and system used in the enterprise. The results of the BIA are then used as input to develop business continuity plans for the enterprise and for the business units. The ISSC is also responsible for reviewing and certifying the BCPs. To ensure adequacy, the BCPs must be exercised at least annually and the exercise reports are presented to the ISSC.

The key responsibilities established for the ISSC include:

- Approval of the enterprise's written information security program.[2]
- Oversee the development, implementation, and maintenance of the information security program.[3]
- Assign specific responsibility for the program implementation.[4]
- Review reports of the state of information security throughout the enterprise.[5]

4   LEGAL REQUIREMENTS

In addition to the national and international standards and laws we have been discussing, there are other requirements that make policies, standards, and procedures a necessity (see Figure 3). Management must demonstrate that a *standard of care* exists within the enterprise and in the manner in which it conducts its affairs. This standard of care requires that management employ a watchful, attentive, cautious, and prudent execution of the business process. Policies are one method that management can use to demonstrate that it is exercising reasonable care.

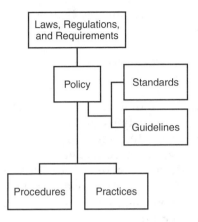

Figure 3. Information Flow Model for Policies, Procedures, and Standards

5   DUTY OF LOYALTY

By assuming office, senior management commits allegiance to the enterprise and acknowledges that the interest of the enterprise must prevail over any personal or individual interest. The basic principle here is that senior management should not use its position to make a personal profit or gain other personal advantage. The duty of loyalty is evident in certain legal concepts, including:

- *Conflict of interest.* Individuals must divulge any interest in outside relationships that might conflict with the enterprise's interests.
- *Duty of fairness.* When presented with a conflict of interest, the individual has an obligation to act in the best interest of all parties.
- *Corporate opportunity.* When presented with "material inside information" (advanced notice on mergers, acquisitions, patents, etc.), the individual will not use this information for personal gain.
- *Confidentiality.* All matters involving the corporation should be kept in confidence until they are made public.

6   DUTY OF CARE

In addition to owing a duty of loyalty to the enterprise, the officers and directors also assume a duty to act carefully in fulfilling the important tasks of monitoring and directing the activities of corporate management. The Model Business Corporation Act established legal standards for compliance. A director shall discharge his or her duties:

- In good faith
- With the care an ordinarily prudent person in a like position would exercise under similar circumstances

- In a manner he or she reasonably believes is in the best interest of the enterprise

7   OTHER LAWS AND REGULATIONS

7.1   Federal Sentencing Guidelines for Criminal Convictions

The Federal Sentencing Guidelines define executive responsibility for fraud, theft, and anti-trust violations, and establish a mandatory point system for federal judges to determine appropriate punishment. Because much fraud and falsifying corporate data involves access to computer-held data, liability established under the Guidelines extends to computer-related crime as well. What has caused many executives concern is that the mandatory punishment could apply even when intruders enter a computer system and perpetrate a crime.

Although the Guidelines have a mandatory scoring system for punishment, they also have an incentive for proactive crime prevention. The requirement here is for management to show "due diligence" in establishing an effective compliance program. There are seven elements that capture the basic functions inherent in most compliance programs:

1. Establish policies, standards, and procedures to guide the workforce.
2. Appoint a high-level manager to oversee compliance with the policies, standards, and procedures.
3. Exercise due care when granting discretionary authority to employees.
4. Ensure that compliance policies are being carried out.
5. Communicate the standards and procedures to all employees and others.
6. Enforce the policies, standards, and procedures consistently through appropriate disciplinary measures.
7. Implement procedures for corrections and modifications in case of violations.

These guidelines reward those organizations that make a good-faith effort to prevent unethical activity; this is done by lowering potential fines if, despite the organization's best efforts, unethical or illegal activities are still committed by the organization or its employees. To be judged effective, a compliance program need not prevent all misconduct; however, it must show due diligence in seeking to prevent and detect inappropriate behavior.

7.2   The Economic Espionage Act of 1996

The Economic Espionage Act (EEA) of 1996 for the first time makes trade secret theft a federal crime, subject to penalties including fines, forfeiture, and imprisonment. The act reinforces the rules governing trade secrets in that businesses must show that they have taken reasonable measures to protect their proprietary trade secrets in order to seek relief under the EEA.

In *Counterintelligence and Law Enforcement: The Economic Espionage Act of 1996 versus Competitive Intelligence,* author Peter F. Kalitka believes that, given the penalties companies face under the EEA, a business hiring outside consultants to gather competitive intelligence should establish a policy on this activity. Included in the contract language with the outside consultant should be definitions of:

- What is hard-to-get information?
- How will the information be obtained?
- Do they adhere to the Society of Competitive Intelligence Professionals Code of Ethics?
- Do they have accounts with clients that may be questioned?

8   BUSINESS REQUIREMENTS

It is a well-accepted fact that it is important to protect the information essential to an organization, in the same way that it is important to protect the financial assets of the organization. Unlike protecting financial assets that have regulations to support their protection, the protection of information is often left to the individual employee. As with protecting financial assets, everyone knows what the solutions are to protecting information resources. However, identifying these requirements is not good enough; to enforce controls, it is necessary to have a formal written policy that can be used as the basis for all standards and procedures.

8.1   The Need for Controls

With requirements to access information both within the campus environment and external through remote access, the need for an organization-wide information security policy with supporting standards and procedures is more important than ever.

The need for non-employees to access corporate information was once less than it is today. There has been a decided change in the processing environment.

8.2   Good Business Practices

Although there are legal and regulatory reasons why policies, standards, and procedures should be implemented, the bottom line is that good controls make good business sense. Failing to implement controls can lead to financial penalties in the form of fines and costs. Such activities can lead to loss of customer confidence, competitive advantage, and, ultimately, jobs.

The avoidance of public criticism, and saving the time on the investigation and subsequent disciplinary process, are very effective benefits to the organization and can be obtained by implementation of proper controls.

Every organization is required to provide its services or products to its customers, either legally or contractually. To ensure that the business objectives are met in a timely and efficient manner, effective policies and standards must be in place. Protecting shareholder interests is a key component in the need to implement effective controls.

When preparing policies, standards, and procedures, tread lightly on the legal reasons (use them when needed), but learn to sell your product as any other product. To be accepted and implemented, the policies and standards will have to help managers meet their business objectives. When developing these documents, it will be necessary to understand what each business needs and then work to fulfill those requirements.

9   WHERE TO BEGIN?

To find out what the business objectives or the mission of the organization are, it will be necessary to search out where these vital concepts are published. Many organizations have published their goals and objectives in an enterprise policy document. One of the first places I check to see what an organization wishes everyone to know about them is the organization Web site.

For publicly held companies, search out the stockholders' Annual Report. The business objectives and commitments to providing return-on-investment are presented and endorsed by the top executives of the organization. A key section of the Annual Report is the "Responsibility for Consolidated Financial Statements." The responsibility for the integrity rests with management and normally contains a statement similar to "The Company maintains systems of internal controls supported by policies and procedures that are communicated throughout the Company."

Understanding the objectives or mission of the organization will help to ensure that the focus of the information security policies, standards, and procedures supports those objectives. Policies that hinder the completion of the business of the organization will be ignored or scrapped. When creating these documents, it will be necessary to keep this key element in mind.

Security, for security's sake, is of no value. The creation of policies, standards, and procedures must be beneficial to the organization. No policy should be created to ensure that the organization is in compliance with audit requirements. Policies, standards, and procedures are developed and implemented to ensure that the organization meets its legal and contractual obligations to its customers, clients, stockholders, and employees.

10   SUMMARY

In this chapter we discussed the need for policies, standards, and procedures and that information security was part of the overall enterprise policy structure.

There are a growing number of laws, regulations, and requirements being established that require management to show that it is practicing due diligence.

There are at least 11 Tier 1 policies that every organization must address. These policies include:

- Employment Practices
- Employee Standards of Conduct
- Conflict of Interest
- Performance Management
- Employee Discipline
- Information Security
- Corporate Communications
- Procurement and Contracts
- Records Management
- Asset Classification
- Workplace Security
- Business Continuity Planning

In an organizationwide policy document, the organization should include a section that presents the mission or charter statements for each organization.

Standing committees are also presented in this document and for an information security program to be successful, an Information Security Steering Committee must be established and act as champion for the program.

The ISSC is charged with four crucial responsibilities and these map to current international standards and national laws.

There are business reasons that policies, standards, and procedures are required.

All policies must be tied to the business objectives or mission of the enterprise.

When you need to write policies, standards, and procedures you will have an overwhelming desire to start writing. But take the time to determine what needs to be done and how you will do it. Do your research. There are no new policies. Whatever you need to write about, you should be able to find an example that can be used to guide you along in your development. However, avoid the temptation of taking an existing policy and just changing the names. It might work, but the odds that this kind of quick fix will meet the specific business objectives of your organization are very small.

In Chapter 2 we discuss handling the writing task as a project.

Notes

1. Examples of Tier 1 policies and a Nondisclosure Agreement can be found in the appendices.
2. Required in ISO 17799, BS 7799, and Gramm–Leach–Bliley.
3. Required in Gramm–Leach–Bliley.
4. Required in ISO 17799, BS 7799, and Gramm–Leach–Bliley.
5. Required in Gramm–Leach–Bliley.

Chapter 2
Why Manage This Process as a Project?

1   INTRODUCTION

Although a project is usually defined as a *one-time* effort that has a definite beginning and end, and the implementation of security policies can be an *ongoing* effort, managing this process as a project will help keep the implementation team focused on the results to be achieved. Applying project management practices will also help with the assessment of those results to ensure they meet the needs of the organization.

Consideration should be given to questions such as:

- What is included within the area of concern, or what is the scope?
- What should be done first?
- How much time will it take?
- Is there a deadline that will act as a constraint on how much can be accomplished?
- How should changing requirements be managed?
- How much will it cost?
- How relevant are the policies and procedures to the environment?
- Who should create them?
- How should they be reviewed?
- How should they be communicated?
- How can opportunities for improvement be maximized?
- How can the potential for resistance by staff be mitigated?
- When should external sources be considered for providing assistance?

Creating and implementing security policies and procedures begins with a thorough understanding of why one's organization is concerned that these policies and procedures exist. Understanding the reasons why the effort was undertaken will help one set goals and objectives when determining how the security needs of the organization will be met. Later, the results of the effort should be reviewed to ensure that they have accomplished what was expected.

2 FIRST THINGS FIRST: IDENTIFY THE SPONSOR

A key factor in successfully implementing policies and procedures is to have commitment from senior-level management. The person with the means to commit resources to this effort should be identified as the project's sponsor. This sponsor will be the final person responsible for all major implementation decisions. Lack of a sponsor of sufficient seniority is a major risk to successful implementation of policies and procedures. Work completed without this sponsor may be subject to rework if the project team proceeds in a direction not supported by management. It is important that support be explicitly obvious. Clear management support will help obtain the cooperation and contributions needed from individuals who may not be direct members of the project team.

The project manager is the individual who leads the work effort and is responsible for the day-to-day planning, management, and control of the project. The successful completion of project deliverables on time, within budget, and to the specified quality standards are included in the project manager's responsibilities.

The project manager can be recruited from any area concerned with security, such as information security or internal auditing. This individual could also be recruited from outside the organization. Superior communication, organization, and team-building skills are among the traits that this individual should possess.

It is best to have only one project manager so that the management and control of project activities can be effectively coordinated. Managing the implementation of policies and procedures requires contributions and feedback from multiple sources, and a project manager fulfills the role of the conductor by ensuring that these contributions are well integrated into the overall project.

Ensure that the project manager possesses a sufficient level of experience and skill to manage the challenges that can be encountered when policies are being implemented. Be conscious of the tendency toward resistance among staff when it comes to documenting business processes or practices that may be perceived as "needing remediation." Review any previous studies or reports that address existing security policies, procedures, or findings. A good place to start is with the internal audit staff or other groups that might perform audit or compliance-tracking functions. Determine if there are any constraints that might inhibit progress and document all assumptions that have been made. Measurable criteria should be established to assess the success of the policy and procedure implementation. If there are quality objectives, quantitative requirements, expected benefits, or cost objectives to consider, document them.

Once the sponsor and project manager have been identified, the project manager should conduct interviews with the sponsor to obtain an understanding of desired outcomes. These interviews are also an opportunity to identify other interested parties, or project stakeholders.

Initiatives to create or revise policies and procedures may be a response to any number of stimuli. Legal requirements, especially in publicly traded or financial organizations, may need to be addressed. An adverse event that has occurred or almost occurred may prompt the effort. Sometimes, the effort is begun to guard against a situation that has occurred at another organization. A change in management can also spur a commitment to implement new or updated policies and procedures. Whatever the reason, the reason itself can be a good starting point for helping to define the overall objectives of this effort. Remember that it is extremely helpful to interview management to gain and document an understanding of its expectations. Clear, concise objectives that are documented and agreed upon by top-level management are a key success factor that should not be overlooked. Strive to obtain explicit confirmation, with a signature if possible, of the major objectives for the project to create and implement the policies and procedures to be producing.

3   DEFINING THE SCOPE OF WORK

Defining the scope of work places boundaries on what is to be accomplished. A Scope Statement should be developed that clearly defines what is and what is not included within the area of work to be completed. For example, one's approach to developing policies might be very different if the scope addresses issues from an enterprise perspective rather than at a more specific departmental position. Whether one is addressing an enterprise or departmental perspective, determine the high-level objectives that the policies and procedures are supposed to address and relate them to the organization's business objectives. Relating the project to the business objectives of the enterprise helps address issues associated with competing demands for limited resources. One needs to demonstrate that the activities associated with the implementation of security policies and procedures provide a positive contribution to the organization's goals.

To help define objectives, consider the types of information security challenges the organization must face. These objectives, or project requirements, lay the foundation for the plan of activities that will be developed to address those requirements. Careful consideration should be given to defining project requirements, and they should always be documented. Requirements that remain floating around in someone's head are subject to ambiguity and misinterpretation. Developing a consistent understanding of the scope and requirements is extremely important in ensuring that the

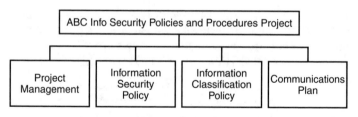

Figure 1. High-Level Work Breakdown Structure

outcomes of the effort meet those requirements. If not sure what the organization needs are, one is not likely to develop policies to address those needs. A clear understanding of requirements will help direct effort toward achieving the project's goals. Keep requirements in mind to guide the activities and as a basis for future decisions as one defines, organizes, and implements the policies and procedures that are created.

Once requirements have been clearly defined, a high-level breakdown of project components or activities can be developed, as shown in Figure 1. This high-level breakdown, or work breakdown structure (WBS), is a deliverable-oriented grouping of elements that help organize and define the total scope of the project. The WBS can be grouped by type of policy or procedure and should also include other supporting elements such as the communications plan. It is a good visual aid for identifying the work that the project will undertake. Work not identified in the WBS is outside the scope of the project.

After a high-level grouping of project deliverables has been defined, each high-level group should be further subdivided into more manageable components until enough detail is obtained to allow for the assignment of estimates of time, cost, and resource requirements to each component. Although the sponsor and project manager can identify the high-level groups, the decomposition into sub-components should be completed with the participation of other team members. See "Time Management" (Section 4) for more details.

Once high-level requirements are defined and agreed upon, a Project Kickoff meeting can be held to officially "begin" the project. This kickoff is a special meeting at which all stakeholders, project participants, and other interested parties are introduced to the project. It is very helpful in terms of obtaining cooperation and buy-in if the project sponsor delivers an overview of the reasons the project was undertaken as well as key expectations.

The kickoff meeting should also include an outline (see Table 1) of the proposed approach to achieving the defined project requirements and provide an opportunity for participants to ask questions of and give feedback to the project team.

Table 1. Sample Project Kick-Off Agenda

Security Policies and Procedures Project
• Date
• Time
• Place

The purpose of this meeting is to begin the Security Policies and Procedures Project.
Invitees: sponsor, project manager, project team members, and other stakeholders
Desired outcomes:
Establish working relationships and lines of communication
Establish and review project scope and objectives
Review project approach
Establish responsibilities
Identify and document issues to be addressed
Identify next steps

Agenda Items	Who
1. Introduction	Project manager
2. Review agenda	Project manager
3. Project briefing: the purpose of this project	Sponsor
4. Project scope and objectives	Project manager
5. Project approach	Team
6. Responsibilities	Team
7. Issues	All
8. Next steps	Project manager

4 TIME MANAGEMENT

Based on the scope, high-level objectives, and constraints of the project, identify the appropriate lower-level steps and tasks to be accomplished. The work breakdown structure (Figure 2) should be reviewed and adjusted to ensure that all necessary tasks are included and that any unnecessary work has been removed. A basic project management tenet is to ensure that the project is controlled so that it includes all the work required and only the work required to bring it to successful completion. This process can be started by the project manager but should be supplemented with contributions from other project participants. Brainstorming techniques can be used when decomposing the high-level elements of the work breakdown structure into its lower-level components. After each element has been broken down, review each one and gain consensus on the validity of its subcomponents.

Each element should be decomposed to a level sufficient to later support an estimate of required time, cost, and resources to complete. The work breakdown structure is intended to organize and define the scope of the project and is not meant to demonstrate the sequence of work to be performed. Sequencing is done during the development of a schedule.

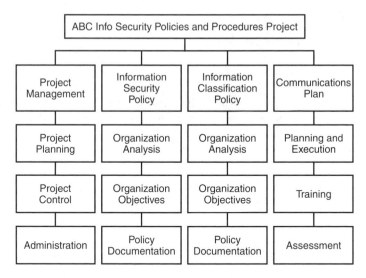

Figure 2.   Sample Work Breakdown Structure Organized by Policy Type

After decomposition, a list of all project activities to be performed can be developed based on the refined work breakdown structure. This list should include descriptions to ensure that the individuals assigned to complete the work understand what is to be delivered. After all activities are identified, they should be analyzed to identify interdependencies. Activities must be sequenced appropriately in order to develop a realistic schedule. Be sure to include activities that are administrative in nature, such as planning and conducting meetings and completing status reports. These activities can be grouped together, but careful consideration to this area will help prevent an over-optimistic estimate. Table 2 displays a sample of a decomposed work breakdown structure.

Estimates for time to complete or effort can be developed after all activities and their interdependencies have been identified. Effort estimates will be influenced by the project manager's prior experience, ability to make judgments based on limited information, and knowledge of the subject matter. The estimating process should include the project team members; estimates developed by obtaining consensus from the team will probably be more accurate. Producing and reviewing estimates with the participation of the people who will do the work will also support team-building and build confidence for the estimates produced.

A bottom-up estimate for the overall project can be produced by allocating effort estimates to each lowest-level component and aggregating them up to obtain an initial estimate for the total project. Effort estimates for each WBS component, together with the identified activities to be performed and their interdependencies, will allow the project manager to

Table 2. Sample Decomposed WBS

Policies and procedures project sample WBS.

I.   Project planning, scheduling, and budgeting
    A.   Project kickoff
    B.   Establish project sponsor
    C.   Identify benefits and costs
    D.   Develop business case
    E.   Establish objectives
    F.   Define project scope
    G.   Define project approach
    H.   Define project activities
    I.   Develop project schedule
    J.   Prepare project budget
    K.   Determine project staffing requirements
    L.   Establish roles and responsibilities
    M.   Conduct project status assessment
II.   Training
    A.   Determine training requirements
    B.   Identify and acquire tools
    C.   Develop training plan
    D.   Manage training activities
    E.   Establish budget status reporting methods
    F.   Establish schedule status reporting methods
    G.   Conduct project status assessment
III.   Project control
    A.   Monitor project progress
    B.   Identify and resolve issues
    C.   Manage exception situations
    D.   Review and revise project plan
    E.   Conduct project status assessment
IV.   Project quality procedures
    A.   Review enterprise documentation standards
    B.   Define quality objectives
    C.   Define product quality control reviews
    D.   Define documentation standards for policies
    E.   Define documentation standards for procedures
    F.   Develop quality plan
    G.   Define policy/procedure review strategies
    H.   Define documentation management plan
    I.   Identify/define support tools and procedures
    J.   Conduct project status assessment
V.   Develop policies
    A.   Document definitions
    B.   Identify required policies
    C.   Identify procedures, standards required

(Continued)

Table 2. Sample Decomposed WBS (Continued)

	D.	Determine formatting
	E.	Outline content
	F.	Develop and define policies
	G.	Develop and define standards
	H.	Develop and define guidelines
	I.	Develop and define procedures
	J.	Conduct project status assessment
VI.		Communications planning
	A.	Identify audiences
	B.	Determine distribution frequency requirements
	C.	Determine information distribution mechanisms
	D.	Develop communications plan
	E.	Define performance reporting requirements
	F.	Conduct project status assessment
VII.		Project closure
	A.	Complete final evaluations
	B.	Initiate maintenance process
	C.	Close outstanding project work
	D.	Collect project feedback
	E.	Compile project closure documents

develop the project schedule. Be sure to record all assumptions and issues identified.

Before beginning the estimating process, review the following questions:

- Who should be involved?
- What units of measure should be used: hours, days, weeks? The unit determined should be appropriate to the level of detail used to define the activities and ideally should be consistent across the entire project.
- How will contingencies be applied?

Two possible approaches to use are consensus-based and weighted average estimating. A consensus-based estimate involves getting a small group of people who are involved in an activity to estimate the effort required for that activity. The estimates produced will vary, based on the differing viewpoints and experiences of the people in the group. Participants are asked to produce estimates and then to explain the reasoning behind the estimates. The estimates can be discussed in reference to these explanations and, eventually, agreement can be reached for a single estimate. A weighted average estimating approach is outlined later in this section. Estimates can be developed using both approaches, with the results compared to refine and develop a single estimate.

To develop a weighted average estimate, have participants estimate each component of the activities list, giving best-case, worst-case, and most likely estimates. This task should be completed individually; then a workshop can be conducted to consolidate and review the initial estimates. A determination of how the weighted average is calculated should be determined by the project manager or by team consensus.

The results should be reviewed, with special attention paid to large variations between the best-case, worst-case, and most likely estimates and different people's estimates for the same activity. Reasons for the large variations should be determined and reconciled. Try to gain agreement among the estimators. The intention is not to arrive at the same value for the best, worst, and most likely cases, but to gain agreement on what are the best, worst, and most likely cases.

Once the estimates have been completed, they should be converted into practical estimates by allowing for nonproductive time, such as sickness and vacation. This might involve the application of a standard percentage value that is used to increase effort estimates. Be careful to avoid double-counting these items and inadvertently inflating the estimates.

As the project progresses, estimates can be revised based on the actual performance to date and due to unplanned events such as scope changes, staff changes, and newly identified activities.

The WBS and activities list (Table 3) can be developed simultaneously and documented as a spreadsheet or used as input to an automated scheduling tool. An automated scheduling tool will allow the project manager to complete "what-if" scenarios such as when the work should be started if an arbitrary deadline is imposed on the project and how the schedule will be impacted if project resources are limited or expanded. The project schedule, or timeline, will serve as a basis for tracking progress against the plan.

5   COST MANAGEMENT

The work breakdown structure (WBS) and sequenced activities list developed during the beginning stages of the project are used to support the development of a cost estimate. A more detailed WBS and activities list will support a more accurate estimate, but the level of detail required depends on the required degree of accuracy and the project manager's estimating experience. Keep in mind that a highly detailed WBS can be used to demonstrate the magnitude of the work involved and will provide support for the cost estimate. Each item on the activities list should include a labor and materials component. The cost of materials can be often overlooked when considering activities that appear to be labor intensive. For example, an activity identified as "training" can be estimated at 200 hours at $60 per

Table 3. Sample Table of Weighted Average Calculations

Category	Item	Best Case in Days (Weight — 15%)	Most Likely Case in Days (Weight — 55%)	Worst Case in Days (Weight — 30%)
Information classification	Establish the team	1	5	15
	Develop the policy	2	10	25
	Determining confidential information	5	20	80
	Identifying information to be declassified or reclassified	10	20	60

Note: Weighted average formula = (BC * 0.15) + (MLC * 0.55) + (WC * 0.30). This weighted average table and its calculations are illustrative only and are not intended to represent the actual experience of any specific project.

hour. The $1,200 estimate will be too low if a graphics software package must be purchased to design the training material, printing and binding services are required, or organizational expectations are that participants will be served food and beverages during training.

See the section on Planning and Preparation for guidance on the types of activities to be included in the WBS and activities list. Also, a checklist can help minimize the risk that certain cost components will be omitted.

6   PLANNING FOR QUALITY

Planning for quality requires that processes be in place to ensure that the policies and procedures created satisfy the needs for which they were developed. These processes include activities such as inspection reviews. These reviews are conducted to critique the policies or procedures to help ensure that management expectations and requirements are met. Reviews also provide an opportunity to reduce the likelihood of errors, omissions, or misunderstandings. Results are documented and corrective action is taken if necessary. Documentation standards, if any, should be reviewed to ensure that the policies and procedures developed are in compliance.

Review participants should include project team members as well as peers from other organization teams who have *not* been closely associated with the project. Management generally should *not* be included at preliminary reviews to ensure that the focus remains on the examination and tuning of the policies or procedures developed and not on the performance or status of the project itself.

7 MANAGING HUMAN RESOURCES

The primary objective of human resource management is to make the most effective use of the people involved with the project. Activities included are planning the organizational structure of the project, acquiring staff, and developing team members. The resources necessary to carry out the project and to ensure its success should be clearly defined and documented in terms of their roles and responsibilities. Reporting relationships can also be documented if necessary. Each person involved in the project should understand his or her responsibilities and should have the time available to carry out those responsibilities.

When determining staffing requirements, the skills required for the activities to be performed and their associated timeframes should be defined. The WBS and activities list should be used during this task. Organizational policies and a description of the existing available resource pool should also be reviewed. If it is determined that resources will be acquired from outside the organization, a plan for how these resources will be brought into and removed from the project may need to be developed. Paying attention to how team members will be transitioned onto and off a project can help reduce costs by eliminating the tendency to create work to fill the time between assignments. See the section on Planning and Preparation for recommended qualities to look for in team members assigned to the development of policies and procedures.

Team development includes activities that support the ability of team members to increase their individual contributions to the project and enhance the ability of the team to function effectively. The capabilities and skills of the project team should be assessed to help establish a plan to train members in any areas of deficiency. The types of training required should be documented so that a training plan can be developed. This training is specific to the project team and is in addition to the awareness training plan that should be developed to introduce the new policies and procedures to the enterprise. The time required to develop team skills should be included in the project schedule.

8 CREATING A COMMUNICATIONS PLAN

Managing security communications effectively ensures that timely and appropriate information is generated, updated, and disseminated to all who have a need to know. Lack of employee awareness will defeat even the most comprehensive policies and procedures. The communications process ensures that critical connections are established among all individuals of an organization. These communication links are absolutely necessary for the successful implementation of security policies and procedures. Creating a communications plan will provide a framework from which to manage the communications process.

An organization's structure will have a major effect on communications requirements. The information delivery mechanisms for an organization that houses staff in one central location can be very different from one that has employees distributed over several remote locations. Take time to determine the information needs for your organization. Consider who needs what information, when and how often they should receive it, and how it will be given to them. An analysis of the policies and procedures and the circumstances that they address will help determine how significant they are to the organization and how often they should be delivered. Analyzing the circumstances that the policies and procedures address will also help identify the intended audience.

8.1   Sample Communications Plan during Development of P & P

Table 4 contains recommended types of communications that can be established during the development of policies and procedures (P & P). The needs of the project and expectations of the project sponsor and stakeholders will influence how adjustments should be made.

8.2   Sample Communications Plan after Deployment

Table 5 contains recommended types of communications to be established once policies and procedures have been approved and are ready for dissemination to the organization. Responsibilities for delivery can be delegated; however, the sponsor should explicitly endorse all communications. The delivery mechanisms or frequencies should be revised to meet the needs of the organization or the urgency of the situations the policy was designed to address. For example, a new policy stating that all company communications are subject to spontaneous monitoring may require more frequent delivery in a large organization with a high contract staff ratio than in an organization with a workforce that is relatively stable.

9   SUMMARY

Managing the development of security policies and procedures as a project involves the application of a variety of skills, tools, experiences, and techniques. Project management processes help guide project activities in order to meet or exceed stakeholder needs and expectations. A primary objective of project management is to efficiently and effectively manage resources to deliver products on time and within budget while attaining a given level of quality. The intent of this chapter was to introduce a few key project management concepts that should be readily adaptable to a policies and procedures development project.

Table 4. Sample Communication Plan (during Planning and Preparation)

Communication Type	Audience	Frequency	Responsibility	Delivery Mechanism
Project kickoff[a]	Project sponsor Stakeholders Project team	At project start	Project manager	Meeting
Overall status report[a]	Project sponsor Stakeholders Project team	Monthly	Project manager	Document attachment via e-mail
Project review milestone assessment[a]	Project sponsor	Quarterly	Project manager	Meeting
Project team meeting[a]	Project team	Weekly	Project manager	Meeting
Project newsletter	All affected (interested) parties	Monthly	Team members	Newsletter document via general mail
Task status	Project team Project manager	Weekly	Team member	Update commitment calendar
Issue identification	Project manager	As needed	All	Issue management process
History/inquiries about project	All	As needed	Project manager	Electronic project notebook accessible via Web page
Problem identification: internal	Project manager	As needed	All	Problem management process

[a] This type of communication should be required.

Table 5. Sample Communications Plan (After Deployment)

Communication Type	Audience	Frequency	Responsibility	Delivery Mechanism
New or revised policy announcement[a]	All	As released, periodically thereafter	Sponsor	Broadcast mail Broadcast e-mail Broadcast voice-mail
New or revised procedure[a]	All affected (interested) parties	As released	Sponsor	Training
Complete policy manual[a]	All	Yearly and at new employee orientation	Sponsor	Manual[a] Intranet Web page
General security awareness	All	Quarterly	Information	
Security team	Broadcast mail Broadcast e-mail Intranet Web page Posters			
Awareness newsletter	All	Semi-annually or quarterly	Information security team	Departmental meetings Broadcast mail
Employee security awareness day	All	Yearly or semi-annually	Information security team	Promotional items Employee contests Topic discussions and demonstrations

[a] This type of communication is required.

Chapter 3
Planning and Preparation

1 INTRODUCTION

Planning and preparation are an integral part of policy, standard, and procedure development, but one that is often neglected. Included in the preparation process is all the work that must be done prior to beginning the actual development process. Discussions in this chapter focus on reference works obtainable, milestones, task checklists, and content level.

2 OBJECTIVES OF POLICIES, STANDARDS, AND PROCEDURES

Policies, standards, and procedures are key elements in ensuring that personnel are trained to handle specific job tasks. The policy will lay out the general requirements, the standard tools required, and the procedures will provide the step-by-step process required in routine activities. They can also be used when employees are required to make decisions. Many 911 operators have a set of tabbed or hypertext drill-down procedures that allow them to understand the situation and make appropriate decisions. This kind of decision tree can be used by all personnel when performing their daily functions.

Well-written procedures will never take the place of supervision, but they can take some of the more mundane tasks and move them out to the employees. These documents are basically management resources that classify and document the organization. The objectives of policies, standards, and procedures are to:

- *State and clarify policy.* When management is unavailable (off-hours or off-site), employees have a resource to which they can refer to assist them in making the correct decision.
- *Define duties, responsibilities, and authority.* The policy can identify who is responsible for which activity and the procedure can provide the step-by-step process needed to complete the task at hand.
- *Formalize duties.* An effective set of desk procedures can assist an organization in meeting two key security requirements: separation of duties and rotation of assignments.

- Separation of duties: the process to ensure that no single individual has complete authority and control of all of the steps in a task. This control concept limits the error, opportunity, and temptation of personnel and can best be defined as segregating incompatible functions (accounts payable from disbursement, test from production, information security from audit or operations). The activities of a process are split among several people. Mistakes made by one person tend to be caught by the next person in the chain, thereby increasing information integrity. Unauthorized activities will be limited because no one person can complete a process without the knowledge and support of someone else. The separation of duties concept is used to thwart fraud.

  The Delegation of Authority policy will support the separation of duties doctrine. An example of a Delegation of Authority Policy can be found in the section entitled "Typical Organization Policies."

- *Rotation of assignments:* individuals should periodically alternate various essential tasks involving business processes or transactions. This doctrine provides many benefits to the organization. These benefits include the ability to discover misuse and fraud, cross training of personnel, and additional support to fix problems. There are always some assignments that can cause an organization to be at risk unless proper controls are in place. To ensure that the task is being completed in an effective and secure manner, each job assignment must develop a set of task or desk procedures. When assignments are switched, the published procedures are to be used by the new person. This will allow for testing as to the adequacy of the procedures and to ensure that the task is being completed properly.

  One of the often-heard knocks against rotation of assignments is that it reduces job efficiency. However, it has been proven that an employee's interest declines over time when doing the same job for an extended period. Additionally, employees sometimes develop shortcuts when they have been in a job too long. By rotating assignments, the organization can compare how the task was being done and where changes should be made.

- *Establish standards.* Once a policy has been implemented, it will be necessary to establish standards that will support the policy. Standards are mandatory requirements that support individual policies. Standards can range from what software or hardware can be used, to what remote access protocol is to be implemented, to who is responsible for approving what.

- *Provide information to employees, customers, etc.* The ability to communicate management directions is what policies, standards, and procedures are all about. Management does not have the luxury of sitting down with each employee, customer, client, vendor, supplier, etc. and telling them what is expected, how they are to perform their assignments, and what tools are to be used. A well-crafted set of policies, standards, and procedures acts as the voice for management when working with personnel.

- *Educate users.* Some organizations have thousands of users accessing various systems and applications. The ability to provide them with the information they need to perform their tasks is an essential element in well-written policies, standards, and procedures. Easy-to-read, current procedures can cut the number of calls to the customer service center (help desk). Recently, users were calling the help desk because the response time on their workstations had slowed. Asked if they had a lot of files on the system, most indicated that they had deleted the files. However, when asked if they had emptied their wastebasket, most were unaware that this function was required.

3   EMPLOYEE BENEFITS

Most organizations attempt to provide all employees with adequate levels of training. While this is the goal, oftentimes constraints do not allow for proper formal training. Effective policies, standards, and procedures can help meet that objective. The adage heard around many offices is: "If I have the time to do it over, why don't I have the time to do it right in the first place?" By making policies, standards, and procedures available, staff members will have the tools and processes necessary to complete their assignments. They will effectively help employees do their jobs better and will provide continuity.

When an employee leaves for a promotion or takes on a new job assignment, the employee replacing them must sometimes jump right into the assignment. Having desk procedures available and current ensures that the level of disruption will be kept to a minimum. Additionally, when a number of employees are performing similar functions, the procedures can assist management in evaluating employee performance. The business unit can guarantee uniform delivery of services and eliminate guesswork.

Probably the biggest benefit to new employees is that they will begin to feel comfortable more quickly. One of the reasons that new employees have a feeling of uneasiness is that many of them were proficient in their old job, and now are faced with a new set of tasks. Where they did not need to ask questions, now they are dependent on someone else to tell them everything they know and can remember about a specific task. Many jobs have different assignments throughout the year. An employee who has to do certain things for year-end activities might not remember to tell a new employee about them. Additionally, when employees leave, they often do

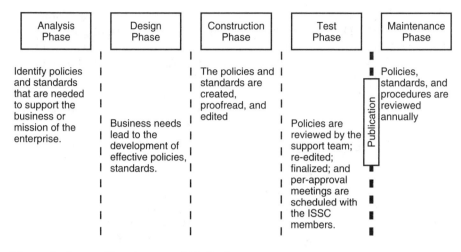

Figure 1. System Development Life Cycle

not have the time to devote to helping someone in their old jobs. Effective procedures are essential during any period of transition.

4 PREPARATION ACTIVITIES

Proper planning will provide the framework on which the activities associated with the design and development of the policies, standards, and procedures documents can be based. As discussed in the project management section, the task of developing written documents must be managed as a project. Each of the phases of a normal system development life cycle (SDLC) (Figure 1) can be used during the company policies, standards, and procedures. In addition to those phases and their deliverables found in an SDLC, the planning and preparation for policy and procedure documents require some extra steps.

5 CORE AND SUPPORT TEAMS

It is strongly recommended that policies, standards, and procedures be developed by teams (see Figure 2). Each one of these activities will have a different team makeup. We will discuss the policy team makeup here and will discuss standards and procedures teams in their respective chapters.

As with any team project, there will be a need to have an established leader. This individual will be responsible for ensuring that content meets the organization's needs and that delivery dates are met. The team responsible for the policy development is the *Core Team.* The Core Team consists of four members and normally includes representatives from:

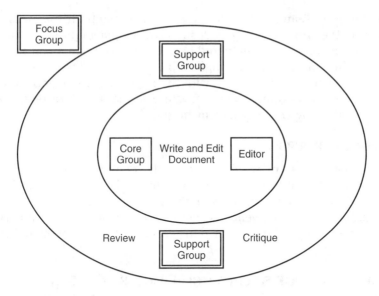

Figure 2. Policy Development Teams

- Information security
- Auditing
- The business units
- The policy approval office or committee

It is very important that this team be composed of individuals who have a number of years with the organization. Although they may not be content experts, they are needed to provide knowledge about the culture of the organization and what pitfalls to avoid. It is their knowledge about the organization and what can cause problems that is needed from them as a member of the Core Team. Use their experience to help create a document that has a chance of being accepted.

Key members of the Core Team will be the writer and the editor. The person who does the writing should not be the same person who does the editing. Choosing these individuals may be the single most important aspect of the preparation process.

The *Support Team* usually consists of representatives from each of the various business units. Their responsibilities will be to review and critique the initial drafts of the policies, standards, and procedures. They will be charged with representing their business unit at each review session and to make sure that the needs of their business unit are expressed and addressed. The Support Team will also be used to gather information on what concerns their senior management has on information security and what the Development Team should be doing to arrest those concerns.

The Support Team is also charged with keeping their business units apprised of the progress being made in the development process. The Core Team will use information gathered by the Support Team members when they schedule individual meetings with the policy approval team members. It will be important to meet with the Support Team members to find out what their management's concerns are so that the Core Team can be prepared with answers to management questions.

6   FOCUS GROUPS

Once the policy has been completed, it is recommended that a Focus Group be established to review the document. This is an important element in ensuring that the message of the policies and procedures is understood by the intended audience. A Focus Group will not be used for critiquing the documents, but can be used to see if the objective of the policy has been met.

7   WHAT TO LOOK FOR IN A GOOD WRITER AND EDITOR

How do we know what to look for in a good writer? To begin with, look for someone who does not require constant supervision. Writers are normally self-starters and have exceptionally good project planning and organizational skills. Any time policies need to be written, there will be a lot of background work to be done before anything of substance can be written. Therefore, it will be necessary to ensure that a timeline of deliverables is established and that the individual(s) chosen to complete the development can meet those dates.

A major portion of the implementation and acceptance process is dealing with people. Not just people — but management. The writer must have the ability to work effectively and pleasantly with personnel from all levels of the organization. It is not uncommon for a writer to interview an entry-level clerk and then have a meeting with the vice president of some business unit (see Figure 3). The ability to write is only a small portion of the writer's job requirements. A writer must be able to work well with individuals within the organization.

The ability to check one's ego is an essential element of this individual's makeup. The ability to conduct an effective interview is another key attribute of the writer. Not only does the writer need to ask good questions, but he must also be able to listen to the answers and follow up when necessary. A good interviewer not only listens to the words, but also watches the body language of the interviewee. Often times, more is learned from watching than from the words that are being said. Many times, the words will state one thing but the body gestures will give a totally different message. So, not only ask and listen, but watch and understand.

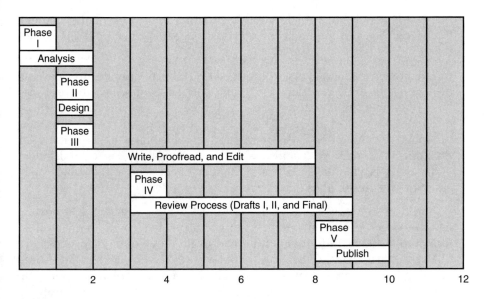

Figure 3. Timeline for Policy Development

Finally, these individuals will need good writing and editing skills. Not everyone can be a writer and even fewer make good editors. The writer must be able to identify the target audience and prepare material to meet the audience's needs. Too many write at their knowledge and comprehension level, and this can often lead to confusion and misunderstanding. Studies financed by the Veterans Administration (VA) indicated that the average informed consent statement is written at a graduate school level and fewer than a third of VA patients have had any college. To be effective, writers must always know the audience for which they are writing.

8   DEVELOPMENT RESPONSIBILITIES

Key responsibilities for the writer or editor include establishing the development plan. As discussed in the project management chapter (Chapter 2), there are a number of tasks and milestones to be established. It is the responsibility of this group to do the research and gather materials that can be used for policy, standards, and procedure development. The research material must be analyzed to determine if it can be used based on the needs and culture of the organization.

Understanding the culture or mental model of the organization is an essential element in creating a set of policies, standards, and procedures that will be accepted and implemented by the organization. As discussed in Chapter 1, there is a business need for these documents. When developing them, the organization mission or business objectives should be posted in the office or cubicle where the writing and editing are being done. Never lose sight of the business reasons that this project is being undertaken.

The project leader and the writer or editor (often the same individual) will have to establish the Development Team. These individuals will be responsible for providing input to the process and subject experts. Procedures will be developed by subject experts. The writers and editors will have to interview prospective candidates (subject writers), establish a scope statement for their specific assignments, and establish delivery dates. (The establishment of due dates is a mutual activity and as much concession to the subject writers' other responsibilities must be made as possible.)

Additional responsibilities for the Project Team leader will be to establish the layout of the document page. For a policy to be a policy, it must look like a policy. Individuals involved in the development process are often thrown for a loop when the document they have spent so many hours creating is summarily dismissed because it does not look like a policy. In business, "form over substance" will win almost every time. Research the layout of existing policy statements and adopt the generally accepted presentation. This includes the page format (the masthead, page number, date, location, and policy number).

9   OTHER CONSIDERATIONS

Taking on the task of writing and implementing policies, standards, and procedures can be a long-term activity, depending on how large or detailed the project needs to be. The involvement of personnel and the number of staff hours required to head up such a project may force the organization to look outside for writers and editors. Another factor in choosing these individuals is how quickly the organization needs to have the documents in place. All too often, organizations are faced with responding to an audit concern before they are willing to expend any resources on creating policies, standards, and procedures. The size and scope of the project, the possibility of a time constraint, and the skill set required may force organizations to look to contractors to fill this need.

10   KEY FACTORS IN ESTABLISHING THE DEVELOPMENT COST

The total cost of developing a quality document will vary from organization to organization. However, regardless of the industry, agency, or business, the components that make up the document development are basically consistent.

10.1   Research, Collect, and Organize the Information

It will be necessary to ferret out all existing policies, procedures, and letters (Chairmen, President, Comptroller, General Letters, Business Unit Vice

President, etc.) relating to the subject. It will be necessary to obtain copies of all laws, regulations, and requirements under which the organization is expected to function. These documents will have to be read to determine if they are still in effect. A good place to begin to create a list of such documents is with the Audit staff. Over the years, they have been writing Audit exceptions to either existing organization policy or good business practices (normally used when no organization policy exists). Once these documents have been located and read, it will be necessary to organize the material to meet the needs of the current project.

10.2 Conduct Interviews

Reading history is only the beginning process. To be effective, it will be necessary to interview senior management, department heads, first line supervisors, and users on how they use the resources and what would happen if the resource was lost, stolen, modified, or destroyed. The interview process should be used to obtain an understanding of where the organization is and how much control will be accepted.

When conducting interviews with management, I normally ask them three key questions:

1. Do you have any information within your business unit that you consider confidential?
2. What is the most important business process of the organization?
3. What one thing that information systems do or permit causes you the most concern?

These three questions can allow management to open up and discuss what it believes is important and what its biggest concerns are. Using this information, the policy writer can then create policies that will alleviate these concerns and answer management's questions.

Included in this process will be interviews with the Audit staff. It is important to know and understand where and what they feel are the biggest areas of concern. The Legal staff must also be included in this activity. They should be able to identify legal concerns (either laws, regulations, or potential litigation exposures). The Human Resources staff can provide information on how personnel information should be handled.

10.3 Write the Initial Draft and Prepare Illustrations

Once the research and reading is finished, the interviews are complete, and the physical layout of the document has been determined, it will be necessary to begin to write the policies, standards, and procedures (usually in that order). How long will it take to write a policy? Well, that depends on many factors. Once all the research has been completed, a good writer should be able to create an initial draft of a policy within eight to sixteen hours. The more experience the writer has in these areas, the better the results and the faster he or she can generally work. What causes the most problems is the desire to have the document perfect before anyone sees it. While this is a very human characteristic, it defeats the role of the proof-reader and editor (their roles are discussed in Section 10.4).

It is during this time that any illustrations will be created. These could be graphs, charts, forms, flowcharts, or other visual aids. Typically, policies and standards do not contain illustrations. It is the procedure that often uses these to help explain the process being described.

10.4 Proofread and Edit

Running the spellchecker is not the same as proofreading a document. It is recommended that different people assume the role of proofreader and editor. The advantage of a "fresh" set of eyes to examine the document can work wonders in creating a document that can be understood, accepted, and implemented.

The proofreader will review the document to ensure that spelling, grammar, and syntax are correct. This is an essential step in the review process. Eventually, the documents will be sent out to be reviewed by the Support Team; and if the document is not correct, the reviewers will spend their time correcting punctuation and spelling and not comment on content.

The individual responsible for editing will prepare the material for publication. Included in these responsibilities is to ensure that the message of the work makes sense. It is recommended that two editors be used — one who understands the technical side of the message and one who is a representative of the target audience. The objective of the policy, standard, or procedure is to take the message to a specific audience.

10.5 Choosing the Medium

Some organizations still require the printed document. If this is the case, then it will be necessary to include time for printing, collating, binding, shipping, and logging all numbered copies. The use of a physical medium is an added expense. Today, many organizations are using the intranet to post policies, standards, and procedures using HTML files or some other hypertext facility. The beauty of this revolution in publishing is that everyone has access to the most current copy of the document; and when an update is made, it only needs to be made once.

10.6 Maintenance

When I first got into information security, one of the sections I created in my own set of desk procedures was one that I titled "Audit and Inventory." This section included a timeline or calendar that identified every activity that needed to be conducted each year within the enterprise. It would include the dates for the inventory of the electronic media, the physical assets of the organization, the output requirements, and a review of policies, standards, and procedures. If the document was not amended or updated during the year, then it was subject to a review by the subject matter owner to ensure that it still met organization requirements.

11   REFERENCE WORKS

When preparing to develop policies, standards, and procedures, it will be advantageous to have access to a set of standard reference materials. These include but are not limited to a dictionary and thesaurus. While most word processor packages have a thesaurus, the spellchecker is not a replacement for the dictionary. The dictionary will be used to understand the meaning of the word. Grammar texts can also be of use; however, the grammar function of most word processor tools is an excellent (although pedantic) way of ensuring proper grammar.

An important reference tool is the *Office Administrator's Guide*. This document provides insight into how documents are constructed within the enterprise. It can also provide the writer with important conventions used within the organization. This guide will provide the writer with the formal and informal ways to identify the enterprise and the business units in print.

For example, General Motors Corporation is the formal name of the automaker. The accepted short form is not GMC (which is a division of General Motors) but GM. It is important that the company be properly identified when writing policies.

The proper way to identify levels of management in print will also be addressed in such a guide. For many organizations, "Management" with a capital "M" designates officers and directors of the organization. Management with a lower case "m" usually refers to line management or supervision.

How to identify employees in print is also found in a guide like this. Most organizations identify employees as "employees." However, I worked for two large corporations that used the singular "employee" as the proper way to identify employees. I have also seen the terms "associate," "customer liaison," and even "cast member" as terms for employees.

12   MILESTONES

When writing, it will be prudent to establish milestones (see Table 1) to help plan the activities, to budget resources, to control the phases, and to set deliverables. These milestones, once tested for implementation of one set of documents, can be used as a template for future writing projects. Publishing a milestone report with dependencies will help management understand how the project is progressing.

Table 1. Milestone Report with Dependencies

Plan Activity #	Description	Comment
37	Develop starter set of standards	Will be completed on June 9, 2003
38	Submit starter set of standards	Dependent on #37
39	Review starter set of standards	Dependent on #38
40	Submit comments	Dependent on #39
41	Edit starter set of standards	Dependent on #40
42	Accept starter set of standards or return to task 39	Dependent on #41
49	Review draft asset classification class material	Will be completed week of June 8, 2003?
50	Submit comments	Dependent on #49
51	Edit draft asset classification class material per client comments	Dependent on #50
52	Accept asset classification class material or return to task 49	Dependent on #51
53	Schedule asset classification workshops	Dependent on #52
54	Deliver asset classification workshops	Dependent on #53
55	Create and update asset classification database	Dependent on #54
56	Deliver asset classification database	Dependent on #55
59	Schedule security awareness classes	
63	Client review of draft security awareness materials	Dependent on #62
64	Submit comments	Dependent on #63
65	Edit draft security awareness material per client comments	Dependent on #64
66	Accept security awareness materials or return to task 62	Dependent on #65
69	Prepare engagement closing presentation	Cannot complete this task while the project is this far behind schedule
70	Schedule engagement closing meeting	
71	Deliver engagement closing material	Dependent on #69
72	Accept security awareness materials or return to task 62	Dependent on #71
73	Submit comments	Dependent on #72
74	Edit engagement closing material	Dependent on #73
75	Accept engagement closing or return to task 71	Dependent on #74

13   RESPONSIBILITIES

Different groups within the organization will have different responsibilities with regard to the development and implementation of policies, standards, and procedures. *Senior Management* has the responsibility to sponsor, fund, and support the development project. They establish the organization's overall program goals, objectives, and priorities in order to support the enterprise business objectives or mission statement. Ultimately, the head of the organization (e.g., the CEO, Chairman, President, Director, etc.) is responsible for ensuring that adequate resources are applied to the program and that it is successful. They are also charged with setting the example that all employees can follow.

13.1   Corporate Responsibilities

- *Chief Information Security Officer (CISO).* The CISO is responsible for the organization's planning, budgeting, and performance, including its information security components. Decisions made in this area should be based on an effective risk management program.
- *System and Information Owner.* These are the business unit managers assigned as functional owners of organization assets; they are responsible for ensuring that proper controls are in place to address integrity, confidentiality, and availability of the information resources to which they are assigned ownership.
- *Business managers.* The managers (AKA owners) are the individuals with the authority and responsibility for making cost-benefit decisions essential to ensure accomplishment of organization mission objectives. Their involvement in the risk management process enables the selection of business-oriented controls.
- *Information Security Administrator (formerly ISSO).* This is the security program manager responsible for the organization's security programs, including risk management.
- *Users.* Users are responsible for following organization policies, standards, and procedures; for reporting security problems; and for attending regular security awareness, education, and training sessions.

14   DEVELOPMENT CHECKLIST

A checklist is an example of items that should be considered when working on a project. Checklists can be misleading in that some people believe that whatever is on the checklist must be all that there is to do. A checklist is a starting point, to be added to or subtracted from. Once a development and implementation cycle is complete, one will have a better idea of the chronology of what events must take place.

1. Research and gather policies, procedures, letters, and documents.
2. Analyze the material and determine which ones are still applicable.
3. Identify and prioritize the policies that must be updated or created.
4. Identify the team members for the Core and Support Teams.
5. Create a Scope Statement and a Statement of Work.
6. Identify list of policies required and prioritize.
7. Establish a schedule, and post a project timeline.
8. Identify the policy approval process.
9. Form a Critique Panel.
10. Determine the physical characteristics of the document (page layout, etc.).
11. Determine the medium for the completed document (if hard copy, there will be additional steps and materials to be ordered).
12. Write the initial policy (first draft).
13. Proofread and correct the first draft.
14. Submit the first draft to the Support Team.
15. Prepare a communication plan.
16. Review and reconcile comments from the Support Team.
17. Prepare a second draft based on critiques.
18. Proofread and edit the second draft.
19. Repeat steps 14 and 15 for the second draft.
20. Prepare final draft based on critiques and schedule management meetings.
21. Obtain formal approval.
22. Prepare cover or transmittal letter.
23. Publish approved policies, standards, and procedures.
24. Create and conduct employee awareness presentations.
25. Establish a calendar to review policies, standards, and procedures on a regular basis.

15 SUMMARY

This chapter determined that the objectives of policies, standards, and procedures are to:

- State and clarify enterprise policy
- Define the duties and responsibilities and authority process
- Formalize duties:
  - Separation of duties
  - Rotation of assignments

The benefits to employees for having well-written policies, standards, and procedures include:

- Preparation activities:
  - Core Group
  - Support Team

- Focus Group
- Writer and editor attributes and development responsibilities

Key factors in establishing the development cost include:

- Researching, collecting, and organizing information
- Conducting interviews
- Writing the initial draft and preparing illustrations
- Proofreading and editing
- Choosing the medium

Reference works were discussed and how they can help the development process.

Employee responsibilities examined include those of:

- Senior management
- CIO
- Application, system, and information owners
- Users

Finally, this chapter reviewed those elements that might make up a development checklist.

Chapter 4
Developing Policies

1 POLICY IS THE CORNERSTONE

The cornerstone of an effective information security architecture is a well-written policy statement. This is the source from which all other directives, standards, procedures, guidelines, and other supporting documents will spring. As with any foundation, it is important to establish a strong footing. As will be discussed, a policy performs two roles: one internal and one external.

A policy is senior management's directives to create an information security program, establish its goals and measures, and target and assign responsibilities. Management is faced with many choices in directing the protection of information resources. Some choices are easy and are based on cost-benefit analysis or return on investment; but others involve granting concessions, questions of enterprise strategic direction versus implementing information security controls. Once these decisions have been made, policy will have been created *de facto*. The task at hand is to take these decisions, common practices, or folklore and fashion them into published policy that can be used as the basis for protecting information resources and guiding employee behavior.

2 WHY IMPLEMENT INFORMATION SECURITY POLICY?

In the absence of an established policy, the organization's current and past activities become the *de facto* policy. Because there is no formal policy to be defended, the organization may be in greater danger of a breach of security, loss of competitive advantage, loss in customer confidence, or an increase in government interference. By implementing policies, the organization takes control of its destiny. In the absence of established policies, the internal and external audit staffs and the courts can step in and set policy. Most organizations would prefer to establish their own policies instead of having some third party impose policy.

The goal of an information security policy is to maintain the integrity, confidentiality, and availability of information resources. The basic threats that can prevent an organization from reaching this goal are unauthorized access, modification, disclosure, or destruction — whether deliberate or accidental — of the information or the systems and applications that process the information.

It is a well-accepted fact that it is important to protect the information resources essential to an organization, in the same manner that it is important to drive on the correct side of the road. Unlike the driving scenario, which has regulations and laws to support it, the protection of information is all too often left to the individual. As with the driving scenario, everyone knows what solutions are available for protecting information. Identifying these requirements is not enough; to enforce controls, it is necessary to have a formal policy. This will form the basis for all necessary controls.

3   SOME MAJOR POINTS FOR ESTABLISHING POLICIES

When developing the policy, there is as much danger in saying too much as there is in saying too little. The policy should provide the direction required by the organization while maintaining business unit management discretion in the actual implementation of the policy. The more intricate and detailed the policy, the more frequent the update requirements and the more complicated the training process for employees.

Although it is important to keep to the facts and keep the document brief, it is also important to include a clear discussion on the proprietary rights of the organization. The employees deserve to know what is expected of them and how they will be apprised with respect to their obligations. By establishing well-written policies, the enterprise can expect that management will (if properly trained) take approximately the same course of action in similar circumstances.

4   WHAT IS A POLICY?

Policy means different things to different people. For our purposes, the term "policy" is defined as a high-level statement of enterprise beliefs, goals, and objectives and the general means for their attainment for a specified subject area. A policy is brief (which is highly recommended) and set at a high level.

Because policy is written at a broad level, organizations must also develop standards, procedures, and guidelines that offer employees, managers, and others a clearer method for implementing the policy and meeting the organization's business objectives or mission.

A policy is not a specific and detailed description of the problem and each step that is needed to implement the policy. A policy on requiring access control for remote users has exceeded its scope if there is a discussion about passwords, password length, password history, etc.

5   DEFINITIONS

5.1   Policy

A policy (see Table 1) is a high-level statement of enterprise beliefs, goals, and objectives and the general means for their attainment for a specified subject area. When we hear discussions on intrusion detection systems (IDSs) monitoring compliance to company policies, these are not the policies we are discussing. The IDS is actually monitoring standards, which we discuss in more detail later) or rules sets or proxies. We will be creating policies like the following policy on information security.

Later in this chapter we examine a number of information security policies and critique them based on an established policy template.

5.2   Standards

Standards are mandatory requirements that support individual policies. Standards can range from what software or hardware can be used, to what remote access protocol is to be implemented, to who is responsible for approving what. We examine standards in more detail later in this book. When developing an information security policy, it will be necessary to establish a set of supporting standards. Table 2 provides an example of what standards for a specific topic might look like.

Table 1. Sample Information Security Policy

Information Security Policy

Business information is an essential asset of the Company. This is true of all business information within the Company, regardless of how it is created, distributed, or stored and whether it is typed, handwritten, printed, filmed, computer generated, or spoken.

All employees are responsible for protecting corporate information from unauthorized access, modification, duplication, destruction, or disclosure, whether accidental or intentional. This responsibility is essential to Company business. When information is not well protected, the Company can be harmed in various ways such as significant loss to market share and a damaged reputation.

Details of each employee's responsibilities for protecting Company information are documented in the Information Protection Policies and Standards Manual. Management is responsible for ensuring that all employees understand and adhere to these policies and standards. Management is also responsible for noting variances from established security practices and for initiating corrective actions.

Internal auditors will perform periodic reviews to ensure ongoing compliance with the Company information protection policy. Violations of this policy will be addressed as prescribed in the Human Resource Policy Guide for Management.

Table 2. Example of Standards

Information Systems Manager/Team Leader

Managers with responsibility for Information Systems must carry out all the appropriate responsibilities as a Manager for their area. In addition, they will act as Custodian of information used by those systems but owned by other managers. They must ensure that these owners are identified, appointed, and made aware of their responsibilities.

All managers, supervisors, directors, and other management-level people also have an advisory and assisting role to IS and non-IS managers in respect of:

- Identifying and assessing threats
- Identifying and implementing protective measures (including compliance with these practices)
- Maintaining a satisfactory level of security awareness
- Monitoring the proper operation of security measures within the unit
- Investigating weaknesses and occurrences
- Raising any new issues or circumstances of which they become aware through their specialist role
- Liaising with internal and external audit

5.3 Procedures

Procedures are mandatory, step-by-step, detailed actions required to successfully complete a task. Procedures can be very detailed. Recently, I was reviewing change management procedures, similar to the one in Table 3, and found one that consisted of 42 pages. It was very thorough, but I found it difficult to believe that anyone has ever read the entire document. We discuss procedures in more detail later in this book.

5.4 Guidelines

Guidelines are more general statements designed to achieve the policy's objectives but by providing a framework within which to implement procedures. Where standards are mandatory, guidelines are recommendations. An everyday example of the difference between a standard and a guideline would be a STOP sign, which is a standard, and a "Please Keep Off the Grass" sign, which would be nice, but it is not a law.

Some organizations issue overall information security policies and standards documents (see Figure 1). These can be a mix of Tier 1, Tier 2, and Tier 3 policies and their supporting standards and guidelines. While it is appropriate to include policies in a document such as this, it is considered impractical to include standards, procedures, or guidelines in Tier 1 policies.

6 POLICY KEY ELEMENTS

To meet the needs of an organization, a good policy should:

- *Be easy to understand.* As discussed in Chapter 1, it is important that the material presented meet the requirements of the intended audience. All too often, policies, standards, and procedures are written by subject experts and given to a general-use audience. The material is often written at a college level when the average reading and comprehension level in the workplace is that of a sixth grader (a 12-year-old).
- *Be applicable.* When creating policy, the writer may research other organizations and copy that document verbatim. What really must be done is to ensure that whatever is written meets the needs of your specific organization.
- *Be do-able.* Can the organization and its employees still meet business objectives if the policy is implemented? I have seen many organizations that have written the ultimate security policy, only to find out that it was so restrictive that the mission of the organization was placed at risk.
- *Be enforceable.* Do not write a self-defeating policy such as "Use of the company-provided telephone is for business calls only." For most organizations, this may, in fact, be the policy, but almost every phone in the facility is used daily for personal calls. What might make a better policy is one that says that "Company-provided telephones are to be used for management-approved functions only." This provides some latitude and still meets the business need.
- *Be phased in.* It may be necessary to allow the organization to read and digest the policy before it takes effect. Many organizations publish a policy and then require the business units to submit a compliance plan within a specific number of days after publication. This provides the business unit managers a period of time to review the policy, determine where their organization might be deficient, and then submit a timetable for compliance. These compliance letters are normally kept on file and are made available to the audit staff.
- *Be proactive.* State what must be done: do not get into the rut of making pronouncements — "Thou shalt not!!!!" Try to state what can be done and what is expected of the employees.
- *Avoid absolutes.* Never say never. Be diplomatic and understand the politically correct way to say things. When discussing sanctions for noncompliance, some organizations have stated that "Employees violating this policy will be subject to disciplinary sanctions up to and including dismissal without warning," when the policy could have something like, "Employees found in noncompliance with this policy will be deemed in violation of the Employee Standards of Conduct." The Standards of Conduct state that employees will suffer disciplinary sanctions up to and including dismissal. Use the kindlier, gentler approach.

Table 3. Sample Application Change Management Procedure

Application Change Management Procedure
General

The System Service Request (SSR) is used to initiate and document all programming activity. It is used to communicate customer needs to Application Development (AD) personnel. An SSR may be initiated and prepared by a customer, a member of the AD staff, or any other individual who has identified a need or requirement, a problem, or an enhancement to an application. No tasks are to be undertaken without a completed SSR.

System Service Request
General

This form, specifying the desired results to be achieved, is completed by the customer and sent, together with supporting documentation, to AD. The request may include the identification of a problem or the documentation of a new request. Customers are encouraged to submit their request in sufficient detail to permit the AD project leader to accurately estimate the effort needed to satisfy the request, but it may be necessary for the project leader to contact the customer and obtain supplementary information. This information should be attached to a copy of the SSR.

After the requested programs have been completed, the agreed-upon Acceptance tests will be conducted. After the customer has verified that the request has been satisfied, the customer will indicate approval on the SSR. This form will also be used to document that the completed project has been placed into production status.

Processing

This section describes the processing of a System Service Request:

1.   The customer initiates the process by completing the SSR and forwarding it to the appropriate Project Manager (PM) or the Director of Application Development.
2.   The SSR is received in the AD department. Regardless of who in AD actually receives the SSR, it must be delivered to the appropriate PM.
3.   If the PM finds the description of requirements on the SSR inadequate or unclear, the PM will directly contact the customer for clarification.

When the PM fully understands the requirements, the PM will prepare an analysis and an estimate of the effort required to satisfy the request. In some cases, the PM may feel that it is either impossible or impractical to satisfy the request. In this case, the PM will discuss with the customer the reasons why the request should not be implemented. If the customer reaffirms the request, the PM and Director of AD will jointly determine whether to appeal the customer's decision to the Information Systems Steering Committee for a final ruling on the SSR.

1.   If the project estimate is forty (40) hours or less, the detailed design should be reviewed with the customer. After design concurrence has been reviewed, the PM will project the tentative target date (TTD) for completion of the SSR. In setting the TTD, the PM will take into consideration the resources available and other project commitments. The TTD will be promptly communicated to the requesting customer.
2.   If the project estimate exceeds forty (40) hours, the SSR and any supplemental project documentation will be forwarded to the ISSC for review, priority determination, and authorization to proceed.

(Continued)

52

Table 3. Sample Application Change Management Procedure (Continued)

The committee will determine whether the requested change is to be scheduled for immediate implementation, scheduled for future implementation, or disapproved. If the request is disapproved, it is immediately returned to the customer, together with an explanation of the reason(s) for disapproval. If it is approved for implementation, a priority designation is made and the SSR is returned to AD for implementation scheduling.

After implementation authorization has been received, the detailed design should be reviewed with the customer. After design concurrence has been received, the PM will project a TTD for completion of the project. In setting a TTD, the PM will take into consideration resources available and other project commitments. The TTD will be promptly communicated to the customer.

1. The PM will coordinate with AD personnel and other IT management and staff personnel (such as Database Administration, User Support Services, Network Administration, etc.) as to the resources that will be required to satisfy this request, or if there will be an operational or procedural impact in the other areas.
2. The PM will contact the customer to discuss, in detail, the test(s) that are to be conducted.
3. When Acceptance Testing (AT) has been completed, and the customer has verified the accuracy of the results obtained, the customer will indicate its approval to place the project into production by signing the SSR.
4. The Production Control Group (PCG) will place the project into production status. The PM will complete the bottom portion of the SSR, documenting that the project has been placed into production. The PM will log the status of the request as "completed" and file a copy of the SSR. The PM will promptly notify the customer that the project has been completed and placed into production.

Retention of Forms and Documentation

All documentation associated with the processing of each SSR will be retained for at least twelve (12) months.

- *Meet business objectives.* Security professionals must learn that the controls must help the organization to an acceptable level of risk. One hundred percent security is zero percent productivity. Whenever controls or policy impact the business objectives or mission of the organization, then the controls and policy will lose. Work to understand that the policy exists to support the business, not the other way round.

The information security policy should cover all forms of information. In 1965 the computer industry introduced the concept of the "paperless office." The advent of the third-generation computers had many in management believing that all information would be stored and secured electronically and that paper would become obsolete. When we talk to management about establishing an information security policy, it will be necessary to discuss with them the need to extend the policy to cover all information wherever it is found and in whatever format it exists. Computer-held

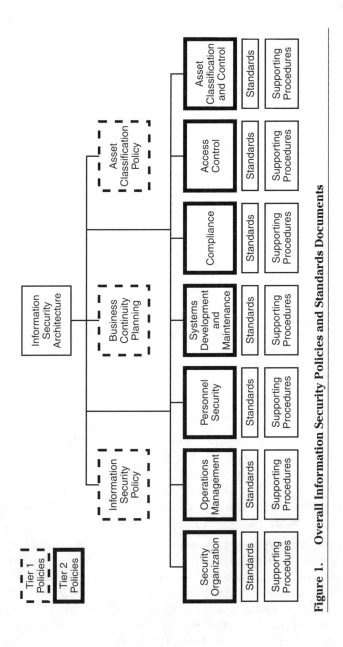

Figure 1. Overall Information Security Policies and Standards Documents

information comprises a small percentage of the organization's entire information resources. Make sure the policy meets the needs of your organization.

7 POLICY FORMAT

The actual physical format (layout) of the policy will depend on what policies look like in your own organization. It is very important that any policy developed look like published policies from the organization. Some members of the review panel will be unable to read and critique the new policy if it does not look like a policy.

Policies are generally brief in comparison to procedures and normally consist of one page of text using both sides of the paper. In my classes I stress the concept of brevity. However, it is important to balance brevity with clarity. Use all the words you need to complete the thought, but fight the urge to add more information.

Years ago we had a young priest visit our parish and his homily that weekend included a discussion of the concept of imprinting. This concept is normally covered in a basic psychology class, is an early social behavior among birds, and is a process that causes the newly hatched birds to become rapidly and strongly attached to social objects such as parents or parental surrogates. While many understood what the priest was talking about, the majority of the parish just stared at him blankly. So he continued to add explanation after explanation until his homily lasted about 45 minutes. When writing a policy, balance the attention span time limit with what needs to be addressed. Keep it brief, but make it understandable.

There are three types of policies, and you will use each type at different times in your information security program and throughout the organization to support the business process or mission. The three types of policies include:

1. *Global policies (Tier 1).* These are used to create the organization's overall vision and direction.
2. *Topic-specific policies (Tier 2).* These address particular subjects of concern. We discuss the information security architecture and each category such as in Figure 2.
3. *Application-specific policies (Tier 3).* These focus on decisions taken by management to control particular applications (financial reporting, payroll, etc.) or systems (budgeting system).

7.1 Global Policy (Tier 1)

Under the Standard of Due Care, and charged with the ultimate responsibility for meeting business objectives or mission requirements, senior management must ensure that necessary resources are effectively applied to develop the capabilities to meet the mission requirements. Management

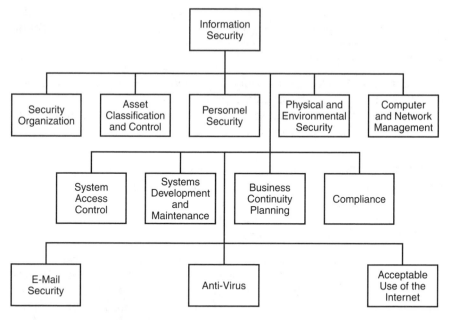

Figure 2. Topic-Specific (Tier 2) Policies

must incorporate the results of the risk analysis process into the decision-making process. Senior management is also responsible for issuing global policies to establish the organization's direction in protecting information assets.

An information security policy will define the intent of management and its sponsoring body with regard to protecting the information assets of the organization. It will include the scope of the program; that is, where it will reach and what information is included in this policy. Finally, the policy will establish who is responsible for what.

The components of a global (Tier 1) policy typically include the following four characteristics.

7.1.1   Topic. The topic portion of the policy defines what the policy is specifically going to address. Because the attention span of readers is limited, the topic must appear quickly, for example, in the opening or topic sentence. I normally suggest (note it is a guideline, not a standard) that the topic sentence also include a "hook." That is, the why me as a reader should continue to read this policy. So, in the opening sentence, we want to convey two important elements: (1) the topic (it should have something to do with the title of the policy), and (2) the hook (why the reader should continue to read the policy).

An opening topic sentence might read as follows: "Information created while employed by the company is the property of the company and must be properly protected."

7.1.2   Scope. The scope can be used to broaden or narrow either the topic or the audience. In an information security policy statement, we could say that "information is an asset and the property of the company and all employees are responsible for protecting that asset." In this sentence we have broadened the audience to include all employees. We can also say something like, "Business information is an essential asset of the Company. This is true of all business information within the Company, regardless of how it is created, distributed, or stored and whether it is typed, handwritten, printed, filmed, computer generated, or spoken." Here, the writer broadened the topic to include all types of information assets.

Another example of broadening the scope might be as follows: "Information of The Company, its subsidiaries and affiliates in electronic form, whether being transmitted, or stored, is a key asset of the Company and must be protected according to its sensitivity, criticality, and value." Here, topic subject is narrowed to "electronic form." However, the audience is broadened to include "subsidiaries and affiliates."

We can also use the scope concept to narrow the topic or audience. In an Employment Agreement policy, the audience is restricted to a specific group such as the following:

- The parties to this Agreement dated (specify) are (Name of Company), a (specify State and type of company) (the "Company"), and (Name of Employee) (the "Executive").
- The Company wishes to employ the Executive, and the Executive wishes to accept employment with the Company, on the terms and subject to the conditions set forth in this Agreement. It is therefore agreed as follows:
- Here, the policy is restricted to Executives and will then go on to discuss what can and cannot be done by the executives. A sample employment agreement policy is contained in the section entitled "Tier 2 Policy Examples."

7.1.3   Responsibilities. Typically, this section of the policy identifies who is responsible for what. When writing, it is better to identify the "who" by job title and not by name. Here again, the Office Administrator's Reference Guide can be of great assistance. The policy will want to identify what is expected from each of the stakeholders.

7.1.4   Compliance or Consequences. When business units or employees are found to be in a noncompliant situation, the policy must spell out the consequences of these actions. For business units or departments, if they are found in noncompliance, they are generally subject to an audit item and will have to prepare a formal compliance response.

For an employee, being found in noncompliance with a company policy will mean they are in violation of the organization's Employee Standards of Conduct and will be subject to consequences described in the Employee Discipline Policy.

7.1.5   Sample Information Security Global Policies. We now examine sample information security policies and then critique them. The written policy should clear up confusion, not generate new problems. When preparing a document for a specific audience, remember that the writer will not have the opportunity to sit down with each reader and explain what each item or sentence means. The writer will not be able to tell every person how the policy will impact the reader's daily assignments. When writing a policy, know your audience. For a global (Tier 1) policy, the audience is the employee base.

Using the general employee population as a base, let us examine a few policies and see if they have the four key elements we should be looking for. We want to see if these policies have:

- A topic (including a topic and a "hook")
- Scope (whether it broadens or narrows the topic or the audience, or both)
- Responsibilities (based on job titles)
- Compliance or consequences

Table 4 addresses the checklist as follows:

- *Topic:* "Information is a valuable corporate asset.... As such, steps will be taken to protect information...."
- *Responsibilities:* "The protection of these assets is a basic management responsibility."
- *Scope:* "Ensuring that all employees understand their obligation to protect these assets."

Compliance: "Noting variance from established security practice and for initiating corrective action." This policy is a good start. However, the topic is vague and that is not acceptable. The most important goal of any writing is to quickly identify the topic. Without the title, we have only a vague idea of where the document is leading us.

When the policy establishes responsibilities, it will work best if you use an active verb. In this example, the writer diminishes the verb and makes it passive by adding the gerund "ing" to the verbs "identify," "ensure," and "note." Try to avoid the passive whenever possible.

Table 4. A Utility Company's Information Security Policy: Example 1

Information Security Policy

Information is a valuable corporate asset. Business continuity is heavily dependent upon the integrity and continued availability of certain critical information and the means by which that information is gathered, stored, processed, communicated, and reported. As such, steps will be taken to protect information assets from unauthorized use, modification, disclosure, or destruction, whether accidental or intentional.

The protection of these assets is a basic management responsibility. Employing officers are responsible for:

• Identifying and protecting computer-related information assets within their assigned area of management control

• Ensuring that these assets are used for management-approved purposes only

• Ensuring that all employees understand their obligation to protect these assets

• Implementing security practices and procedures that are consistent with the Company Information Asset Security Manual and the value of the asset

• Noting variance from established security practice and for initiating corrective action

When identifying levels of management, most organizations have established a scheme for how differing levels are referred to in print. Normally, *Management*, with an uppercase M, refers to senior management and lowercase *management* refers to line management or supervision.

In Table 4, the writer referred to the "employing officer." For many enterprises, an officer is the most senior level of management. Officers may rank up there with the board of directors. The Chief Executive Officer, Chief Financial Officer, etc. are examples of this level of management. It is pretty safe to assume that the writer was not intending for such a high-ranking individual to be involved in this policy.

Table 5 addresses the checklist as follows:

• *Topic.* The policy statement establishes that "company information... that would violate company commitments... or compromise...competitive stance..." must be protected.

• *Responsibilities.* The policy does establish "employee responsibilities;" however, if there is to be a reference to another document, there are two standards and one guideline that must be followed:
  – The referenced document must exist.
  – The reader must be able to easily access the referenced document.
  – Referencing other documents should be used judiciously.

• *Scope.* Here, the policy makes a mistake in the first section; the policy actually narrows the scope of the material to be protected

Table 5. A Power Company's Information Security Policy: Example 2

Information Security
Policy Statement

It is the policy of the Power and Light Company to protect all company information from disclosures that would violate company commitments to others or would compromise the competitive stance of the company.

Employee Responsibilities

Employee responsibilities are defined in Company Procedure AUT 15. Violations of these responsibilities are subject to appropriate disciplinary action up to and including discharge, legal action, or having the matter referred to law enforcement agencies.

---

by stating that "company information...that would violate company commitments...or compromise...competitive stance...." This statement, in fact, narrows the overall policy direction to only that information that meets this specific criterion.

Compliance. Straight out: you violate, you pay the penalty. This may be a bit harsh. Remember that part of policy implementation is acceptance. A better way to state this consequence might be: "Employees found to be in violation of this policy will be subject to the measures described in the Employee Discipline Policy."

This policy does meet one of the main requirements of a policy: that it be brief. It appears to be too brief. Some very important elements are left out, especially what role management will play in this policy and how compliance will be monitored. The policy also seems to exclude information about personnel.

The opening sentence discusses the "policy" of the company. The document was drafted as a policy statement, so it is not necessary to add the term "policy" to the text. Let the words establish what the policy is.

Now let us take a look at the policy statement we used as an example earlier in this chapter (Table 6).

For this critique we will examine the policy line-by-line. The initial line starts out as:

1. Business information is an essential asset of the Company.
   - This starts out as a topic sentence, but it leaves out the hook.
2. This is true of all business information within the Company, regardless of how it is created, distributed, or stored and whether it is typed, handwritten, printed, filmed, computer generated, or spoken.
   - This is scope; it addresses all the various types of information that could be included.

Table 6. Information Security Policy for a Healthcare Provider: Example 3

Information Security Policy

Business information is an essential asset of the Company. This is true of all business information within the Company, regardless of how it is created, distributed, or stored and whether it is typed, handwritten, printed, filmed, computer generated, or spoken.

All employees are responsible for protecting corporate information from unauthorized access, modification, duplication, destruction, or disclosure, whether accidental or intentional. This responsibility is essential to Company business. When information is not well-protected, the Company can be harmed in various ways, such as significant loss in market share and a damaged reputation.

Details of each employee's responsibilities for protecting Company information are documented in the Information Protection Policies and Standards Manual. Management is responsible for ensuring that all employees understand and adhere to these policies and standards. Management is also responsible for noting variances from established security practices and for initiating corrective actions.

Internal auditors will perform periodic reviews to ensure ongoing compliance with the Company information protection policy. Violations of this policy will be addressed as prescribed in the Human Resource Policy Guide for Management.

3. All employees are responsible for protecting corporate information from unauthorized access, modification, duplication, destruction, or disclosure, whether accidental or intentional.
   - Here, finally, is the hook. It also has scope in that in includes all employees.
4. This responsibility is essential to Company business.
   - This is probably additional scope, but appears to be part of an explanation. When developing a policy, it is not necessary to include why the policy was created. Explaining the "why" will be handled in the policy awareness program.
5. When information is not well protected, the Company can be harmed in various ways, such as significant loss to market share and a damaged reputation.
   - This is definitely why the policy is important. To be clear on this point, the policy needs to be as clear and concise as possible. Try to avoid adding why the policy was created. After the policy has been around for a few years and become part of the culture of the organization, it will seem superfluous to have these words in the policy.
6. Details of each employee's responsibilities for protecting Company information are documented in the Information Protection Policies and Standards Manual.
   - Remember our two standards and one guideline about referencing other works: (1) the document has to exist; (2) it has to be

easily accessible to the reader; and (3) use this tactic infrequently. Note in line six that the author changes information type from "business" information to "company" information. This could add confusion for the reader. Strive to be consistent throughout the policy.

7. Management is responsible for ensuring that all employees understand and adhere to these policies and standards.
   - Here, the sentence begins with "Management." Is the capital "M" for the beginning of the sentence, or is it there to identify a level of management? When writing a sentence like this, it is better to start with an adjective such as "Company Management." This will reduce the confusion for the reader.

8. Management is also responsible for noting variances from established security practices and for initiating corrective actions.
   - The same critique as sentence seven. This is a reference to responsibilities and also what to do if a business unit is found to be in a noncompliant condition.

9. Internal auditors will perform periodic reviews to ensure ongoing compliance with the Company information protection policy.
   - This sentence causes me the greatest concern. This is what auditors do, so it is not necessary to include a statement like this in the policy. Additionally, if this sentence remains, then the policy requires that only internal auditors can conduct reviews of this policy. Remember when writing anything, be very careful with what you say. The words will be interpreted by each reader in the manner that best meets their needs.

10. Violations of this policy will be addressed as prescribed in the Human Resource Policy Guide for Management.
    - As we discussed in the review of sentence seven, the rules on other documents apply. This is the final compliance issue as it addresses what occurs when employees are in a noncompliant condition.

We now examine one last sample policy (Table 7). This one appears to have all of the elements. I recommend that when you critique something you read it through completely. Then go back and dissect it line by line. We will look for our four key elements: (1) topic, (2) scope, (3) responsibilities, and (4) compliance.

The opening paragraph is captioned "policy"; this should give us the information we need. It does contain some of the topic sentences we discussed earlier. It has half the requirements we would like to see, and it lacks the "hook." The second sentence contains the scope.

Under "Responsibilities," we find the "hook" in the first item. Item numbers two, three, and four appear to be elements that we would normally

Table 7. A Utility Company's Information Protection Policy: Example 4

Information Protection

Policy

Information is a company asset and is the property of Your Company. Your Company information includes information that is electronically generated, printed, filmed, typed, stored, or verbally communicated. Information must be protected according to its sensitivity, criticality, and value, regardless of the media on which it is stored, the manual or automated systems that process it, or the methods by which it is distributed.

Responsibilities

1.   Employees are responsible for protecting corporate information from unauthorized access, modification, duplication, destruction, or disclosure.

2.   Employees responsible for creating, administering, or using corporate information are identified as information **owners, custodians,** and **users** with responsibilities to protect information under their control.

   a.   *Owner:* Employees responsible for the creation or use of the information resource. **Owners** are responsible to define safeguards that assure the confidentiality, availability, and integrity of the information assets. **Owners** are also responsible to place information in the proper classification so that it can be obtained by those who need the information to perform their assigned duties (see section 4 below).

   b.   *Custodian:* Employees responsible for maintaining the safeguards established by the **owner.** The **custodian** is designated by the **owner.**

   c.   *Users:* Employees responsible for using and safeguarding information under their control according to the directions of the **owner. Users** are authorized access to information assets by the **owner.**

3.   Access to information will be granted by the **owner** to those with an approved business need.

4.   All corporate information shall be classified by the **owner** into one of three classification categories:

   a.   *Confidential:* Information that, if disclosed, could violate the privacy of individuals, reduces the company's competitive advantage, or could cause damage to the company.

   b.   *Public:* Information that has been made available for public distribution through authorized company channels. (See Corporate Communications Policy.)

   c.   *Internal Use:* Information that is intended for use by employees when conducting company business. Information that does not qualify as **Confidential** or **Public** is classified as **Internal Use.**

Compliance

1.   Each Manager shall:

   a.   Develop and administer an information protection program that appropriately classifies and protects corporate information under their control.

(Continued)

Table 7. A Utility Company's Information Protection Policy: Example 4 (Continued)

     b.   Implement an employee awareness program to ensure that all employees are aware of the importance of information and the methods employed for its protection.

     c.   Establish an information records retention schedule in compliance with applicable laws and regulations.

2.   Employees who fail to comply with the policies will be considered in violation of Your Company's *Employee Standards of Conduct* and will be subject to appropriate corrective action.

---

find in an Asset Classification policy. When I talked to the people who developed this policy, I was told that the company had gone through a paper-reduction process during the past couple of years and had streamlined its operating documents quite a bit. The new philosophy was that no new policies would be created. After about a year of campaigning and audit comments, the management approval team authorized one new policy. The team took advantage and combined the Information Security Policy and the Asset Classification Policy into the Information Protection Policy. What they did was correct, based on the current climate of their organization.

The final section discusses the compliance issues and includes some interesting requirements that management must implement to be compliant with this policy. The Information Protection Group developed a set of policies, standards, and guidelines that could be used by the various departments as a template for their own supporting documents. A sample of this type of document is included in the book under the section "Information Security Reference Guide."

7.2   Topic-Specific Policy (Tier 2)

Whereas the global (Tier 1) policy is intended to address the broad organizationwide issues, the topic-specific policy is developed to focus on areas of current relevance and concern to the organization. Management may find it appropriate to issue a policy on how an organization will approach Internet usage or the use of the company-provided e-mail system. Topic-specific policies may also be appropriate when new issues arise, such as when implementing a recently enacted law requiring protection of particular information (GLBA, HIPAA, etc.). The global (Tier 1) policy is usually broad enough so that it does not require modification over time, whereas topic-specific (Tier 2) policies are likely to require more frequent revisions as changes in technology and other factors dictate.

Topic-specific policies (see Figure 3) will be created most often by an organization. We will examine the key elements in the topic-specific policy. When creating an *Information Security Policies and Standards* document,

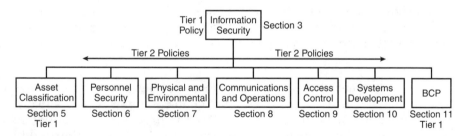

Figure 3. Topic-Specific Policies by Section

each section in the document will normally begin with a topic-specific policy. The topic-specific policy will narrow the focus to one issue at a time. This will allow the writer to focus on one area and then develop a set of standards to support this particular subject.

Where the Tier 1 policies are approved by the Information Security Steering Committee, the topic-specific (Tier 2) policies are issued by a single senior manager or director.

As with the Tier 1 policies, Tier 2 policies will address management's position on relevant issues. It is necessary to interview management to determine what their concerns are and what is it that they want to have occur. The writer will take this information and incorporate it into the following structure.

7.2.1   Thesis Statement. This is similar to the Topic section discussed in the Tier 1 policies, but it also adds more information to support the goals and objectives of the policy and management's directives. This section will be used to discuss the issue in relevant terms and what conditions are included. If appropriate, it may be useful to specify the goal or justification for the policy. This can be useful in gaining compliance with the policy.

When developing a Workstation Standards document, a topic-specific policy on appropriate software, with supporting standards, would include a discussion of "company-approved" software. This policy would define what is meant by "company-approved" software, which could be "any software not approved, purchased, screened, managed, and owned by the organization." The policy would also discuss the conditions necessary to have software approved.

Once the terms and conditions have been discussed, the remainder of this section would be used to state management's position on the issue.

7.2.2   Relevance. The Tier 2 policy also needs to establish to whom the policy applies. In addition to whom, the policy will want to clarify where, how, and when the policy is applicable. Is the policy only enforced when employees are in the work-site campus, or will it extend to off-site activities? It is necessary to identify as many of the conditions and terms as possible.

7.2.3   Responsibilities. The assignment of roles and responsibilities is also included in Tier 2 policies. For example, the policy on company-approved software will have to identify the process to get software approved. This would include the authority (by job title) authorized to grant approval and a reference to where this process is documented.

This is a good time to discuss deviations from policy requirements. I have established a personal standard in that I never discuss how an entity can gain a dispensation from the policy. I do not like to state that "this is the policy and all employees must comply, except those of you who can find a way around the policy." Most organizations have a process to gain an approved deviation from a policy or standard. This normally requires the petitioner to submit a business case for the deviation, along with alternative controls that would satisfy the spirit of the policy. If some organization or person wants a deviation from the policy, let them discover what the process is.

7.2.4   Compliance. For a Tier 2 policy, it may be appropriate to describe, in some detail, the infractions that are unacceptable, and the consequences of such behavior. Penalties may be explicitly stated and should be consistent with the Tier 1 Employee Discipline Policy. Remember that when an employee is found in a noncompliant situation, it is management and Human Resources that are responsible for disciplining the individual.

7.2.5   Supplementary Information. For any Tier 2 policy, the appropriate individuals in the organization to contact for additional information, guidance, and compliance should be indicated. Typically, the contact information would be specified by job title — not by individual name. It may also be prudent to identify the owner of this policy. This information will provide readers with the appropriate information if they have suggestions on how to improve the policy.

To be effective, a policy requires visibility. Visibility aids implementation of the policy by helping to ensure that it is fully communicated throughout the organization. Management presentations, videos, panel discussions, guest speakers, question-and-answer forums, and newsletters will increase visibility. The organization's Information Security Awareness Program can effectively notify users of new policies. The New Employee Orientation Program can also be used to familiarize new employees with the organization's policies.

When introducing policies, it is important to ensure that management's support is clear, especially in areas where employees feel inundated with directives, regulations, or other requirements. Organization policies are the vehicles used to emphasize management's commitment to effective internal controls and their expectations for employee support and compliance.

Table 8 is an example of a Tier 2 (topic-specific) policy.

The Senate policy discusses what is allowed and what is not allowed. It identifies where a member can go to get additional information on proper usage. In the section indicated by "Scope and Responsibility," item 1 establishes the Topic or *Thesis Statement* of this policy.

Item 3 assigns Responsibilities and major headings B and C provide *Supplemental Information*. The only area not apparently covered by this policy is *Compliance*. It also identifies who is responsible to oversee or monitor activities. Item 1 under Scope and Responsibility discusses the Thesis Statement or Topic. Under the circumstances, it may be appropriate to leave out the compliance or consequences in the policy.

Let us examine another sample Internet Usage Policy (see Table 9). This is an interesting Tier 2 policy, in that it adds a Statement of Compliance section that the Internet user is to read and sign. I have encountered a number of policies that use this tactic. A word of warning about usage and responsibility statements: they must be revisited annually to ensure employees remember that they signed such a document. It is important that this reminder be part of an annual information security awareness program. This will ensure that the desired effect remains active.

A typical Usage and Responsibility Statement might look like the one in Table 10.

Another area that requires a Tier 2 policy is the proper use of electronic mail (e-mail). We will examine two existing e-mail policies and compare them to the criteria we have established for these types of policies.

The opening paragraph in Table 11 spells out what this policy is about, what is unacceptable behavior, that activities are subject to monitoring, and that noncompliance will be referred to management. This is a good, strong opening statement. The remainder of the policy supports the other objectives of proper e-mail usage.

Items 1, 2, 8, and 9 discuss compliance issues. Item 4 discusses the relevance issues, and items 4, 5, and 7 handle responsibility concerns. I have only one real problem with this policy and that is the use of the term "guideline." Over the years, my research into policy writing has led me to believe that in many instances the term "guideline," when used in a policy like the one above, really means "standard."

Table 8. Tier 2 Sample Internet Usage Policy

U.S. Senate Internet Services Usage Rules and Policies
Policy for Internet Services

A. Scope and Responsibility

1. Senate Internet Services ("FTP Server, Gopher, World Wide Web and electronic mail") may only be used for official purposes. The use of Senate Internet Services for personal, promotional, commercial, or partisan political/campaign purposes is prohibited.

2. Members of the Senate, as well as Committee Chairmen and Officers of the Senate, may post to the Internet Servers information files which contain matter relating to their official business, activities, and duties. All other offices must request approval from the Committee on Rules and Administration before posting material on the Internet Information Servers.

3. It is the responsibility of each Senator, Committee Chairman, Officer of the Senate, or office head to oversee the use of the Internet Services by his or her office and to ensure that the use of the services is consistent with the requirements established by this policy and applicable laws and regulations.

4. Official records may not be placed on the Internet Servers unless otherwise approved by the Secretary of the Senate and prepared in accordance with Section 501 of Title 44 of the United States Code. Such records include, but are not limited to: bills, public laws, committee reports, and other legislative materials.

B. Posting or Linking to the Following Matter Is Prohibited

1. Political Matter

    a. Matter which specifically solicits political support for the sender or any other person or political party, or a vote or financial assistance for any candidate for any political office is prohibited.

    b. Matter which mentions a Senator or an employee of a Senator as a candidate for political office, or which constitutes electioneering, or which advocates the election or defeat of any individuals, or a political party is prohibited.

2. Personal Matter

    a. Matter which by its nature is purely personal and is unrelated to the official business activities and duties of the sender is prohibited.

    b. Matter which constitutes or includes any article, account, sketch, narration, or other text laudatory and complimentary of any Senator on a purely personal or political basis rather than on the basis of performance of official duties as a Senator is prohibited.

    c. Reports of how or when a Senator, the Senator's spouse, or any other member of the Senator's family spends time other than in the performance of, or in connection with, the legislative, representative, and other official functions of such Senator is prohibited.

    d. Any transmission expressing holiday greetings from a Senator is prohibited. This prohibition does not preclude an expression of holiday greetings at the commencement or conclusion of an otherwise proper transmission.

(Continued)

Table 8. Tier 2 Sample Internet Usage Policy (Continued)

3.   Promotional Matter
    a.   The solicitation of funds for any purpose is prohibited.
    b.   The placement of logos or links used for personal, promotional, commercial, or partisan political/campaign purposes is prohibited.
C.   Restrictions on the Use of Internet Services
1.   During the 60-day period immediately preceding the date of any primary or general election (whether regular, special, or runoff) for any national, state, or local office in which the Senator is a candidate, no Member may place, update, or transmit information using a Senate Internet Server ("FTP Server, Gopher, and World Wide Web") unless the candidacy of the Senator in such election is uncontested.
2.   Electronic mail may not be transmitted by a Member during the 60-day period before the date of the Member's primary or general election unless it is in response to a direct inquiry.
3.   During the 60-day period immediately before the date of a biennial general Federal election, no Member may place or update on the Internet Server any matter on behalf of a Senator who is a candidate for election, unless the candidacy of the Senator in such election is uncontested.
4.   An uncontested candidacy is established when the Rules Committee receives written certification from the appropriate state official that the Senator's candidacy may not be contested under state law. Since the candidacy of a Senator who is running for re-election from a state which permits write-in votes on election day without prior registration or other advance qualification by the candidate may be contested, such a Member is subject to the above restrictions.
5.   If a Member is under the restrictions as defined in subtitle C, paragraph (1), above, the following statement must appear on the homepage: ("Pursuant to Senate policy this homepage may not be updated for the 60-day period immediately before the date of a primary or general election"). The words "Senate Policy" must be hypertext linked to the Internet services policy on the Senate Home Page.
6.   A Senator's homepage may not refer or be hypertext linked to another Member's site or electronic mail address without authorization from that Member.
7.   Any Links to Information not located on a Senate Internet Server must be identified as a link to a non-Senate server.

When writing policies, it is important to use the language that is accepted at your organization. When I worked for a global manufacturing corporation, we learned that the term "should" meant "must." It was known as a "Company should." That meant that whenever you saw the word "should" in a policy, standard, or procedure, you were to consider it to be mandatory. The company felt that use of the term "must" was harsh. So, it would substitute a less harsh term to make the requirement more palatable. The term "shall" meant that the reader had an option to use whatever was discussed or not. So, for this company, "should" meant "standard" and "shall" meant "guideline."

Table 9. Sample Internet Usage Policy 2

Internet Usage Policy
Overview

The Brother's Institute will provide access to the information resources of the Internet to assist in supporting teaching and learning, research, and information handling skills. This represents a considerable commitment of Institute resources in the areas of telecommunications, networking, software, storage, and cost.

This Internet Usage Policy is designed to outline for staff and students the conditions of use for these resources.

General

Internet access is provided as an information and learning tool and is to be used for Institute- and curriculum-related purposes only.

All existing Institute policies and regulations apply to a user's conduct on the Internet, especially (but not exclusively) those that deal with unacceptable behavior, privacy, misuse of Institute resources, sexual harassment, information and data security, and confidentiality.

The Institute has software systems that can monitor and record all Internet usage, and record each chat, newsgroup, or e-mail message. The Institute reserves the right to do this at any time. No user should have any expectation of privacy as to his or her Internet usage.

The Institute reserves the right to inspect any and all files stored on the network in order to ensure compliance with Institute policies.

The Institute will use independently supplied software and data to identify inappropriate or sexually explicit Internet sites. We will block access from within our networks to all such sites that we know of.

If you find yourself connected accidentally to a site that contains sexually explicit or offensive material, you must disconnect from that site immediately, regardless of whether that site had been previously deemed acceptable by any screening or rating program.

No user may use the Institute's Internet facilities to deliberately disable or overload any computer system or network, or to circumvent any system intended to protect the privacy or security of another user.

File Downloading

Any software or files downloaded via the Internet onto the Institute network become the property of the Institute.

Any such files or software may be used only in ways that are consistent with their licenses or copyrights.

No user may use Institute facilities knowingly to download or distribute illegal software or data. The use of Institute resources for illegal activity will be grounds for immediate dismissal.

Any file that is downloaded must be scanned for viruses before it is run or accessed.

No user may use the Institute's Internet facilities to deliberately propagate any virus.

Video and audio streaming and downloading represent significant data traffic, which can cause local network congestion. Video and audio downloading are prohibited unless for agreed demonstration purposes.

(Continued)

Table 9. Sample Internet Usage Policy 2 (Continued)

Chats, Newsgroups, and E-Mail

Each user of the Internet facilities must identify him or herself honestly, accurately, and completely (including Institute status and function if requested) when participating in chats or newsgroups, or when setting up accounts on outside computer systems.

Only those users who are duly authorized to speak to the media on behalf of the Institute may speak or write in the name of the Institute to any newsgroup or Web site.

Other users may participate in newsgroups or chats in the course of information research when relevant to their duties, but they do so as individuals, speaking only for themselves.

The Institute retains the copyright to any material posted to any forum, newsgroup, chat, or World Wide Web page by any employee in the course of his or her duties.

Users are reminded that chats and newsgroups are public forums and it is inappropriate to reveal confidential Institute information.

Offensive material should not be e-mailed. Anyone found doing this will be subject to severe disciplinary action.

Passwords and IDs

Any user who obtains a password or ID for an Internet resource must keep that password confidential.

User IDs and passwords will help maintain individual accountability for Internet resource usage.

The sharing of user IDs or passwords obtained for access to Internet sites is prohibited.

Security

The Institute has installed routers, firewalls, proxies, Internet address screening programs, and other security systems to assure the safety and security of the Institute's networks. Any user who attempts to disable, defeat, or circumvent any Institute security facility will be subject to disciplinary action.

Only those Internet services and functions which have been documented for education purposes within the Institute will be enabled at the Internet firewall.

Computers that use their own modems to create independent data connections sidestep our network security mechanisms. Therefore, any computer used for independent dial-up or leased-line connections to any outside computer or network must be physically isolated from the Institute's internal networks.

Any machine used for FTP must not contain any sensitive applications or data, and Java will be disabled for users or networks running mission-critical applications such as the production of core financial and student information.

Statement of Compliance

"I have read the Institute's Internet usage policy. I fully understand the terms of this policy and agree to abide by them. I realize that the Institute's security software may record for management use the Internet address of any site I visit and keep a record of any network activity in which I transmit or receive any kind of file. I acknowledge that any message I send or receive may be recorded and stored in an archive file for management use. I know that any violation of this policy may lead to disciplinary action being taken."

Table 10. Sample Internet Usage and Responsibility Statement

Internet Usage and Responsibility Statement

I, _____, acknowledge and understand that access to the Internet, as provided by the Company, is for management-approved use only. This supports Peltier Associates policies on *Employee Standards of Conduct* and *Information Classification*, and among other things, prohibits the downloading of games, viruses, inappropriate materials or picture files, and unlicensed software from the Internet.

I recognize and accept that while accessing the Internet, I am responsible for maintaining the highest professional and ethical standards, as outlined in the Company policy on *Employee Standards of Conduct*.

I have read and understand the policies mentioned above and accept my responsibility to protect the Company's information and reputation.

Name _____ Date _____

Research the writing requirements of your organization and make certain you incorporate any idiosyncrasies into your writing. By understanding the form, you will be better able to ensure that the substance is read and accepted.

The sample e-mail policy in Table 12 has some problems. The opening paragraph is not as strong as the one contained in sample 1 (Table 11). Items 1 and 7 discuss business need for using the e-mail system. I strongly recommend that when writing a policy, try to avoid the term "for company business only." We all know that e-mail and Internet access will be used at times for personal communications or research. The real intent is to prohibit the improper use of these business tools. Look at these forms of communications as you would the use of company-provided phones. Be consistent in your requirements. If the phone on an employee's desk is to be used for company business only and this policy is enforced, then it is safe to use that language for other forms of communications. However, if the phone system use policy allows for limited employee personal use, then the other communication-related policies should reflect this concept. A better term would be "for management-approved activities."

Items 3, 6, and 8 discuss privacy issues for the company and the company's right to monitor activities. When developing this kind of concept, be sure to include the legal staff and human resources in the review of the policy language.

I have to admit that I do not care for item 5. It goes against all that we know about passwords and defeats any attempt to bring individual accountability into the company culture. If employees are to create confidential passwords that are required to be given to "the Company," then there is no individual accountability. Breaching the confidentiality of the password makes it now public domain.

Table 11. E-Mail Usage Policy: Sample 1

Company E-Mail Usage Policy
Policy
Company e-mail services are provided for official Company business use. Personal e-mail is not official Company business, although minimal use of e-mail for personal communication is acceptable. E-mail may be monitored by authorized system administrators. Abuse of the Company e-mail policy, outlined herein, will be brought to the attention of the department director and may result in disciplinary action.

E-Mail Guidelines
1. All users of the Company e-mail system are expected to conduct themselves in a legal, professional, and ethical manner.
2. Users are responsible for their information technology accounts, and may be held accountable if someone uses their account with permission and violates policy.
3. The Company e-mail system shall be used in accordance with Federal and State law and Company policies, and may not be used as a vehicle to harass or intimidate.
4. Company information technology resources are provided to employees for the purpose of business, research, service, and other work-related activities. Access to information technology resources is granted to an individual by the Company for that individual's sole use, the use of which must be in furtherance of the mission and purpose of the Company. Information technology resources must be shared among users in an equitable manner. The user may not participate in any behavior that unreasonably interferes with the fair use of information technology resources by another.
5. The Company reserves the right, without notice, to temporarily limit or restrict any individual's use and to inspect, copy, remove, or otherwise alter any data, file, or system resource which may undermine the authorized use of any information technology facility. This is intended to protect the integrity of the Company's information technology facilities and its users against unauthorized or improper use.
6. Users must use only those information technology resources that the Company has authorized for their individual use. Users are authorized to access, use, copy, modify, or delete files and data on their own account. Users are not authorized to perform any of these functions on another user's account or a Company system.
7. User privacy is not to be violated. It is the responsibility of the user to protect their privacy. Users should not leave a password where it can be easily found, give a password to someone else, leave confidential information on a screen where it could be viewed by an unauthorized person, or leave a public PC or terminal signed on and unattended.

(continued)

Table 11. E-Mail Usage Policy: Sample 1 (Continued)

8. Non-business-related chain e-mail messages are not to be forwarded using any Company resource. Chain e-mail is defined as any message sent to one or more people that instructs the recipient to forward it to multiple others and contains some promise of reward for forwarding it or threat of punishment for not doing so. Chain e-mail messages can have technological, social, and legal ramifications. Chain e-mail messages have the ability to clog an entire network and degrade the ability of employees to do their work. Heavy traffic due to chain mail messages can disrupt not only the e-mail service by other network activities as well.

9. Users may not intentionally obscure, change, or forge the date, time, physical source, logical source, or other label or header information on electronic mail, files, or reports.

Departments should contact the ISD Help Desk to report all problems with e-mail.

In the section titled "Sample Topic-Specific Policies," we have assembled draft copies of Tier 2 policies that support the ISO 17799 areas of concern. These sample Tier 2 policies are intended to be used as a guide for language and possible content. As with any policy examples, please read them carefully and make certain that they are appropriate for your organization.

7.3 Application-Specific Policy (Tier 3)

Global-level (Tier 1) and topic-specific (Tier 2) policies address policy on a broad level; they usually encompass the entire enterprise (see Figure 4). The application-specific (Tier 3) policy focuses on one specific system or application. As the construction of an organization information security architecture takes shape, the final element will be the translation of Tier 1 and Tier 2 policies down to the application and system level.

Many security issue decisions apply only at the application or system level. Some examples of these issues include:

- Who has the authority to read or modify data?
- Under what circumstances can data be read or modified?
- How is remote access controlled?

To develop a comprehensive set of Tier 3 policies, use a process that determines security requirements from a business or mission objective. Try to avoid implementing requirements based on security issues and concerns. Remember that the security staff has been empowered to support the business process of the organization. Typically, the Tier 3 policy is more free-form than Tier 1 and Tier 2 policies. As you prepare to create Tier 3 policies, keep in mind the following concepts:

- Understand the overall business objectives or mission of the enterprise.

Table 12. E-Mail Usage Policy: Sample 2

Electronic Mail Policy

Every company employee is responsible for ensuring that the electronic mail ("e-mail")
system is used properly and in accordance with this policy. Any questions about this
policy should be directed either to the Human Resources department or to the
Company's E-Mail Administrator.

1. The E-Mail system of the Company is part of the business equipment and
technology platform and should be used for Company purposes only. Personal
business should not be conducted by means of the E-Mail system.
2. Employees should disclose information or messages from the E-Mail system only
to authorized employees.
3. Employees do not have a personal privacy right in any matter created on,
received through, or sent from the Company E-Mail system. Employees should
not enter personal matters into the E-Mail system. The Company, in its
discretion, reserves the right to monitor and to access any matter created on,
received through, or sent from the E-Mail system.
4. No messages or information should be entered into the Company E-Mail system
without a good business reason for doing so. Copies of e-mail messages should
be sent only for good business reasons.
5. Even if you have a password for the E-Mail system, it is impossible to assure the
confidentiality of any message created on, received through, or sent from the
Company E-Mail system. Any password you use must be known to the Company,
as the Company may need to access this information in your absence.
6. The provisions of the Company's no solicitation-no distribution policy (see
Employee Handbook) apply fully to the E-Mail system.
7. No e-mail message should be created or sent that may constitute intimidating,
hostile, or offensive material on the basis of sex, race, color, religion, national
origin, sexual orientation, or disability. The Company's Policy against sexual or
other harassment applies fully to the E-Mail system, and any violation of that
policy is grounds for discipline up to and including discharge.
8. The Company expressly reserves the right to access, retrieve, read, and delete
any communication that is created on, received through, or sent in the E-Mail
system to assure compliance with this or any other Company policy.
9. Any employee who becomes aware of misuse of the E-Mail system should
promptly contact either the Human Resources department or the E-Mail
Administrator.
10. Your signature indicates your understanding of this policy and your consent to its
contents.

- Understand the mission of the application or system.
- Establish requirements that support both sets of objectives.

Typical Tier 3 polices may be as brief as the example in Table 13.

The Tier 3 policy in Table 14 is brief and to the point. It establishes what
is required, who is responsible, and where to go for additional information
and help.

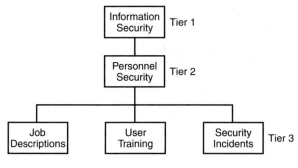

Figure 4. Tiers 1, 2, and 3

Table 13. Sample Application-Specific Policy

Accounts Payable Policy

Accounts payable checks are issued on Friday only. This will promote efficiency in the accounts payable function. To ensure your check is available, please have your check request and/or invoice to the Financial Affairs office by the close of business on Monday.

For access to the online portion of the Accounts Payable System (APS), please contact the APS System Administrator.

The APS Customer Help Desk is available to answer any additional questions.

We appreciate your cooperation.

We can use this (Table 14) policy to point out a few items that typically make for bad reading in a policy. When writing, try to avoid making words stand out. This is particularly true of words that cause people to react negatively. In this policy, the writer likes to use bold words for emphasis. "MUST," "LATE TIMECARDS," "YOU MUST BE ACCURATE." I find that when words appear like this, the writer was in an agitated state and was taking out his or her personal frustration on the policy. Although what was said in this policy was fairly good, the tone was very negative. The person who wrote this policy probably has a sign posted in his work area that reads "Poor planning on your part does not make it a crisis on my part."

When I do network vulnerability assessments for companies, I like to do a physical walk-though of the work area. I am on the lookout for what I call the "Dilbert factor." This comic strip has given us many a great laugh because we realize that it is our working environment that Scott Adams is identifying. However, be on the lookout for areas that have a high number of Dilbert cartoons posted. This is usually an area of employees who are unhappy with someone or something in the work area. These are the people who might write a policy like the one above.

Table 14. Sample Timecard Policy and Instructions

Timecard Policy and Instructions

An original timecard/timesheet MUST be turned in before your hours can be processed. Hours MUST be turned in before 10:00 a.m. on Monday to have your paycheck/direct deposit slip available on Thursday. If your time card is turned in after noon on Wednesday, you will be paid the following week. We CANNOT guarantee paycheck availability for LATE TIMECARDS.

The timecard is our invoice; YOU MUST BE ACCURATE!

As with most BOX Group clients, you must work 40 straight time hours in a week before you can get overtime pay. All hours should be listed in the regular hours column until you reach 40. After you have worked 40, all hours should go in the overtime column. Overtime (premium rates) are based upon the terms of BOX Group's purchase order and any applicable tax codes. Because of this, policy may vary from company to company or depending upon your position, pay rate, etc. Specific overtime rates will be discussed and agreed upon prior to starting your assignment. If you have any questions regarding overtime, contact your branch office.

When you do not work a full 40 hours straight time during the week, Saturday's hours must go toward straight time until you reach the necessary 40 hours.

ONLY write the hours you actually work on the timecard.

When you have a week in which a holiday occurs, you should leave the space blank instead of hours in the regular hours column. The hours for a holiday are not counted toward your total hours worked for that week. If no overtime hours are worked this week, your timecard total would be 32 hours. During a week in which a holiday occurs, most BOX Group clients pay overtime over 32 hours in that week.

If you miss a day of work, hours should not be entered for that day.

Copies of timecard: (Client timecard copies differ.)

Yellow/White Copies: Payroll/Invoice copies. Return to BOX Group

Pink Copy: Branch copy. Return to BOX Group

Blue Copy: Customer copy. Company you are working for/Supervisor

Goldenrod Copy: Employee copy. Keep your copy.

IMPORTANT! Please note that your check will not be generated without the original timecard.

This policy is written in a condescending manner and gives the impression that these highly skilled contractors are dummies. Write in a positive tone and instruct the reader as to what is expected. It is important to identify the consequences of noncompliance, but channel that into a specific subsection that identifies "Noncompliance."

8   ADDITIONAL HINTS

To have even the slightest hope of being successful, the policy must receive some level of visibility. Visibility takes a number of forms. The first, and probably most important form, will be management support. The issue of information security is not contained within the Information Systems organization. It is an enterprisewide concern and, thus, any policy relating to the protection and security of organization information must come from the highest possible level within the enterprise. In Chapter 9, "Understanding How to Sell the Policies, Standards, and Procedures," strategies used to gain management and employee support are discussed. For now, one should begin to formulate a plan on how to get senior management support.

As discussed in Chapter 2, one needs a communication plan to take the message policy and all of its ramifications to the employees. This plan should include an employee awareness program. The program should include all existing and incoming (new hires) employees. If the organization wants contract personnel to be compliant with the policies, then this must first be negotiated through the language of the contract. It is permissible to include contract personnel in the list of those who must comply with the policy; however, the actual compliance piece must be included in the language of the purchase order and the contract.

9 PITFALLS TO AVOID

"Effective policy statement" is not an oxymoron. If properly drafted, a policy statement can actually improve productivity rather than add to organizational overhead. The following is a ten-step approach to help improve the likelihood of having a successful policy implementation process.

1. *Review existing policies.* Before writing a new policy, review what already exists. It is easier to update an existing policy than to gain acceptance of a totally new concept.
2. *Make the organization's business objectives or mission an active part of the policy.* There is a reason that policies are created, and that is to support the activities of the enterprise. To help gain acceptance, use the language in your organization's "Shared Beliefs" or "Corporate Vision" section of the policy statement.
3. *Make policies look like policies.* Take the time to ensure that whatever is created looks like existing policies. All too often, the message gets lost because the format is unfamiliar. Save the development team some grief and research the policy format of the organization.
4. *Watch out for grammar and spelling.* The worst thing that one can do is send out a draft document that has not been edited for spelling and grammar. Show the user community that proper care has been taken, by looking out for the "little" things; the chances of success will be increased.
5. *Streamline the language.* Most advanced writing courses have the students explore all the elements of language. Painting pictures through the use of prose: while this might be effective in a class in writing fiction, it will not help in a policy document.

6. *Security is not attainable.* Be realistic about policy implementation. The most secure computer system is one that is turned off, locked away, and unplugged. A computer in this condition is secure but productivity is probably going to be impacted. Seek out an acceptable level of security.

7. *Remember the audience.* Whenever writing, remember who the intended audience is. The majority of the readers will not be technical or security professionals. Ensure that the words are understandable.

8. *Sell the policy prior to introduction.* This is discussed later; but for now, remember that senior management must be fully aware of the policy and understand how it applies to their organization before it is submitted to them for approval.

9. *Keep the message brief.* Long-winded or complicated policies often lead to trouble. Keep the policy as simple as possible. This will allow for a limited variation on interpretation and, by being brief, there will be a better chance that someone will actually read the policy.

10. *Take the message to the people.* Be prepared to develop employee awareness programs for the implementation of the policy.

10 SUMMARY

The policy is the cornerstone of an organization's information security architecture. A policy is important to establish, both internally and externally, what an organization's position on a particular topic might be.

This chapter defined what a policy is and what it is not. Also included were definitions for:

- Policy
- Standard
- Guideline
- Procedure

Next, there was an examination of the key elements of a policy:

- Be easy to understand
- Be applicable
- Be do-able
- Be enforceable
- Be phased in
- Be proactive
- Avoid absolutes
- Meet business objectives

This chapter also provided a review of what the policy format might be and then discussed the three basic types of policy:

INFORMATION SECURITY POLICIES AND PROCEDURES

1. Program policy
2. Topic-specific policy
3. Application-specific policy

The chapter also looked at the policy content and a checklist based on the elements found in a journalism class:

- *What:* the intent of the policy
- *Who:* employee responsibilities and obligations
- *Where:* the scope of the policy
- *How:* compliance
- *When:* when the policy takes effect
- *Why:* the selling of the policy

Finally, five actual policy statements were examined and critiqued, based on the checklist and some helpful hints and pitfalls to avoid.

Chapter 5
Asset Classification Policy

1   INTRODUCTION

With the U.S. Congress on full alert regarding the protection of information assets and the international community certifying organizations to information security standards, the requirement for an asset classification policy is at hand. As a security professional, it is important to know that an asset or information classification policy is only one element in the overall information management process. The Information Classification Policy must be coupled with a Records Management Policy.

Any security standard or best practice must be founded on a solid foundation of an asset classification. To ensure proper protection of our information resources, it is necessary to define what an owner is and how that entity has ultimate responsibility for the information assets within its business unit; this includes classification and assigning retention requirements. By implementing an asset management scheme and supporting methodology, we are able to determine required controls commensurate with the sensitivity of the information as classified by the owner.

This chapter explores the need for both policies, examines the contents of these policies, and then critiques various examples of these policies.

2   OVERVIEW

Information is an asset and the property of the organization. All employees are to protect information from unauthorized access, modification, disclosure, and destruction. Before employees can be expected to protect information, they must first understand what they have. An information classification policy and methodology will provide them with the help they need.

There are four essential aspects of information classification: (1) information classification from a legal standpoint, (2) responsibility for care and control of information, (3) integrity of the information, and (4) the criticality of the information and systems processing the information. Examples of how the classification process fits into the application and system development life cycle are presented to assist you in the development of your own information classification process.

As discussed later in this chapter, information classification is only one of the elements in an effective information management program. Knowing what we have and how important it is to the organization is key to the success for the information security program. The implementation of this program will require that representatives of the organization be charged with exercising the organization's proprietary rights. In addition, a full inventory of these assets must be conducted with a requirement for annual review established.

3   WHY CLASSIFY INFORMATION?

Organizations classify information in an effort to establish the appropriate levels of protection for these resources (see Figure 1). Because resources are limited, it will be necessary to prioritize and identify what really needs protection. One of the reasons to classify information is to ensure that scarce resources exist where they will do the most good. The return on investment for implementing an encryption system to protect public domain information would not be considered a sound business decision. All information is created equal, but not all information is of equal value.

Of all the information found within an enterprise, only about ten percent of it is actually competitive advantage, trade secret, or personal information. The biggest portion of organization information is that which employees must access in order to do their assigned tasks. The remaining information is that which has been available to the public through authorized channels. Information resources that are classified as public would include annual stockholders' reports, press releases, and other authorized public announcements.

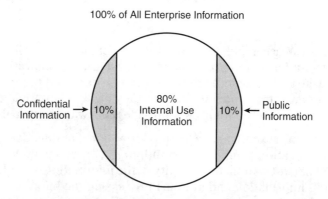

Figure 1. Information Classification Breakdown

An effective way of understanding the difference between internal use information and public information is to picture your organization's connection to the Internet. The Web site and information contained on it that is outside your zone of protection is your public information. Remember that posting information to the public Web site is only done by the Webmaster and with approval of the owner of the information. This is your organization's Internet connection.

The portion of Internet access that is behind your zone of protection and contains information for use by employees is your intranet connection. This area contains information that is unavailable to the outside world but has been made accessible to employees for use while performing their assigned tasks.

For years the information handling standard was that all information is closed until the owner opens it. This worked well in the mainframe environment when access control packages ruled the single platform of information processing. With the introduction of the client/server environment and the multiple platforms operating situation, no one access control package could handle all the needs. With decentralized processing and then the move to connect to the Internet, the restrictions on information closure began to weaken. The operating concept during this period was that all information was open until the owner classified it and closed access to it.

Now we have gone full circle. As the decentralized processing environment matures and national and international laws, statutes, and privacy concerns become stronger, the information protection concept was reverted to all information access is closed until the owner opens access. For this to be effective and to allow the organization to demonstrate due diligence, it is incumbent for the organization to establish an effective information classification policy and support handling standards.

Most organizations do not have information that is all the same value or sensitivity. It is necessary to at least develop an initial high-level attempt at classification. This should be done if for no other reason than to ensure that budgeted resources are not misused in over-protecting nonsensitive, noncritical information assets. Before employees can protect information assets, they must first have a policy that identifies classification levels and then a methodology to implement the policy requirements. An information classification policy that is not overly complex and a methodology that relies on common sense and is facilitated by either information security or records management will make acceptance possible.

4 WHAT IS INFORMATION CLASSIFICATION?

An information or asset classification process is a business decision process. Information is an asset of the organization and managers have been charged with protecting and accounting for proper use of all assets. An information classification process will allow managers to meet this fiduciary responsibility. The role of the information security professional or even information systems personnel is one of advice and consulting. The final decision is made by the business unit managers or, as we will define soon, the asset owner.

When preparing to develop the information classification policy, it is important to get input from the management team. As discussed in previous chapters, knowing what management really wants will improve the quality of the overall policy. It is important that you ask questions to find out what they mean. When my daughter was about seven or eight years old, she came to me and asked, "Pa (that is what she calls me), where do we come from?" Well, I pretended to not hear her so I could research my answer. The next day I sat down with her and discussed the "facts of life" with her. She looked at me and said, "I know all that. What I want to know is where we come from. Terri Lynn comes from Tennessee and Pam comes from Kentucky." So before you develop an answer, make sure you understand the question.

When conducting interviews with management and other key personnel, develop a set of questions to ensure a consistency in the direction of the responses. These questions might include some of the following:

- What are the mission-critical or sensitive activities or operations?
- Where is mission-critical or sensitive information stored?
- Where is this information processed?
- Who requires access to this information?

There are no hard-and-fast rules for determining what constitutes sensitive information. In some instances, it may be that the number of people who require access may affect the classification. The real test of an information classification system is how easy is it for the reader to understand what constitutes sensitive information and what organization-approved label should be affixed to the information asset resource.

5   WHERE TO BEGIN?

After you have a clearer idea of what management is expecting, it is time to do some research. I like to contact my fellow information security professionals and find out what they have done to answer the problems I have been assigned. By being a member of the Computer Security Institute (CSI), the Information System Security Association (ISSA), and the Information Systems Audit and Control Association (ISACA), I have a ready access to people in my area who are usually willing to share examples of their work.

When developing classification levels, I prefer to discuss the topic with fellow professionals. I recommend that you cultivate contacts in similar business environments and see what your peers are doing. The Internet can generate some examples of classification policies, but many of them are university or government-agency-related. Be careful of what you uncover in your research; while there are many good ideas and terms out there, they are only good if they are applicable to your specific needs.

Use the information you gather from fellow professionals as a starting point. Your organization will have its own unique variation on the classification policy and categories. We examine a number of examples of information categories in the subsequent subsection. If you are a government agency, or do work for a government agency, be sure to check with your regulatory affairs group to see if there are any government-imposed requirements.

5.1   Information Classification Category Examples

Using the information in Tables 1 and 2, the manager can determine the level of criticality of an information asset.

The service provider shown in Table 3 has established five categories to be used by managers in classifying information assets. Part of the reason for their use of these categories is that they have experience with Department of Defense contracts and have become accustomed to certain classification levels. The concern I have with patterning a policy after a government standard is that there might be confusion regarding what is government contact information and what is normal business information. Also, the number of employees exposed to the government standards may impact the drafting of these standards.

I recently discussed the classification scheme shown in Table 4 with the company that created it to find out how they use the color coding. The sample "Information Security Handbook" included in this book also uses color codes for information classification. The company does not actually use the colors to color-code the documents. Instead, the company identifies the level of classification but requires the footer to contain "Company Red" or whatever color. It gives a good visual for the employees.

The company in Table 5 also requires that specific levels of information contain appropriate markings to identify it as classified information. We discuss an Information Handling Matrix later in this chapter. When you create your organization's handling requirements, use the following as thought starters:

- MAKE NO COPIES
- THIRD-PARTY CONFIDENTIAL
- ATTORNEY–CLIENT PRIVILEGED DOCUMENT
- DISTRIBUTION LIMITED TO _____
- COVERED BY A NON-ANALYSIS AGREEMENT

INFORMATION SECURITY POLICIES AND PROCEDURES

Table 1. Information Classification Category Example 1

Mega Oil Corporation

HIGHLY CONFIDENTIAL — Information whose unauthorized disclosure will cause the corporation severe financial, legal, or reputation damage. Examples: acquisitions data, bid details, and contract negotiation strategies.

CONFIDENTIAL — Information whose unauthorized disclosure may cause the corporation financial, legal, or reputation damage. Examples: employee personnel and payroll files, and competitive advantage information.

GENERAL — Information that, because of its personal, technical, or business sensitivity, is restricted for use within the company. Unless otherwise classified, all information within Mega Oil Corporation is in this category.

At this point in the classification scheme, this company has included a mechanism to establish the criticality of the information. It has established its three information classification categories and now adds three impact categories. Using these sets of definitions, the manager of the information resources will be able to determine how critical the asset is to the company.

MAXIMUM — Information whose unauthorized modification and destruction will cause the company severe financial, legal, or reputation damage.

MEDIUM — Information whose unauthorized modification and destruction may cause the company financial, legal, or reputation damage. Examples: electronic funds, transfer, payroll, and commercial checks.

MINIMUM — Although an error in this data would be of minimal consequence, this is still important company information and therefore will require some minimal controls to ensure a minimal level of assurance that the integrity of the data is maintained. This applies to all data that is not placed in one of the above classifications. Examples: lease production data, expense data, financial data, and exploration data.

CRITICAL — It is important to assess the availability requirements of data, applications, and systems. A business decision will be required to determine the length of unavailability that can be tolerated prior to expending additional resources to ensure the information availability that is required. Information should be labeled "CRITICAL" if it is determined that special procedures should be used to ensure its availability.

Table 2. Criticality Matrix

		Clasification Level		
		Highly Confidential	**Confidential**	**General**
Business Impact	Maximum	1	2	3
	Medium	2	2	3
	Minimum	2	3	4

1: Availability safeguards must be implemented.

2: Availability safeguards should be implemented.

3: Continue to monitor availability requirements.

4: No additional action is required at this time.

Table 3. Information Classification Category Example 2

International Service Provider

Top Secret — Information that, if disclosed, could cause severe impact to the company's competitive advantage or business strategies.

Confidential — Information that, if disclosed, could violate the privacy of individuals, reduce competitive advantage, or damage the company.

Restricted — Information that is available to a specific subset of the employee population when conducting company business.

Internal Use — Information that is intended for use by all employees when conducting company business.

Public — Information that has been made available to the public through authorized company channels.

Table 4. Information Classification Category Example 3

Global Manufacturer

Company Confidential Red — Provides a significant competitive advantage. Disclosure would cause severe damage to operations. Relates to or describes a long-term strategy or critical business plans. Disclosure would cause regulatory or contractual liability. Disclosure would cause severe damage to our reputation or the public image. Disclosure would cause a severe loss of market share or the ability to be first to market. Disclosure would cause a loss of an important customer, shareholder, or business partner. Disclosure would cause a long-term or severe drop in stock value. Strong likelihood somebody is seeking to acquire this information.

Company Confidential Yellow — Provides a competitive advantage. Disclosure could cause moderate damage to the company or an individual. Relates to or describes an important part of the operational direction of the company over time. Provides important technical or financial aspects of a product line or a business unit. Disclosure could cause a loss of Customer or Shareholder confidence. Disclosure could cause a temporary drop in stock value. Very likely that some third party would seek to acquire this information.

Company Confidential Green — Might provide a business advantage over those who do not have access to the same information. Might be useful to a competitor. Not easily identifiable by inspection of a product. Not generally known outside the company or available from public sources. Generally available internally. Little competitive interest.

Company Public — Would not provide a business or competitive advantage. Routinely made available to interested members of the General Public. Little or no competitive interest.

6   RESIST THE URGE TO ADD CATEGORIES

Keep the number of information classification categories to a minimum. If two possible categories do not require substantially different treatment, then combine them. The more categories available, the greater the chance

Table 5. Information Classification Category Example 4

Company CONFIDENTIAL — A subset of Company Internal information, the
  unauthorized disclosure or compromise of which would likely have an adverse
  impact on the company's competitive position, tarnish its reputation, or embarrass
  an individual. Examples: customer, financial, pricing, or personnel data;
  merger/acquisition, product, or marketing plans; new product designs, proprietary
  processes, and systems.

Company INTERNAL — All forms of proprietary information originated or owned by
  the Company, or entrusted to it by others. Examples: organization charts, policies,
  procedures, phone directories, some types of training materials.

Company PUBLIC — Information officially released by the Company for widespread
  public disclosure. Example: press releases, public marketing materials, employment
  advertising, annual reports, product brochures, the public Web site, etc.

---

for confusion among managers and employees. Normally, three or four categories should be sufficient to meet the organization's needs.

Additionally, avoid the impulse to classify everything the same. To simplify the classification process, some organizations have flirted with having everything classified as confidential. The problem with this concept is that confidential information requires special handling. This would violate the concept of placing controls only where they are actually needed, and would require the organization to waste limited resources protecting assets that do not really require that level of control.

Another pitfall to avoid is to take the information classification categories developed by another enterprise and adopt them verbatim as one's own. Use the information created by other organizations to assist in the creation of the organization's unique set of categories and definitions.

In some government sectors, there are five categories for information classification (Top Secret, Secret, Confidential, Restricted, and Unclassified). In addition to these categories, there are additional impact levels of Sensitive and Nonsensitive. Using this scheme, it would be possible to have an information asset of higher concern if it is classified *Restricted/Sensitive* compared to one that was classified *Confidential/Nonsensitive*. In addition, information labeled as *Unclassified* has the classification level of *Unclassified*, so it has actually been classified. Sometimes I think Joseph Heller in *Catch 22* actually established a guideline for government and industry to use when developing standards and policies.

7   WHAT CONSTITUTES CONFIDENTIAL INFORMATION?

There are a number of ways to look at information that may be classified as confidential. A number of statements relating to confidential information are examined below. The first is a general statement about sensitive information.

For a general definition of what might constitute confidential information, it may be sufficient to define such information as:

Information if disclosed could violate the privacy of individuals, reduce the company's competitive advantage, or cause damage to the organization.

The Economic Espionage Act of 1996 (EEA) defines "trade secret" information to include "all forms and types of financial, business, scientific, technical, economic, or engineering information," regardless of "how it is stored, complied, or memorialized." The EEA criminalizes the actions of anyone who:

- Steals or, without authorization, appropriates, takes, carries away, or conceals, or by fraud, artifice, or deception obtains a trade secret
- Without authorization, copies, duplicates, sketches, draws, photographs, downloads, uploads, alters, destroys, photocopies, replicates, transmits, delivers, sends, mails, communicates, or conveys a trade secret
- Receives, buys, or possesses a trade secret, knowing the same to have been stolen or appropriated, obtained, or converted without authorization
- Conspires with one or more other persons to commit any offense described in any part of the EEA under the heading "conspiracy"

The information classification policy that you will be developing will discuss organization-confidential information. Typically, this type of information will consist of either competitive-advantage or trade secret information or personal information.

The laws regarding trade secret information were developed from the duty of good faith imposed generally in commercial dealings. A trade secret is commonly defined as information deriving actual or potential economic value by virtue of its not being readily ascertainable through proper means by the public, and which is the subject of reasonable efforts to maintain its secrecy. The legal system protects the owner (in our case, the organization) from someone who uses improper means to learn the trade secret, either directly or indirectly. Therefore, anyone using improper means to learn the trade secret has breached a duty of good faith dealing with the trade secret owner.

The breach of that duty of good faith usually takes the form of an abuse of a confidence, the use of improper means to ascertain the secret, or a breach of contract. Anyone involved in the breach of that duty is liable for trade secret stealing.

The laws are requirements governing trade secret and competitive-advantage information, are well established, and offer substantial penalties for noncompliance (see Figure 2). The area of personal information has

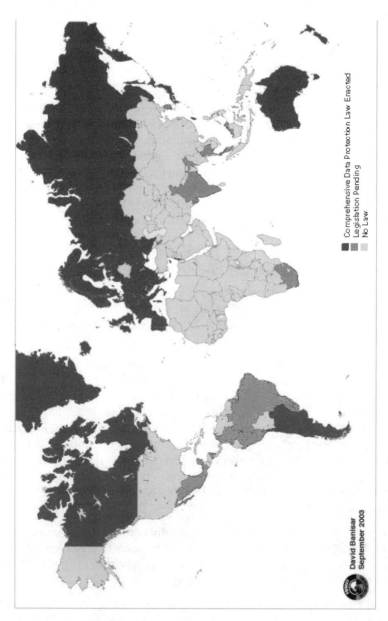

Figure 2. Data Protection Laws around the World. *Source:* Privacy International. Used with permission.

become hotter during the past couple of years. The passage of the Health Insurance Portability and Accountability Act (HIPAA), Gramm–Leach–Bliley Act (GLBA), European Union privacy laws, and organizations such as Privacy International are working to increase the safeguards required for personal information.

Any policy and supporting standards on information classification levels must take into account not only the trade secret and competitive-advantage information, but must also include any personal information about employees, customers, clients, and other third parties.

Earlier in this chapter we examined a number of examples of information classification categories. Now we discuss one other important element: the role of employees in the information classification process.

8 EMPLOYEE RESPONSIBILITIES

When I was doing research for this section of the book, I came across the following policy statement:

> The **"Information Owner"** means the party who <u>confides</u> the referenced <u>Confidential Information</u> to the other party, the <u>Confidant</u>. Despite the name, the Information Owner benefits from a <u>Confidentiality Engagement</u> with respect to <u>Confidential Information</u> that it owns or possesses.

These two sentences have five terms that require the reader to get further definitions. As I attempted to determine exactly what it means to "confide," I was sent to a hypertext page that explained that it meant to "entrust" the information to a "confidant," which means the "party receiving the information," and at that point I started looking elsewhere for examples.

The two lines of policy above provide a good example of what should be avoided when you are writing a policy — or writing anything. The document just referenced came from an organization with strong roots in the legal and government sector. If this is your audience, then this is the language for you. If not, try to think like Henry David Thoreau and simplify.

There are typically three areas of employee responsibility: owner, user, and custodian. We discuss each of these concepts and examine how other organizations have defined these responsibilities.

8.1 Owner

The information owner is the entity within the organization that has been assigned the responsibility to exercise the organization's proprietary rights and grant access privileges to those with a true business need. This role is normally assigned to the senior level manager within the business unit where the information asset was created, or is the primary user of that asset. The manager will have the ultimate responsibility for compliance, but will probably delegate the day-to-day activities to some individual who reports to him or her.

> *Information owner: the person who creates or initiates the creation or storage of the information is the initial owner. In an organization, possibly with divisions, departments, and sections, the owner becomes the unit itself with the person responsible being designated as the "head" of the unit.*

The Information owner is responsible for ensuring that:

- A classification hierarchy is agreed upon and it is appropriate for the types of information processed for that business unit.
- Classify all information stored into the agreed types and create an inventory (listing) of each type.
- For each document or file within each of the classification categories, append its agreed (confidentiality) classification. Its availability should be determined by the respective classification.
- Ensure that, for each classification type, the appropriate level of information security safeguards is available; for example, the log-on controls and access permissions applied by the Information Custodian provide the required levels of confidentiality.
- Periodically check to ensure that information continues to be classified appropriately and that the safeguards remain valid and operative.

I am not certain what being designated "head" actually means, but I do not believe I would want that title. The term "initial owner" may also lead the reader to believe that someone else may come along and become the "final" or "ultimate" leader.

We now review the owner definition from a global media organization.

> *Owners are authorized employees to whom responsibility has been delegated for the creation and/or use of specific business data by the business unit that "owns" the data. Owners are responsible for defining requirements for safeguards that assure the confidentiality, availability, and integrity of the information. Owners are also responsible for placing information in the proper classification so that those who need the information to perform their assigned duties can obtain it. The owner provides requirements for security for the information to the custodian. The custodian implements the controls to meet the owner's requirements.*

This is a fairly good definition. The only element that I might add is the requirement that the owner monitor the safeguards to ensure custodian compliance. Let us examine one more example.

A. **Owner:** the Company management of an organizational unit, department, etc. where the information is created, or that is the primary user of the information. **Owners** have the responsibility to:

Identify the classification level of all corporate information within
their organizational unit

Define and implement appropriate safeguards to ensure the confidentiality, integrity, and availability of the information resource

Monitor safeguards to ensure their compliance and report situations
of non-compliance

Authorize access to those who have a business need for the information

Remove access from those who no longer have a business need for
the information

We see variations on this definition in the following section.

8.2 Custodian

The next responsibility we have to create is that of the information custodian. This entity is responsible for protecting the information asset based
on the requirements established by the owner. In an organization that has
an information systems organization, the operations group might be considered the custodian of client data and information. They do not have the
right to permit anyone access to the information asset, nor can they alter
that information in any way without approval from the owner. This would
include any programming or system upgrades that would modify the information or the output from applications and transactions.

> *An Information Custodian is the person responsible for overseeing and
> implementing the necessary safeguards to protect assets, at the level clas-
> sified by the Information Owner.*

> *This could be the System Administrator, controlling access to a computer
> network; or a specific application program or even a standard filing cabinet.*

This example started out well but finished oddly. Giving examples of
what might be considered a custodian is good. Trying to liken a filing cabinet to the opening sentence where the policy identifies the custodian as a
"person" is not. Remember that when you are writing, go back and read
what you just wrote to make sure the concepts match from beginning to
end. Do not try to be cute. Stick to what the subject is, and make sure you
say exactly what needs to be said.

> *Custodians are authorized system support persons or organizations
> (employees, contractors, consultants, vendors, etc.) responsible for main-
> taining the safeguards established by owners. The owner designates the
> custodian. The Custodian is the "steward of the data" for the owner; that
> is, the Data Center may be the Custodian for business applications
> "owned" by a Business Unit.*

The use of the term "steward of the data" brings out a point that needs
to be made. Some organizations and cultures prefer other terms than the
ones discussed here. When I was younger, I played Pony League baseball

for a team called the "Custodians." Our uniforms were the most realistic because we had the name on the front and number on the back. The other teams had names like "Tigers" and "Braves" but had some advertisement about their sponsor on the back. It was not until we played a few games that the other team started calling us the janitors. Custodian to some is a noble name; to others, maybe not so noble. So choose your terms wisely. Curator, Keeper, and Guardian are other terms that might work.

Recently we were doing work for HIPAA compliance. While developing policies for a hospital, we discussed the definition for "user." The hospital staff started to chuckle and told us that the term "user" had a totally different meaning there and we needed to find another term.

B. **Custodian:** employees designated by the Owner to be responsible for maintaining the safeguards established by the Owner.

It is important to remember that when we use the term "employee," we are actually discussing the virtual employee. We can only write policy for employees; for all third parties, a contract must contain compliance language. So it is perfectly acceptable to identify "employees" even if we know that someone other than an employee may actually perform the function. This is true for all employee responsibilities except "owner." The owner must be an employee; after all, it is the organization's information.

8.3   User

The final element is the user. The owner grants permission to access the information asset to this individual. The user must use the information in the manner agreed upon with the owner. The user has no other rights. When granting access, the owner should use the concept of "least privilege." This means that users are granted only the access they specifically need to perform their business task, and no more.

> *An Information User is the person responsible for viewing, amending, or updating the content of the information assets. This can be any user of the information in the inventory created by the Information Owner.*

The inventory discussed here will be addressed in both the classification policy and the records management policy. Including who has been assigned access needs to be tracked. The Custodian is generally responsible for providing the tools to monitor the user list.

> *Users are authorized system users (employees, contractors, consultants, vendors, etc.) responsible for using and safeguarding information under their control according to the directions of the Owner. Users are authorized access to information by the Owner.*

The final example is similar to the definition used above.

C. **User:** employees authorized by the Owner to access information and use the safeguards established by the Owner.

9   CLASSIFICATION EXAMPLES

In this section we examine attributes and examples of different classification categories. We also present examples of organization information classification policies.

9.1   Example 1

Critique of Example 1 (Table 6): This is an actual classification policy (very high level) for the executive branch of a national government. There is little here to help the average user. This is an example of a Program or General Policy Statement; however, a Topic-Specific Policy Statement might have been more beneficial. Perhaps the next two examples will provide more information.

9.2   Example 2

Critique of Example 2 (Table 7): The policy seems to stress competitive advantage information in its opening paragraphs. It does not appear to address personal information about employees or customers. It does provide for these topics as categories under Confidential but it never really mentions them by name. This appears to be a policy that is somewhat limited in scope. Additionally, it does not establish the scope of the information (is it computer generated only, or exactly what information is being addressed). The employee responsibilities are missing. What is management's responsibility with respect to information classification, and what is expected of the employees? Finally, what are the consequences of non-compliance?

Table 6. Information Classification Policy Example 1

Information Classification

Policy: Security classifications should be used to indicate the need and priorities for security protection.

Objective: To ensure that information assets receive an appropriate level of protection.

Statement: Information has varying degrees of sensitivity and criticality. Some items may require an additional level of security protection or special handling. A security classification system should be used to define an appropriate set of security protection levels, and to communicate the need for special handling measures to users.

Table 7. Information Classification Policy Example 2

Classification Requirements

Classified data is information developed by the organization with some effort and some expense or investment that provides the organization with a competitive advantage in its relevant industry and that the organization wishes to protect from disclosure.

While defining information protection is a difficult task, four elements serve as the basis for a classification scheme:

The information must be of some value to the organization and its competitors so that it provides some demonstrable competitive advantage.

The information must be the result of some minimal expense or investment by the organization.

The information is somewhat unique in that it is not generally known in the industry or to the public or may not be readily ascertained.

The information must be maintained as a relative secret, both within and outside the organization, with reasonable precautions against disclosure of the information. Access to such information could only result from disregarding established standards or from using illegal means.

Top Secret (Secret, Highly Confidential)

Attributes:

Provides the organization with a very significant competitive edge

Is of such a nature that unauthorized disclosure would cause severe damage to the organization

Shows specific business strategies and major directions

Is essential to the technical or financial success of a product

Examples:

Specific operating plans, marketing strategies

Specific descriptions of unique parts or materials, technology intent statements, new technologies, and research

Specific business strategies and major directions

Confidential (Sensitive, Personal, Privileged)

Attributes:

Provides the organization with a significant competitive edge

Is of such a nature that unauthorized disclosure would cause damage to the organization

It shows operational direction over extended period of time

Is extremely important to the technical or financial success of a product

Examples:

Consolidated revenue, cost, profit, or other financial results

Operating plans, marketing strategies

Descriptions of unique parts or materials, technology intent statements, new technological studies, and research

Market requirements, technologies, product plans, revenues

(continued)

Table 7. Information Classification Policy Example 2 (Continued)

Restricted (Internal Use)

Attributes:

All business-related information requiring baseline security protection, but failing to meet the specified criteria for higher classification

Information that is intended for use by employees when conducting company business

Examples:

Business information

Organization policies, standards, procedures

Internal organization announcements

Public (Unclassified)

Attributes:

Information that, due to its content and context, requires no special protection, or

Information that has been made available to the public distribution through authorized company channels

Examples:

Online public information, Web site information

Internal correspondence, memoranda, and documentation that do not merit special controls

Public corporate announcements

9.3   Example 3

Critique of Example 3 (Table 8): Examples 2 and 3 are very similar; this one does address the role of the Owner but it fails to define what an Owner is. The issue of noncompliance is not addressed and the scope of the policy is vague.

9.4   Example 4

Critique of Example 4 (Table 9): The intent of the policy is stated as "Information is a corporate asset and is the property of Corporation." The scope of the policy is "Corporate information includes electronically generated, printed, filmed, typed, or stored." The responsibilities are well established. The issue of compliance is the only policy element that appears to be lacking.

10   DECLASSIFICATION OR RECLASSIFICATION OF INFORMATION

Classified information normally declines in sensitivity with the passage of time. Downgrading should be as automatic as possible. If the information owner knows the date that the information should be reclassified, then it might be labeled as *Confidential until (date)*. There should be an established review process for all information classified as Confidential, and reclassified when it no longer meets the criteria established for such information.

Table 8. Information Classification Example 3

Information Classification

Introduction

Information, wherever it is handled or stored (for example, in computers, file cabinets, desktops, fax machines, voice-mail), needs to be protected from unauthorized access, modification, disclosure, and destruction. All information is not created equal. Consequently, segmentation or classification of information into categories is necessary to help identify a framework for evaluating the information's relative value and the appropriate controls required to preserve its value to the company.

Three basic classifications of information have been established. Organizations may define additional sub-classifications as necessary to complete their framework for evaluating and preserving information under their control.

When information does require protection, the protection must be consistent. Often, strict access controls are applied to data stored in the mainframe computers but not applied to office workstations. Whether in a mainframe, client/server, workstation, file cabinet, desk drawer, waste basket, or in the mail, information should be subject to appropriate and consistent protection.

The definitions and responsibilities described below represent the minimum level of detail necessary for all organizations across the company. Each organization may decide that additional detail is necessary to adequately implement information classification within their organization.

Corporate Policy:

All information must be classified by the **owner** into one of three classifications: **Confidential, Internal Use,** or **Public**. (From: Company Policy on Information Management)

Confidential

Definition

Information that, if disclosed, could:

Violate the privacy of individuals

Reduce the company's competitive advantage

Cause damage to the company

Examples

Some examples of **Confidential** information are:

Personnel records (including name, address, phone, salary, performance rating, social security number, date of birth, marital status, career path, number of dependents, etc.)

Customer information (including name, address, phone number, energy consumption, credit history, social security number, etc.)

Shareholder information (including name, address, phone number, number of shares held, social security number, etc.)

Vendor information (name, address, product pricing specific to the company, etc.)

Health insurance records (including medical, prescription and psychological records)

Specific operating plans, marketing plans, or strategies

Consolidated revenue, cost, profit, or other financial results that are not public record

Descriptions of unique parts or materials, technology intent statements, or new technologies and research that are not public record

(continued)

Table 8. Information Classification Example 3 (Continued)

Specific business strategies and directions

Major changes in the company's management structure

Information that requires special skill or training to interpret and employ correctly, such as design or specification files

If any of these items can be found freely and openly in public records, the company's obligation to protect from disclosure is waived.

Internal Use

Definition

Classify information as **Internal Use** when the information is intended for use by employees when conducting company business.

Examples

Some examples of **Internal Use** information are:

Operational business information/reports

Non-company information that is subject to a non-disclosure agreement with another company

Company phone book

Corporate policies, standards, and procedures

Internal company announcements

Public

Definition

Classify information as **Public** if the information has been made available for public distribution through authorized company channels. **Public** information is not sensitive in context or content, and requires no special protection.

Examples

The following are examples of **Public** information:

Corporate Annual Report

Information specifically generated for public consumption, such as public service bulletins, marketing brochures, and advertisements

---

Part of an effective information classification program is the ability to combine the requirements with a Records Management Policy. Information assets must be protected, stored, and then destroyed based on a policy and a set of standards. The information classification policy will ensure that an owner is assigned to each asset, that a proper classification is assigned, and that an information handling set of standards will help maintain control of information copies.

The Records Management Policy will require that the owner provide a brief description of the information record and the record retention requirements. These requirements will be a set of standards that support the Records Management Policy.

We next briefly examine what is typically part of a Records Management Policy.

Table 9. Information Classification Policy Example 4

Information Management

General

Corporate information includes electronically generated, printed, filmed, typed, or stored.

Information is a corporate asset and is the property of Corporation.

Information Retention

Each organization shall retain information necessary to the conduct of business.

Each organizational unit shall establish and administer a records management schedule in compliance with applicable laws and regulations, and professional standards and practices, and be compatible with Corporate goals and expectations.

Information Protection

Information must be protected according to its sensitivity, criticality, and value, regardless of the media on which it is stored, the manual or automated systems that process it, or the methods by which it is distributed.

Employees are responsible for protecting corporate information from unauthorized access, modification, destruction, or disclosure, whether accidental or intentional. To facilitate the protection of corporate information, employee responsibilities have been established at three levels: **Owner, Custodian,** and **User.**

Owner: Company management of the organizational unit where the information is created, or management of the organizational unit that is the primary user of the information. **Owners** are responsible to:

Identify the classification level of all corporate information within their organizational unit

Define appropriate safeguards to ensure the confidentiality, integrity, and availability of the information resource

Monitor safeguards to ensure they are properly implemented

Authorize access to those who have a business need for the information

Remove access from those who no longer have a business need for the information

Custodian: Employees designated by the owner to be responsible for maintaining the safeguards established by the owner.

User: Employees authorized by the owner to access information and use the safeguards established by the owner.

Each Vice President shall appoint an Organization Information Protection Coordinator who will administer an information protection program that appropriately classifies and protects corporate information under the Vice President's control and makes employees aware of the importance of information and methods for its protection.

Information Classification: To ensure the proper protection of corporate information, the owner shall use a formal review process to classify information into one of the following classifications:

Public: Information that has been made available for public distribution through authorized company channels. (Refer to Communication Policy for more information.)

(continued)

100

Table 9. Information Classification Policy Example 4 (Continued)

Confidential: Information that, if disclosed, could violate the privacy of individuals, reduce the company's competitive advantage, or could cause significant damage to the company.

Internal Use: Information that is intended for use by all employees when conducting company business. Most information used in the company would be classified Internal use.

11 RECORDS MANAGEMENT POLICY

An organization's records are one of its most important and valuable assets. Almost every employee is responsible for creating or maintaining organization records of some kind, whether in the form of paper, computer data, optical disk, electronic mail, or voice-mail. Letters, memoranda, and contracts are obviously information records, as are things such as a desk calendar, an appointment book, or an expense record.

Organizations are required by law to maintain certain types of records, usually for a specified period of time. The failure to retain such documents for these minimum time periods can subject an organization to penalties, fines, or other sanctions, or could put it at a serious disadvantage in litigation. Therefore, every organization should implement a Records Management Policy to provide standards for maintaining complete and accurate records in order to ensure that employees are aware of what records to keep and for how long, what records to dispose of, and how to dispose of them.

Cost of storage and administration problems involved in retaining material beyond its useful life are a few important reasons to establish a Records Management Policy. Consideration should also be given to the impact that a failure to produce subpoenaed records might have on the organization when defending itself against a lawsuit. Determining the proper retention periods for information records is a requirement in today's operating environment. Information records should be kept only as long as they serve a useful purpose, or until legal requirements are met. At the end of the retention period, records should be destroyed in a verifiable manner. Implementing effective information classification and records management policies makes sound business sense and shows that management is practicing its due diligence.

Before drafting a Records Management Policy, consult with your legal staff to ensure that the policy reflects any relevant statutes. The retention standards that support the policy should be reviewed annually when an information asset inventory is conducted organizationwide.

11.1 Sample Records Management Policy

See Table 10.

12 INFORMATION HANDLING STANDARDS MATRIX

Later in the book we discuss standards and how they support the implementation of the policy. Because information classification and records management are unique in their standards requirements, I thought it appropriate to give examples now of what these standards might look like. When you are developing your standards, use these as a guideline — not a standard.

12.1 Printed Material

See Table 11.

12.2 Electronically Stored Information

See Table 12.

12.3 Electronically Transmitted Information

See Table 13.

12.4 Records Management Retention Schedule

See Table 14.

13 INFORMATION CLASSIFICATION METHODOLOGY

The final element in an effective information classification process is to provide management and employees with a method with which to evaluate information and provide them with an indication of where the information should be classified. To accomplish this, it may be necessary to create an information classification worksheet (see Exhibit 8). These worksheets can be used by the business units to determine what classification of information they have within their organization.

To complete this worksheet, the employee would fill in the information requested at the top of the sheet:

- *Organization:* the department designated as the information owner.
- *Group:* the reporting group of the individual performing the information classification process.
- *Review performed by/Phone:* the name and phone number of the individual performing the review.
- *Date:* the date of the review.
- *Information Name/Description:* an identifier and description of the information being reviewed.

Table 10. Sample Records Management Policy

Records Management Policy

Introduction

It is the policy of the Company to accommodate the timely storage, retrieval, and disposition of records created, utilized, and maintained by the various departments. The period of time that records are maintained is based on the minimum requirements set forth in State and Federal retention schedules.

1. Role of Retention Center

The role of the Retention Center is to receive, maintain, destroy, and service inactive records that have not met their disposition date. Each business unit is to establish schedules to comply with the minimum amount of time records should be maintained in compliance with State and Federal guidelines. Retention requirements apply whether or not the records are transferred to the Retention Center. Copies of the schedules must be maintained by the business unit and available for inspection.

2. Role of Records Manager

The role of the Records Manager is to administer the Records Management program. The Records Manager is well acquainted with all records and/or record groups within an agency and has expertise in all aspects of records management. The duties of the Records Manager include planning, development, and administration of records management policies. These duties also include the annual organization-wide inventory of all information assets to be conducted by the business unit manager with reports sent to the Records Manager.

3. Role of Management Personnel

Management Personnel are responsible for records under their control.

4. Role of Departmental Records Coordinator

The Departmental Records Coordinator is to be a liaison between the department and the Retention Center. It is recommended that each department appoint a Records Coordinator in writing. The letter of appointment should include the Records Coordinator's full name, department, and telephone extension. The letter should be forwarded to the Retention Center and maintained on file.

5. Type of Documents Maintained in Retention Center

    5.1 Record Retention accepts only public records that are referenced in the State Retention Schedule, except student transcripts. Copies of student transcripts may be obtained from Records and Admissions located at the Student Service Center.

    5.2 Record Retention does not accept personal, active, or non-records.

    5.3 Record Retention stores only inactive and permanent records until final disposition according to State and Federal retention schedules. Examples include personnel files, purchase orders, grade books, or surveys.

    5.4 Record Retention receives and stores inactive permanent records from TVI departments until final disposition according to State and Federal retention guidelines.

    5.5 Record Retention ensures records are classified according to State and Retention guidelines.

    5.6 Record Retention ensures records are tracked and entered into an electronic records management software system that tracks record boxes, assigns retention schedules, permanent box numbers, destruction dates, and shelf locations.

(continued)

Table 10. Sample Records Management Policy (Continued)

6. Services
   6.1 If a department has obsolete records that are deemed confidential or sensitive, or copies of non-records, a special request for shredding may be sent to the Record Retention Center. The records can be shredded by the Record Retention Center staff or transferred to the State Record Center for destruction.
   6.2 Departments must complete a Request for Destruction form for confidential or non-records to be shredded. Departments are required to purchase forms from Central Stores at Shipping & Receiving.
   6.3 The Record Retention Center provides consulting services to departments on filing systems and maintenance of records.
7. Transferring Records
   7.1 Departments should transfer records in January, July, and October to Record Retention for storage.
   7.2 Records with a retention period of two years or more should be transferred to Record Retention.
8. Record Retrieval
   8.1 Records are retrieved and delivered to customers by request, given a 24-hour notice.
   8.2 Records can be retrieved for customers on an emergency basis, as requested.
   8.3 Management personnel, the records coordinator, or the requester will sign for receipt of records. Records are to be checked out for no longer than 30 days. If a longer period is required, a written request should be sent to the Retention Center. If records are checked out for more than a year, the records will be permanently withdrawn from inventory.
   8.4 Permanent Withdrawal: If a department wishes to withdraw a record permanently from storage, forward a request to Record Retention by phone, fax, or inter-office mail. The department will complete a Withdrawal Request form and the records will be deleted from inventory.
   8.5 Second-Party Withdrawal: If a department requests a record originating from another department, then the requesting department must contact the department of origin to obtain authorization. The department of origin will contact Record Retention for records withdrawal. The department requester must view the requested records at the Record Retention Center.
   8.6 Records should not be returned via inter-office mail due to the confidential nature of the documents.
9. Record Destruction
   9.1 Record Retention destroys records in January, July, and October according to State guidelines.

(continued)

Table 10. Sample Records Management Policy (Continued)

9.2   Records are destroyed by Record Retention according to State and Federal guidelines when legal requirements are met. A Destruction Request form will be sent to the originating department for review and signature by the Departmental Records Coordinator and by management personnel. Only when the Destruction Request has been reviewed, signed, and returned to Record Retention will the expired records be destroyed. Authorized personnel will shred confidential records. If departments wish to keep the records past their assigned destruction date, management personnel can extend the date no longer than one year unless a litigation, audit, or investigation is pending. Records kept by the department past the retention date of destruction will be permanently withdrawn from inventory.

9.3   All records scheduled for destruction are reviewed by the Institute's Records Manager and by State Records Analysts for approval.

10.   Supplies

10.1   Records must be stored in the appropriate record retention boxes, which are obtained from Central Stores at Shipping & Receiving.

10.2   Storage Ticket forms and Request for Destruction forms are obtained from Central Stores at Shipping & Receiving.

In the section for Information Name/Description, it will be necessary to enter the information type. For example:

- Employee Records:
  - Employee performance review records
  - Timecards
  - Employee discipline documents
  - Pay records
  - Medical records
- Group Administrative Records:
  - Monthly status reports
  - Yearly status reports
  - Yearly business objectives
- Business Process Records:
  - Purchasing contracts
  - Quarterly financial reports
  - Project management tasks, schedules
  - Reference manuals
  - Contract negotiations
- Operations Information:
  - Business partner information
  - Asset allocation
  - Trading activities

Table 11. Information Handling Matrix for Printed Material

	Confidential	Internal Use	Public
Labeling of documents	Document should identify owner and be marked "CONFIDENTIAL" on cover or title page	No special requirements	Document may be marked "PUBLIC" on cover or title page
Duplication of documents	Information owner to determine permissions	Duplication for business purposes only	No special requirements
Mailing of documents	No classification marking on external envelope; "CONFIDENTIAL" marking on cover sheet; confirmation of receipt at discretion of information owner	Mailing requirements determined by information owner	No special requirements
Disposal of documents	Owner observed physical destruction beyond ability to recover	Controlled physical destruction	No special requirements
Storage of documents	Locked up when not in use	Master copy secured against destruction	Master copy secured against destruction
Read access to documents	Owner establishes user access rules; generally highly restricted	Owner establishes user access rules; generally widely available	No special requirements; generally available within and outside company
Review of document classification level	Information owner to establish specific review date (not to exceed one year)	Information owner to review at least annually	No special requirements

- Production formulas
- Production cost information
- Customer lists
• Distribution Records:
  - Distribution models
  - Inventory records
  - Parts supplies

Using the definitions, the person(s) performing the review would place a checkmark in the appropriate column — only one check for each item being reviewed. This process would allow the user department to identify

Table 12. Information Handling Matrix for Electronically Stored Information

	Confidential	Internal Use	Public
Storage on fixed media (access controlled)	Unencrypted	Unencrypted	Unencrypted
Storage on fixed media (not access controlled)	Encrypted	Unencrypted	Unencrypted
Storage on removable media	Encrypted	Unencrypted	Unencrypted
Read access to information (includes duplication)	Information owner to authorize individual users	Information owner to define permissions on user, group, or function basis	No special requirements
Update access to information	Information owner to authorize individual users	Information owner to define permissions on user, group, or function basis	Information owners to define permissions
Delete access to information	Information owner to authorize individual users; user confirmation required	Information owner to define permissions on user, group, or function basis; user confirmation required	Information owner to define permissions
Print hardcopy report of information	Output to be routed to a predefined, monitored printer	Information owner to define permissions	No special requirements
Internal labeling of information at the application or screen/display level	Notification of "CONFIDENTIAL" to appear at top of display	No special requirements	Notification of "PUBLIC" may optionally appear at top of display
External labeling of exchangeable media	Media must identify owner and be marked CONFIDENTIAL	Marking at discretion of owner	No special requirements
Disposal of electronic media (diskettes, tapes, hard disks, etc.)	Owner observed physical destruction beyond ability to recover	Physical destruction	No special requirements

(continued)

Table 12. Information Handling Matrix for Electronically Stored Information (Continued)

	Confidential	Internal Use	Public
Disposal of information	Delete by fully writing over information	Delete files through normal platform delete command, option, or facility	No special requirements
Review of classified information for reclassification	Information owner to establish specific review date (not to exceed one year)	Information owner to review annually	Information owner to review annually
Logging access activity	Log all access attempts; information owner to review all access and violation attempts	Log all violation attempts; information owner reviews as appropriate	No special requirements
Access report retention requirements	Information owner to determine retention of access logs (not to exceed one year)	Information owner to determine retention of violation logs (not to exceed six months)	No special requirements

all the various types of information found in their department and then be able to determine into which classification they probably fall.

14   AUTHORIZATION FOR ACCESS

To establish a clear line of authority, some key concepts must be established. As discussed above, there are typically three categories of employee responsibilities. Depending on the specific information being accessed, an individual may fall into more than one category. For example, an employee with a desktop workstation becomes the owner, custodian, and user. To better understand the concepts, the responsibilities of each category are listed below.

14.1   Owners

Minimally, the information owner is responsible for:

- Judging the value of the information resource and assigning the proper classification level
- Periodically reviewing the classification level to determine if the status should be changed

Table 13. Information Handling Matrix for Electronically Transmitted Information

	Confidential	Internal Use	Public
By FAX	Attended at receiving FAX	Information owner to define requirements	No special requirements
By WAN	Confirmation of receipt required; encryption optional	No special requirements; encryption optional	No special requirements
By LAN	Confirmation of receipt required; encryption optional	No special requirements; encryption optional	No special requirements
By Inter-office mail	No external labeling on envelope; normal labeling on document	No special requirements	No special requirements
By voice-mail	Confirmation of receipt required (sender); remove message after receipt (recipient)	No special requirements	No special requirements
By electronic messaging (e-mail)	Confirmation of receipt required; encryption optional	No special requirements	No special requirements
By wireless or cellular phone	Do not transmit	No special requirements	No special requirements

- Assessing and defining appropriate controls to assure that information created is properly safeguarded from unauthorized access, modification, disclosure, and destruction
- Communicating access and safeguard requirements to the information custodian and users
- Providing access to those individuals with a demonstrated business need for access
- Assessing the risk of loss of the information and assuring that adequate safeguards are in place to mitigate the risk to information integrity, confidentiality, and availability
- Monitoring safeguard requirements to ensure that information is being adequately protected
- Assuring a business continuity plan has been implemented and tested to protect information availability

14.2 Custodians

At a minimum, the custodian is responsible for:

- Providing proper safeguards for processing equipment, information storage, backup, and recovery

Table 14. Sample Record Retention Schedule

Record	Retain
Accounts payable schedules	Permanent
Accounts receivables schedules	Permanent
Bank drafts and paid notices	10 Years
Bank statements and reconciliations	10 Years
Bills of lading	7 Years
Cancelled checks	10 Years
Cash disbursements journals	Permanent
Cash receipts journals	Permanent
Claims register	7 Years
Corporate minutes book	Permanent
Correspondence	10 Years
Counter tickets	7 Years
CPA audit reports	Permanent
Credit memos	7 Years
Customer files	7 Years
Customer repair orders (both office and hard copy)	7 Years
Documents pertaining to litigation	Permanent
Duplicate deposit slips	10 Years
Employee earning and history record	Permanent
Employment contracts	Permanent
Federal revenue agents' reports and related papers	Permanent
Federal tax returns	Permanent
Financial statements	Permanent
General journals	Permanent
General ledgers	Permanent
Insurance policies	Until Expiration
Internal repair orders (hard copy only)	7 Years
Internal sales journals	Permanent
Journal vouchers	Permanent
Miscellaneous schedules	Permanent
New and used vehicle records	7 Years
New vehicle sales journals	Permanent
Office receipts	7 Years
Parts, accessories, and service sales journals	Permanent
Payroll journals	Permanent
Prepaid and accrued expense schedule	2 Years
Property tax returns	Permanent
Purchase journals	Permanent
Purchase orders	7 Years
Receiving reports	7 Years
Repair order check sheet	2 Years
Repair orders — internal (office copy only)	2 Years

(continued)

Table 14. Sample Record Retention Schedule (Continued)

Record	Retain
Sales invoices	7 Years
Salesperson's commission reports	Permanent
Social security tax returns	Permanent
State and local sales tax returns	Permanent
State annual reports	Permanent
State franchise tax returns	Permanent
Sundry invoices	7 Years
Time cards	2 Years
U.S. and state unemployment tax returns	Permanent
Used and repossessed vehicles journals	Permanent
Vehicle invoices	7 Years
Vendor invoices	7 Years
Withholding tax returns	Permanent

- Providing a secure processing environment that can adequately protect the integrity, confidentiality, and availability of information
- Administering access requests to information properly authorized by the owner

14.3 User

The user must:

- Use the information only for the purpose intended.
- Maintain the integrity, confidentiality, and availability of information accessed.

Being granted access to information does not imply or confer authority to grant other users access to that information. This is true whether the information is electronically held, printed, hardcopy, manually prepared, copied, or transmitted.

15 SUMMARY

Information classification drives the protection control requirements and this allows information to be protected to a level commensurate with its value to the organization. The costs of overprotection are eliminated and exceptions are minimized. With a policy and methodology, specifications are clear and accountability is established.

There are costs associated with implementing a classification system. The most identifiable costs include labeling classified information, implementing and monitoring controls and safeguards, and proper handling of confidential information.

INFORMATION SECURITY POLICIES AND PROCEDURES

Information, wherever it is handled or stored, must be protected from unauthorized access, modification, disclosure, and destruction. All information is not created equal. Consequently, segmentation or classification of information into categories is necessary to help identify a framework for evaluating the information's relative value. By establishing this relative value, it will be possible to establish cost-effective controls that will preserve the information asset for the organization.

The information classification program will require the identification of the record type, the owner, and the classification level. Two thirds of this information may already be gathered by the record management program. Link these two vital processes together to ensure that employee time is not wasted on redundant activities. By combining the effort, the organization will have a better overall information security program.

Chapter 6
Developing Standards

1 INTRODUCTION

There are many existing sources for information security supporting standards. The banking industry has many that have been established by regulations and requirements from the federal government. The healthcare industry also has standards that are required. We will explore where to find industry-specific standards and how to make them apply to your organization.

Standards — we have standards. We have stacks and stacks of standards. We asked for them and we got them. The computer and information security industry worked for years developing standards that would be accepted throughout the industry. We did not do too well. We could not even decide whether we should slash the alphabetic "O" or the numeric "0." The industry leaders met in Gaithersburg, Maryland, at the invitation of the National Institute of Standards and Technology (NIST) to establish a "taxonomy" for the information security industry. The results of this work were the Generally Accepted System Security Principles (GASSP) that were generally ignored by the industry.

Even without the GASSP, organizations are faced with an explosion of third-party standards. Organizations face complex requirements to comply with a host of standards. Even within specific industries such as financial services, the complexity to meet security requirements is brought on by new legislation (e.g., the U.S. Gramm–Leach–Bliley Act of 1999 [GLBA], Basel Accords, Securities and Exchange Commission [SEC] requirements, and USA Patriot Act). No longer is it about meeting one compliance obligation, but a complex web of requirements that grows exponentially as organizations cross international boundaries.

In this section we examine the development of supporting standards that will reflect the prevailing requirements. When you develop your set of standards, focus on those that support your current business environment. Standards are easier to update and modify than a Tier 1 policy. Review them at least annually to see if the technology and need have remained the same.

2   OVERVIEW

You will use standards to flesh out supporting documents such as an Information Security Handbook or a Network Standards document or Application Programming Standards and Practices. You will use the standards to identify what is expected of the reader. There will also be a place for the guidelines in these documents.

Standards for each phase or section of an information security handbook must be developed. Almost everyone in the enterprise recognizes the need for standards. However, developing them, adhering to them, and monitoring them is a logistical problem.

Two things are necessary to achieve success with standards:

1. There must be a commitment to the standards by all personnel.
2. The standards must be:
    - Reasonable
    - Flexible
    - Current

These two necessities are interdependent. Commitment must start with senior management and then move throughout the enterprise. If line management does not get the proper message from senior management, then the standards have no chance of surviving. On the other hand, if the employees see that their management is committed to the standards, there is a better chance that the employees will be committed. It is very much a two-way street, and therefore standards must be:

- Practical
- Applicable
- Up-to-date
- Reviewed regularly

3   WHERE DO STANDARDS BELONG?

Policies, standards, and procedures fit into a hierarchy (see Figure 1):

- A *policy* states a goal in general terms.
- *Standards* define what is to be accomplished in specific terms.

Procedures tell us how to meet the standards.

A Tier 1 policy is written at a broad level and as such will require the support of standards, procedures, and guidelines that will offer the user community a more detailed approach to implementing policy and meeting enterprise objectives. Standards specify technologies and methodologies to be used to secure systems. Procedures are the detailed steps required to accomplish a particular task or process.

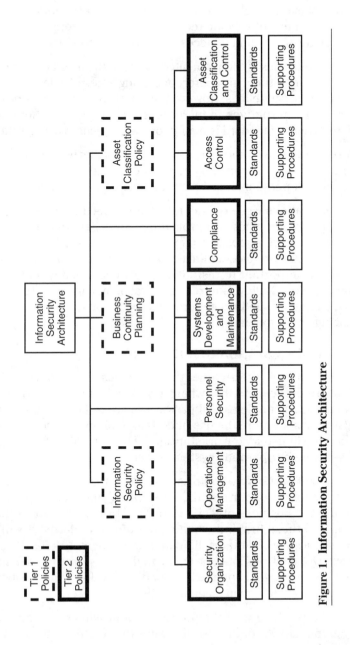

Figure 1. Information Security Architecture

Enterprise standards (not to be confused with British Standards 7799 [BS 7799], the ISO 17799, the Australian-New Zealand 44 44 [ANZ 44 44], the Generally Accepted System Security Principles [GASSP], HIPAA, GLBA, Sarbanes–Oxley, Basil Accords, or other national or international standards) specify a uniform use of specific technologies, parameters, or procedures to be used by those wishing to access enterprise resources.

Enterprise guidelines are implemented to assist the user community, support personnel, and others in securely accessing enterprise information and system resources. Guidelines, however, attempt to provide business units and others with alternatives to increase levels of control where deemed appropriate. Where a standard is mandatory, a guideline is a suggestion.

Enterprise procedures normally assist in complying with applicable policies, standards, and guidelines. They are the detailed steps to be followed by users, support personnel, or others to accomplish a particular task.

Many organizations issue overall information security manuals, regulations, handbooks, practices and procedures, or other similar documents. These documents are a mix of policy, standards, guidelines, and procedures because they are closely linked. While such documents serve as a useful tool, it is important to distinguish between a policy and its implementation elements. Policy requires approval of management teams, while standards, guidelines, and procedures can be modified as needed to support changing environments.

4 WHAT DOES A STANDARD LOOK LIKE?

Standards have no set pattern other than they must have a verb that relays the message to the readers that what they have just read is required. The standard can be as simple as "All passwords are to be kept confidential." Standards can also require the use of certain equipment, such as "Marketing personnel will use Mac workstations." They can also require certain forms of software or operating system levels.

The important part of developing standards is to make certain that they meet the needs of the organization. Just as when you develop policies you keep in mind the business objectives and mission of the enterprise, you must also keep these in mind when developing standards. It will do no good to create a standard that is difficult to implement. "All data contained on company workstations must be encrypted when stored or transmitted." This might be a great goal but it will probably slow down the business process and be abandoned by management and staff.

The standards, along with the policies, will provide the business units with a reference document that will permit them to develop local procedures to be implemented in a consistent framework. Even if you are a multinational organization, the standards manual will provide for a consistent structure upon which to build the security program.

It will be necessary to instruct the user community as to what is expected of them when using the standards. Typically, the standards manual will have a section on how to use the standards and this is where you identify the standards on standards usage. The process might read as follows:

In implementing the standards, the following process is to be used:

Review existing procedures and practices against company standard.

Document business unit's current compliance level.

Document deficiencies.

Create a compliance plan.

Implement compliance plan.

Check compliance annually.

The remainder of this section is an Information Security Standards Manual that can be used as a template for building your own standards manual or to do a gap analysis for your existing document. I recommend that each section of the document begin with a Tier 2 policy outlining the overall objectives of the section. Examples of Tier 2 policies are also included in this book in Chapter 4.

Standards must be reviewed at least annually to ensure that they are still meeting the business needs and operating environment. Information security personnel are often looked upon as the group that puts roadblocks in the way of getting business completed. For example, one morning, my wife and I were having a discussion about her current job assignment (to implement a single sign-on solution). One of the problems she was having was that there was a requirement to change user passwords every 30 days. I asked her why they were required to do so, and she told me, "Because it is a standard." I asked her why was that a standard to change a password every 30 days, and she told me, "Because it has always been that way."

Well, being ten years older than my wife, I knew that it really was a standard that we began to implement when access control packages were being installed in the mid-1970s. These new packages allowed us to make it so the user could change his or her own password. Prior to that we had to run a batch job to manually change the passwords and have the employees or their supervisors sign for the new passwords (I usually did this once a quarter). Well, with ACF2, RACF, and Top-Secret, we could now have the users do this task. It also allowed us to establish the timeframe, and many of us began to establish a *de facto* standard of 30 days.

So here they were attempting to install a single sign-on package that was running smack-dab against an outdated standard. The mid-1970s saw the processing environment of TSO and IMS; those really advanced had CICS. There was not a terminal on every desk, but a terminal room where you signed up to use the terminals. Remote job entry meant a card reader on another floor. The environment had changed but the standard remained the same. When it was first introduced, we told employees not to write down their password. Now, because of the proliferation of accounts, we tell them not to leave the card containing their account information lying around. To be effective, standards must keep pace with the changing environment and technology.

5 WHERE DO I GET THE STANDARDS?

As previously discussed, there are many places to obtain sample standards. For those working in healthcare, the HIPAA requirements are available; and for financial institutions, the GLBA requirements should be used. I suggest that you develop a document like the sample below that will help you identify what is expected by the specific requirements placed on your industry or organization. Map these requirements to your own organization and, where possible, determine your current level of compliance. The one in Table 1 uses ISO 17799 and BS 7799 as reference documents, with a partial review of GLBA requirements included.

6 SAMPLE INFORMATION SECURITY MANUAL

A Sample Standards Manual is provided in Appendix 1C. It was designed to give you the feel and flavor of what you might want to include in a standards document that will support your information security program. The manual contains a series of information security standards that would be commonly implemented throughout an organization. The standards will then form a baseline against which compliance can be measured. This compliance measurement can subsequently be used to report to management on the state of information security within the organization.

It will be important to work with the subject matter experts (SMEs) to determine which standards meet the current level of technology throughout the organization. It may become necessary to establish a baseline operating environment for the organization. This might mean that in some areas of the standards document, the business units might first have to upgrade their operating environment to meet minimum compliance levels. If you encounter pockets of back-level operating environments or groups that are using non-standard equipment, it will be necessary for the business unit to create a compliance plan.

Table 1. Information Security Architecture Based on ISO 17799 and Partial GLBA

Security Architecture
Based on ISO 17799
(With GLBA partially included)

Overview

This document identifies the policies, standards, and procedures that are part of an effective information security program. The International Standard for Information Security (ISO 17799) is used as the basis for the security architecture. The Generally Accepted Systems Security Principles (GASSP) and the National Institute of Standards and Technology (NIST) Computer Security Handbook (800-12) were also used as reference documents. In this example, I used a GLBA overview document to identify those sections or specific topics that are also addressed in GLBA for compliance purposes.

How to Use

Column one identifies the information security requirement; column two is a description of the requirement; column three is where you indicate if the identified activity has been completed; and column four identifies who is responsible for this requirement.

3. SECURITY POLICY
Note: Reference numbers are for ISO 17799 and BS 77 99.

3.1	Information Security Policy	Management direction and support for information security must be clearly established.	
3.1.1	Information Security Policy Document Development (GLBA)	Develop an Information Security Policy.	Y ___ N ___ Information Security Organization
3.1.2	Information Security Policy Document Publication (GLBA)	Implement an Information Security Policy.	Y ___ N ___ IS Steering Committee

4. ORGANIZATIONAL SECURITY

4.1	Information Security Infrastructure	A management framework must be established to initiate and control the implementation of information security within the organization.	
4.1.1	Management Information Security Forum (GLBA)	Establish a corporate committee to oversee information security.	Y ___ N ___ IS Steering Committee
4.1.2	Information Security Coordination (GLBA)	Develop and implement an Information Security organization mission statement.	Y ___ N ___ IS Mission Statement
4.1.3	Allocation of Information Security Responsibilities (GLBA)	Identify the roles and responsibilities of the IS organization.	Y ___ N ___ IS Organization

(continued)

Table 1. Information Security Architecture Based on ISO 17799 and Partial GLBA (Continued)

4.1.4	Authorization Process for Information Processing Facilities	Establish a management approval process to authorize new IT facilities from both a business and technical standpoint.	Y ___ N ___	IS Steering Committee
4.1.5	Specialist Information Security Advice	Charge the IS organization with providing specialized information security advice.	Y ___ N ___	IS Organization
4.1.6	Cooperation between Organizations	Establish a liaison requirement with external information security personnel and organizations including industry and/or government security specialists; law enforcement authorities; IT service providers; telecommunications authorities.	Y ___ N ___	IS Organization
4.1.7	Independent Review of Information Security	Identify that independent reviews of information security practices are conducted to ensure feasibility, effectiveness, and compliance with written policies.	Y ___ N ___	Audit Mission Statement
4.2	Security of Third-Party Access	The organizational IT facilities and information assets that control the access of nonorganizational third parties must be kept secure.		
4.2.1	Identification of Risks from Third-Party Access (GLBA)	Implement a process to analyze third-party connection risks.	Y ___ N ___	IS Organization
	Combating Risks from Third-Party Connections	Implement specific security standards to combat third-party connection risks.	Y ___ N ___	
4.2.2	Security Conditions in Third-Party Contracts	Ensure that security requirements are included in formal third-party contracts.	Y ___ N ___	Procurement
4.3	Outsourcing	The security of information should be maintained even when the responsibility for the processing has been outsourced to another organization.		
4.3.1	Security Requirements in Outsourcing Contracts	Implement standards to address security requirements if the information owners are in a contract between the owners and any outsourcing organization.	Y ___ N ___	Procurement

(continued)

Table 1. Information Security Architecture Based on ISO 17799 and Partial GLBA (Continued)

5. ASSET CLASSIFICATION and CONTROL

5.1	Accounting of Assets	Appropriate accounting of organizational assets must be established.		
5.1.1	Inventory of Assets	Establish an inventory of major assets associated with each information system.	Y ___ N ___	Asset Classification Policy
5.2	Information Classification	Security classifications should be used to indicate the need for, and priorities for, security protection of information assets.		
5.2.1	Classification Guidelines	Implement standards for security classification of the level of protection required for information assets.	Y ___ N ___	Asset Classification Policy
5.2.2	Information Labeling and Handling	Implement standards to ensure the proper handling of information assets.	Y ___ N ___	Asset Classification Policy

6. PERSONNEL SECURITY (GLBA)

6.1	Security in Job Definitions and Resourcing	Security should be addressed at the recruitment stage, included in job descriptions and contracts, and monitored during an individual's employment.		
6.1.1	Security in Job Descriptions	Ensure that security responsibilities are included in employee job descriptions.	Y ___ N ___	Employment (HR)
6.1.2	Personnel Screening and Policy	Implement standards to ensure that employment applications are screened for jobs that require access to sensitive information.	Y ___ N ___	Employment (HR)
6.1.3	Confidentiality Agreement	Implement nondisclosure agreements for all employees and third parties.	Y ___ N ___	Procurement
6.1.4	Terms and Conditions of Employment	Implement standards to ensure that employee terms and conditions of employment include the employee's responsibility for information security, including duration after employment and consequences of failure to fulfill these terms.	Y ___ N ___	Procurement
6.2	User Training	Users should be trained in security procedures and the correct use of IT facilities.		

(continued)

Table 1. Information Security Architecture Based on ISO 17799 and Partial GLBA (Continued)

6.2.1	Information Security Education and Training	Implement training standards to ensure that users are trained in information security policies and procedures, security requirements, business controls, and the correct use of IT facilities.	Y ___ N ___	HR and IS User Training
6.3	Responding to Security Incidents and Malfunctions	Incidents affecting security should be reported through management channels as quickly as possible.		
6.3.1	Reporting of Security Incidents	Implement procedures and standards for formal reporting and incident response action to be taken on receipt of an incident report.	Y ___ N ___	Emergency Response Team (ERT)
6.3.2	Reporting of Security Weaknesses	Implement standards and procedures to ensure that users are aware of the requirement to note and report all observed or suspected security weaknesses in or threats to systems or services.	Y ___ N ___	ERT
6.3.3	Reporting of Software Malfunctions	Implement standards and user training to ensure that users note and report to the proper location any software that does not function correctly.	Y ___ N ___	ERT
6.3.4	Learning from Incidents	Implement standards to ensure mechanisms are in place to monitor the types, volumes, and costs of incidents and malfunctions.	Y ___ N ___	ERT
6.3.5	Disciplinary Process	Update corporate discipline policies to include dealing with employees who violate security policies and procedures.	Y ___ N ___	ERT & HR Discipline Policy

7. PHYSICAL and ENVIRONMENTAL SECURITY (GLBA)

7.1	Secure Areas	IT facilities supporting critical or sensitive business activities belong in secure areas.		

(continued)

Table 1. Information Security Architecture Based on ISO 17799 and Partial GLBA (Continued)

7.1.1	Physical Security Perimeter	Implement standards to ensure that physical security protection exists, based on defined perimeters through strategically located barriers throughout the organization.	Y ___ N ___	Physical Security
7.1.2	Physical Entry Controls	Implement entry procedures to secure areas to ensure that only authorized personnel can gain access.	Y ___ N ___	Physical Security
7.1.3	Securing Offices, Rooms, and Facilities	Implement procedures for physical security for data centers and computer rooms that are commensurate with threats.	Y ___ N ___	Physical Security
7.1.4	Working in Secure Areas	Implement standards and procedures to control personnel or third parties working in the secure area.	Y ___ N ___	Physical Security
7.1.5	Isolated Delivery and Loading Areas	Implement standards to ensure that the computer room/data center delivery and loading areas are isolated to prevent unauthorized access.	Y ___ N ___	Physical Security
7.2	Equipment Security	Equipment must be physically protected from security threats and environmental hazards.		
7.2.1	Equipment Location and Protection	Implement standards to ensure that equipment is located properly to reduce risks of environmental hazards and unauthorized access.	Y ___ N ___	Operations
7.2.2	Power Supplies	Implement procedures for electronic equipment to protect them from power failures and other electrical anomalies.	Y ___ N ___	Operations
7.2.3	Cabling Security	Implement standards to protect power and telecommunications cabling from interception or damage.	Y ___ N ___	Operations

(continued)

Table 1. Information Security Architecture Based on ISO 17799 and Partial GLBA (Continued)

7.2.4	Equipment Maintenance	Implement procedures to establish and correctly maintain IT equipment to ensure its continued availability and integrity.	Y ___ N ___	Operations
7.2.5	Security of Equipment Off-premises	Implement standards and procedures to ensure that equipment used off-site, regardless of ownership, provides the same degree of protection afforded on-site IT equipment.	Y ___ N ___	Physical Security
7.3	General Controls	Information and information processing facilities should be protected from disclosure to, modification of, or theft by, unauthorized persons, and controls should be in place to minimize loss or damage.		
7.3.1	Clear Desk and Clear Screen Policy	Implement a clear desk/clear screen policy for sensitive material to reduce risks of unauthorized access, loss, or damage outside normal working hours.	Y ___ N ___	Physical Security
7.3.2	Removal of Property	Implement procedures to ensure that personnel are required to have documented management authorization to take equipment, data, or software off-site.	Y ___ N ___	Physical Security

8. COMMUNICATIONS AND OPERATIONS MANAGEMENT

8.1	Operational Procedures and Responsibilities	Responsibilities and procedures must be established for the management and operation of all computers and networks.		
8.1.1	Documented Operating Procedures (GLBA)	Implement operating procedures to clearly document that all operational computer systems are being operated in a correct, secure manner.	Y ___ N ___	Operations
8.1.2	Operational Change Control (GLBA)	Implement procedures for controlling changes to IT facilities and systems to ensure satisfactory control of all changes to equipment, software, or procedures.	Y ___ N ___	Systems

(continued)

124

Table 1. Information Security Architecture Based on ISO 17799 and Partial GLBA (Continued)

8.1.3	Incident Management Procedures (GLBA)	Implement standards and procedures to identify incident management responsibilities and to ensure a quick, effective, orderly response to security incidents.	Y ___ N ___	ERT
8.1.4	Segregation of Duties (GLBA)	Implement standards and user training to ensure that sensitive duties or areas of responsibility are kept separate to reduce opportunities for unauthorized modification or misuse of data or services.	Y ___ N ___	Operations and Employment Policy
8.1.5	Separation of Development and Operational Facilities (GLBA)	Implement procedures to segregate development and production facilities to reduce the risk of accidental changes or unauthorized access to production software and data.	Y ___ N ___	Operations
8.2	System Planning and Acceptance	Advance planning and preparation can ensure the availability of adequate capacity and resources.		
8.2.1	Capacity Planning	Implement standards to ensure that capacity requirements are monitored, and future requirements projected, to reduce the risk of system overload.	Y ___ N ___	Systems and Operations
8.2.2	System Acceptance	Implement procedures to establish acceptance criteria for new systems, and that adequate tests have been performed prior to acceptance.	Y ___ N ___	Systems
8.3	Protection from Malicious Software	Applying precautions to prevent and detect the introduction of malicious software can safeguard the integrity of software and data.		
8.3.1	Controls against Malicious Software	Implement standards and user training to ensure that virus detection and prevention measures are adequate.	Y ___ N ___	Operations
8.4	Housekeeping	Routine procedures should be established for making backup copies of data, logging events and faults, and where appropriate, monitoring the equipment environment.		

(continued)

Table 1. Information Security Architecture Based on ISO 17799 and Partial GLBA (Continued)

8.4.1	Information Backup	Establish procedures for making regular backup copies of essential business data and software to ensure that it can be recovered following a computer disaster or media failure.	Y ___ N ___	Operations
8.4.2	Operator Logs	Implement standards and procedures such that computer operators are required to maintain a log of all work performed.	Y ___ N ___	Operations
8.4.3	Fault Logging	Implement procedures for logging faults reported by users regarding problems with computer or communications systems.	Y ___ N ___	Operations
8.5	Network Management	The security of computer networks that may span organizational boundaries must be managed to safeguard information and to protect the supporting infrastructure.		
8.5.1	Network Controls	Implement appropriate standards to ensure the security of data in networks and the protection of connected services from unauthorized access.	Y ___ N ___	Network
8.6	Media Handling and Security	Computer media should be controlled and physically protected to prevent damage to assets and interruptions to business activities.		
8.6.1	Management of Removable Computer Media	Implement procedures exist for the management of removable computer media such as tapes, disks, cassettes, and printed reports.	Y ___ N ___	Operations and Physical Security
8.6.2	Disposal of Media	Implement standards and procedures to ensure that computer media are disposed of securely and safely when no longer required.	Y ___ N ___	Operations and Physical Security
8.6.3	Information Handling Procedures	Implement procedures for handling sensitive data to protect such data from unauthorized disclosure or misuse.	Y ___ N ___	Asset Classification

(continued)

126

Table 1. Information Security Architecture Based on ISO 17799 and Partial GLBA (Continued)

8.6.4	Security of System Documentation	Implement standards to protect system documentation from unauthorized access.	Y ___ N ___	Asset Classification
8.7	Exchanges of Information and Software	Exchanges of data and software between organizations should be controlled to prevent loss, modification, or misuse of data.		
8.7.1	Information and Software Exchange Agreements	Implement procedures to establish that formal agreements exist, including software escrow agreements when appropriate, for exchanging data and software (whether electronically or manually) between organizations.	Y ___ N ___	Operations
8.7.2	Security of Media in Transit	Implement standards to safeguard computer media being transported between sites to minimize its vulnerability to unauthorized access, misuse, or corruption during transportation.	Y ___ N ___	Operations
8.7.3	Electronic Commerce Security	Implement standards to protect electronic commerce (electronic data interchange, electronic mail, and online transactions across a public network such as the Internet) against unauthorized interception or modification.	Y ___ N ___	Operations
8.7.4	Security of Electronic Mail	Implement standards and user training to reduce the business and security risks associated with electronic mail, to include interception, modification, and errors.	Y ___ N ___	Operations & Network
8.7.5	Security of Electronic Office Systems	Implement a risk analysis process and resultant standards to control business and security risks associated with electronic office systems.	Y ___ N ___	IS Organization

(continued)

Table 1. Information Security Architecture Based on ISO 17799 and Partial GLBA (Continued)

8.7.6	Publicly Available Systems	Implement a formal policy to establish an authorization process for information that is to be made publicly available.	Y ___ N ___	Corporate Communications
8.7.7	Other Forms of Information Exchange	Implement procedures and standards to protect the exchange of information through the use of voice, facsimile, and video communications facilities.	Y ___ N ___	Network

9. ACCESS CONTROL (GLBA)

9.1	Business Requirement for System Access	Policies for information dissemination and entitlement should control access to computer services and data on the basis of business requirements.		
9.1.1	Access Control Policy	Implement a risk analysis process to gather business requirements to document access control levels.	Y ___ N ___	Access Control
9.2	User Access Management	Formal procedures are needed to control allocation of access rights to IT services.		
9.2.1	User Registration	Implement procedures for user registration and deregistration access to all multi-use IT services.	Y ___ N ___	Access Control
9.2.2	Privilege Management	Implement standards to protect against the use of any feature or facility of a multi-user IT system that enables a user to override system or application controls.	Y ___ N ___	Access Control
9.2.3	User Password Management	Implement standards to address password management.	Y ___ N ___	Access Control
9.2.4	Review of User Access Rights	Implement procedures to conduct periodic reviews of users' access rights.	Y ___ N ___	Access Control
9.3	User Responsibilities	Users should be made aware of their responsibilities for maintaining effective access controls, particularly regarding the use of passwords and security of user equipment.		

(continued)

Table 1. Information Security Architecture Based on ISO 17799 and Partial GLBA (Continued)

9.3.1	Password Use	Implement user training to ensure users are taught good security practices in the selection and use of passwords.	Y ___ N ___	IS User Training
9.3.2	Unattended User Equipment	Implement policies and procedures to ensure that all users and contractors are made aware of the security requirements and procedures for protecting unattended equipment.	Y ___ N ___	IS User Training
		Implement standards to log that all users and contractors have been made aware of their responsibilities for implementing such protection.	Y ___ N ___	IS User Training
9.4	Network Access Control	Connections to network services should be controlled to ensure that connected users or computer services do not compromise the security of any other networked services.		
9.4.1	Policy on Use of Network Services	Implement procedures to ensure that network and computer services that can be accessed by an individual user or from a particular terminal are consistent with business access control policy.	Y ___ N ___	Network
9.4.2	Enforced Path	Implement standards that restrict the route between a user terminal and the computer services that its user is authorized to access.	Y ___ N ___	Network
9.4.3	User Authentication for External Connections	Implement standards to ensure that connections by remote users via public or non-organization networks are authenticated to prevent unauthorized access to business applications.	Y ___ N ___	Network

(continued)

Table 1. Information Security Architecture Based on ISO 17799 and Partial GLBA (Continued)

9.4.4	Node Authentication	Implement standards to ensure that connections by remote computer systems are authenticated to prevent unauthorized access to a business application.	Y ___ N ___	Network
9.4.5	Remote Diagnostic Port Protection	Implement procedures to control access to diagnostic ports designed for remote use by maintenance engineers.	Y ___ N ___	Network
9.4.6	Network Segregation	Implement standards to have large networks divided into separate domains to mitigate the risk of unauthorized access to existing computer systems that use the network.	Y ___ N ___	Network
9.4.7	Network Connection Control	Implement standards to restrict the connection capability of users, in support of access policy requirements of business applications that extend across organizational boundaries.	Y ___ N ___	Network
9.4.8	Network Routing Control	Implement standards that identify routing controls over shared networks across organizational boundaries to ensure those computer connections and information flows conform to the access policy of business units.	Y ___ N ___	Network
9.4.9	Security in Network Services	Implement standards to capture network providers to clearly define security attributes of all services used, and use this information to establish the security controls to protect the confidentiality, integrity, and availability of business applications.	Y ___ N ___	Network

(continued)

Table 1. Information Security Architecture Based on ISO 17799 and Partial GLBA (Continued)

9.5	Operating System Access Control	Access to computers should be strictly limited through the use of: • Automatic terminal identification • Terminal log-on procedures • User IDs • Password management • A duress alarm • Terminal time out • Limited connection time		
9.5.1	Automatic Terminal Identification	Implement standards for automatic terminal identification to authenticate connections to specific locations.	Y ___ N ___	Operations
9.5.2	Terminal Log on Procedures	Implement procedures for logging into a computer system to minimize the opportunity for unauthorized access.	Y ___ N ___	Operations
9.5.3	User Identification and Authentication	Establish standards to ensure all users have a unique identifier (user ID) for their personal and sole use, to ensure that their activities can be traced to them.	Y ___ N ___	Access Control
9.5.4	Password Management System	Implement standards to ensure an effective password management system is employed to authenticate users.	Y ___ N ___	Access Control
9.5.5	Use of System Utilities	Implement standards to restrict access to system utility programs that could be used to override system and application controls.	Y ___ N ___	Operations
9.5.6	Duress Alarm to Safeguard Users	Conduct a risk analysis to determine if a duress alarm needs to be provided for users who might be the target of coercion.	Y ___ N ___	Physical Security
		Implement standards to define responsibilities for responding to duress alarms.	Y ___ N ___	Physical Security

(continued)

Table 1. Information Security Architecture Based on ISO 17799 and Partial GLBA (Continued)

9.5.7	Terminal Timeout	Implement standards to ensure that terminals in high-risk locations are set to time out when inactive to prevent access by unauthorized persons.	Y ___ N ___	Network
9.5.8	Limitation of Connection Time	Implement standards to identify the period during which terminals may be connected to sensitive application systems.	Y ___ N ___	Access Control
9.6	Application Access Control	Logical access controls should be enacted to protect application systems and data from unauthorized access.		
9.6.1	Information Access Restriction	Implement procedures to restrict access to applications system data and functions in accordance with defined access policy and based on individual requirements.	Y ___ N ___	Applications
9.6.2	Isolation of Sensitive Systems	Implement standards to isolate sensitive application systems processing environment.	Y ___ N ___	Operations
9.7	Monitoring System Access and Use	Systems should be monitored to ensure conformity with access policy and standards, to detect unauthorized activities, and to determine the effectiveness of security measures adopted.		
9.7.1	Event Logging	Implement standards to have audit trails record exceptions and other security-relevant events, and to ensure that they are maintained to assist in future investigations and in access control monitoring.	Y ___ N ___	Operations
9.7.2	Monitoring System Use	Implement procedures for monitoring system use to ensure that users are only performing processes that have been explicitly authorized.	Y ___ N ___	Operations
9.7.3	Clock Synchronization	Implement standards to ensure computer or communications device clocks are correct and in synchronization.	Y ___ N ___	Operations

(continued)

Table 1. Information Security Architecture Based on ISO 17799 and Partial GLBA (Continued)

9.8	Mobile Commuting and Telecommuting	When using mobile computing and telecommuting, the organization should examine the risks and apply appropriate protection to the equipment or site.		
9.8.1	Mobile Commuting	Implement a formal policy and supporting standards that address the risks of working with mobile computing facilities, including requirements for physical protection, access controls, cryptographic techniques, backup, and virus protection.	Y ___ N ___	Network
9.8.2	Telecommuting	Implement policies and procedures to control telecommuting, to include existing facilities, the proposed telecommuting environment, communications security requirements, and the threat of unauthorized access to equipment or the network.	Y ___ N ___	Employment (HR Policies)

10. SYSTEMS DEVELOPMENT and MAINTENANCE

10.1	Security Requirements of Systems	To ensure that security is built into IT systems, security requirements should be identified, justified, agreed to, and documented as part of the requirements definition stage of all IT system development projects.		
10.1.1	Security Requirements Analysis and Specification	Implement standards to ensure that analysis of security requirements is part of the requirement analysis stage of each development project.	Y ___ N ___	Systems
10.2	Security in Application Systems	Security controls that conform to commonly accepted industry standards of good security practice should be designed into applications systems to prevent loss, modification, or misuse of user data.		
10.2.1	Input Data Validation	Implement standards to ensure that data input into applications systems is validated to ensure that it is correct and appropriate.	Y ___ N ___	Applications

(continued)

133

INFORMATION SECURITY POLICIES AND PROCEDURES

Table 1. Information Security Architecture Based on ISO 17799 and Partial GLBA (Continued)

10.2.2	Control of Internal Processing	Implement standards to ensure that validation checks are incorporated into systems to detect corruption caused by processing errors or through deliberate acts.	Y ___ N ___	Applications
10.2.3	Message Authentication	Implement standards to ensure that message authentication is considered for applications that involve the transmission of sensitive data.	Y ___ N ___	Applications
10.2.4	Output Data Validation	Implement standards to ensure that data output from applications systems is validated to ensure that it is correct and appropriate.	Y ___ N ___	Applications
10.3	Cryptographic Controls (GLBA)	To protect the confidentiality, authenticity, or integrity of information, cryptographic systems and techniques should be used for complete protection of information that is considered at risk.		
10.3.1	Policy on the Use of Cryptographic Controls	Implement policies and standards on the use of cryptographic controls, including management of encryption keys and effective implementation.	Y ___ N ___	Asset Classification
10.3.2	Encryption	Implement standards to ensure that data encryption is used to protect highly sensitive data during transmission or in storage.	Y ___ N ___	Operations
10.3.3	Digital Signatures	Implement standards for the use of digital signatures to protect the authenticity and integrity of electronic documents.	Y ___ N ___	Operations
10.3.4	Non-Repudiation Services	Implement standards for non-repudiation services where disputes might arise based on the use of encryption or digital signatures.	Y ___ N ___	Operations
10.3.5	Key Management	Implement standards for use of cryptographic techniques, including secret key techniques and public key techniques.	Y ___ N ___	Operations

(continued)

134

Table 1. Information Security Architecture Based on ISO 17799 and Partial GLBA (Continued)

10.4	Security of System Files	To ensure that IT projects and support activities are conducted in a secure manner, the responsibility for controlling access to application system files should be assigned to and carried out by the owning user function or development group.		
10.4.1	Control of Operational Software	Implement standards. Is strict control exercised over the implementation of software on operational systems?	Y ___ N ___	Systems
10.4.2	Protection of System Test Data	Implement standards to ensure that all application system test data is protected and controlled.	Y ___ N ___	Applications
10.4.3	Access Control to Program Source Library	Implement standards and procedures to restrict access to program source libraries to reduce the potential for corruption of computer programs.	Y ___ N ___	Applications
10.5	Security in Development and Support Environments	Project and support environments must be strictly controlled to maintain the security of application system software and data.		
10.5.1	Change Control Procedures	Implement standards and procedures for formal change control procedures.	Y ___ N ___	Systems
10.5.2	Technical Review of Operating System Changes	Implement procedures to review application systems when changes to the operating systems occur.	Y ___ N ___	Systems
10.5.3	Restrictions on Changes to Software Packages	Implement standards to restrict modifications to vendor-supplied software.	Y ___ N ___	Systems and Applications
10.5.4	Covert Channels and Trojan Code	Implement standards and procedures to avoid covert channels or Trojan codes; these standards and procedures should address at a minimum that the organization: • Buy programs only from a reputable source • Buy programs in source code that is verifiable • Use only evaluated products	Y ___ N ___	Systems

(continued)

135

Table 1. Information Security Architecture Based on ISO 17799 and Partial GLBA (Continued)

		• Inspect all source code before operational use •Control access to, and modification of, installed code •Use trusted staff to work on key systems		
10.5.5	Outsourced Software Development	Implement standards to address when software development is outsourced, that controls are in place to address the ownership of intellectual property throughout the project life cycle.	Y ___ N ___	Procurement and Applications

11. BUSINESS CONTINUITY MANAGEMENT (GLBA)

11.1	Aspects of Business Continuity Planning	Business continuity plans should be available to counteract interruptions to business activities.		
11.1.1	Business Continuity Management Process	Implement procedures for the development and maintenance of business continuity plans across the organization.	Y ___ N ___	BCP
11.1.2	Business Continuity and Impact Analysis	Implement standards for corporate business continuity, and ensure that management endorses the plan.	Y ___ N ___	BCP and IS Steering Committee
11.1.3	Writing and Implementing Continuity Plans	Implement standards and procedures for business continuity planning to encompass the identification of all responsibilities and emergency procedures.	Y ___ N ___	BCP
11.1.4	Business Continuity Planning Framework	Implement a single business continuity plan framework, maintained to ensure that all levels of the plan are consistent.	Y ___ N ___	BCP
11.1.5	Testing, Maintaining, and Reassessing Business Continuity Plans	Implement standards to ensure regular testing of the BCPs.	Y ___ N ___	BCP

(continued)

Table 1. Information Security Architecture Based on ISO 17799 and Partial GLBA (Continued)

12. COMPLIANCE

12.1	Compliance with Legal Requirements	All relevant requirements for each IT system should be identified and documented.		
12.1.1	Identification of Applicable Legislation	Implement standards to ensure that all relevant statutory, regulatory, and contractual requirements are specifically defined and documented for each information system.	Y ___ N ___	Applications and Systems
12.1.2	Intellectual Property Rights	Implement standards to ensure there is compliance with legal restrictions on the use of copyright material, ensuring that only software developed by the organization, or licensed or provided by the developer to the organization, is used.	Y ___ N ___	IS Organization
12.1.3	Safeguarding of Organizational Records	Implement policies and standards to ensure that important organizational records are securely maintained to meet statutory requirements, as well as to support essential business activities.	Y ___ N ___	Records Management
12.1.4	Data Protection and Privacy of Personal Information	Implement standards to ensure that applications that process personal data on individuals comply with applicable data protection legislation.	Y ___ N ___	Applications and IS Organization
12.1.5	Prevention of Misuse of Information Processing Facilities	Implement policies to ensure that IT facilities are used only for business purposes.	Y ___ N ___	Operations
12.1.6	Regulation of Cryptographic Controls	Implement standards and procedures to ensure that legal advice is sought on the organization's compliance with national and international laws on cryptographic controls.	Y ___ N ___	IS Organization

(continued)

Table 1. Information Security Architecture Based on ISO 17799 and Partial GLBA (Continued)

12.1.7	Collection of Evidence	Implement standards and procedures to ensure that when conducting an investigation, the rules for evidence are followed for admissibility, quality, and completeness.	Y ___ N ___	Physical Security and ERT
12.2	Reviews of Security Policy and Technical Compliance	To ensure compliance of IT systems with organizational security policies and standards, compliance reviews should be conducted regularly.		
12.2.1	Compliance with Security Policy	Implement standards to ensure that all areas within the organization are considered for regular review to ensure compliance with security policies and standards.	Y ___ N ___	IS Steering Committee and Mission Statements
12.2.2	Technical Compliance Checking	Implement standards to ensure that IT facilities are regularly checked for compliance with security implementation standards.	Y ___ N ___	Mission Statements and IS Organization
12.3	System Audit Considerations	There should be controls over operational systems and audit tools during system audits to minimize interference to and from the system audit process, and to protect the integrity and prevent the misuse of audit tools.		
12.3.1	System Audit Controls	Implement standards to ensure audits and activities involving checks on operational systems are carefully planned and arranged.	Y ___ N ___	Mission Statements
12.3.2	Protection of System Audit Tools	Implement standards and procedures to restrict access to system audit tools.	Y ___ N ___	Operations

This compliance plan will include the movement to the standard operating systems. However, there may be areas (marketing, for one) that may present to management a business case why they need to remain outside the organization's operating requirements. If this is approved, then it will be necessary to meet with the non-standard business unit or group and perform a gap analysis on their environment and the organization's requirements.

Just because a unit or group is not using standard equipment or current-level operating systems does not absolve them of the responsibility to be compliant with the information security standards. If there are standards that they cannot meet based on their hardware or software, then they must present alternative controls and standards. All activities must be documented so that all business units can be audited or reviewed for compliance to agreed-upon standards.

Your information security standards document is intended to be a living, dynamic instrument. It is to be managed by the Information Security staff, and all requests for changes, amendments, and additions must be made in writing to the IS Manager.

It will be necessary to implement version control and, where sufficient changes have been received, a full reissue should occur. All requests for changes must be circulated to the specific SME for review and comment. Once approval has been received from the SME, the standard should be updated and sent to the user community. To help with version control, an online document available on the enterprise intranet is highly recommended. It will be necessary to notify the user community when changes are made; however, this may become a daily occurrence. It is recommended that regularly scheduled update procedures be established to send notification of the changes to the users. This is typically done quarterly, but in some instances it can be done immediately if conditions warrant.

7 SUMMARY

Standards are used to support the Tier 1 and Tier 2 policies. They must have support from management to be effective and they must be practical. Use the existing national and international standards and business or agency regulations to form the basis for standards. It is much easier to get standards accepted if you can track them to a specific regulation.

When writing the standard, it often becomes difficult because the language is at times severe. "Managers must..." or "failure to comply will result in disciplinary action." We live in an era of political correctness and we often want to soften the language so as not to offend anyone. The only entity that will be offended is the organization if the standards are not properly implemented and supported by management. Make certain that the readers know exactly what is expected and what the consequences will be if they or the business units are found to be noncompliant.

Remember that standards are mandatory, and will impact the organization and the way it conducts its affairs. Use them to support the policies — not to punish the user community. Check standards to make certain they are still effective.

All standards will "cost" the organization something. It could be budget dollars to implement or it could be turn-around time or system response time. All standards will cost the organization, so select only the level of controls necessary to allow the organization to meet its objectives in a safe operating environment. Many times, we discuss the concept of "least privilege," meaning that a user is granted only the minimum level of access necessary to perform his or her job function. A variation on this concept is the implementation of a "least intrusive" standard: implement only that level of standard necessary to secure the information or transaction.

The most secure computer system is one that is turned off, unplugged, locked away, and encased in cement. While a system like this is secure, it will probably impact department productivity in some manner. The security professional must understand that for information to be of any value, it must be available and shared with those having a business need. Standards must support the objectives of sharing information as securely as possible.

Chapter 7
Developing Procedures

1 INTRODUCTION

Procedures are as unique as the organization. There is no generally accepted standard for the proper way to write a procedure. What will determine how your procedures look will be how they currently look or what will work best to provide the target audience with what it needs. This means that it may be necessary to use a number of different styles. This chapter examines what some of those procedure styles look like and how they are used.

2 OVERVIEW

Procedure writing is different than policy writing in that it is not useful to have teams develop the procedures (see Figure 1). Procedures will not have to be approved by a management team; thus, the process is quicker but will require some work.

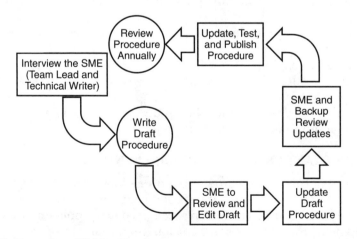

Figure 1. Procedure Writing Process

Unlike the policy development process, the use of a team to develop procedures will actually slow down the process. Many security professionals reach this stage of the information security program and believe that the bulk of their work is complete and now it will be up to the subject matter experts (SMEs) to write the procedures. This is probably not going to work. The SMEs are usually the same groups of people required now to provide documentation for the work they perform. They are busy with their day-to-day functions and are already hard-pressed to find the time to worry about existing paperwork, let alone adding the requirement that they write procedures.

When developing procedures, use a technical writer to gather the relevant information from the SME and put that information into one of the procedure formats. We will discuss formats in this chapter. I recommend that you schedule an interview with the SMEs and let them know in advance what the topic will be. Ask them to bring any written procedures they may have created on the subject and any other visual aid (perhaps a flowchart or an information flow model).

Schedule the meeting for 45 minutes. This should be long enough to get the information necessary, but not so long as to impact the SME's busy schedule. Remember to treat the SMEs with respect and to listen to what they have to say, but keep them on track. After you have gathered all the information you can about the subject, inform the SMEs as to what the next steps will be.

1. The material just discussed will be put into procedure format.
2. A draft procedure will be sent to the SME for review and content editing.
3. The technical writer will update the procedure based on the SME's remarks.
4. The updated procedure will be sent to the SME and the SME backup for a final review.
5. Any additional updates will be incorporated into the procedure.
6. The procedure will be tested (either with the backup or some other person).
7. If the procedure provides the proper results, it will be published in the appropriate procedure document.

3   IMPORTANT PROCEDURE REQUIREMENTS

When putting the SME's words into a procedure, it will be necessary to ensure that the procedure is developed properly. There are procedure-writing requirements just as we have examined in the policy and standards development process. For some reason, requirements seem to come in tens. So let us examine the ten requirements for procedure writing.

1. Write to the Audience. Procedures are created and implemented with the sole intention to be read and used by the user community. Always keep the audience in mind when writing procedures. When you interview the SME, you will get a flavor for the language that is used in that area. Write the procedure to reflect this level of technology. However, when writing procedures to support business continuity planning (BCP) activities, the audience has changed. Instead of the SME, the audience may be someone filling in for the SME. So before any procedure can be written, it will be necessary to know who the audience is and what its level of knowledge of the subject at hand is.

Every department has its own language. Therefore, the procedures must be developed using the terms to which the department members are accustomed. If you write procedures using the wrong "language," the procedure may as well be written in Sanskrit. The intended audience will not be able to understand it, or they will find it difficult to follow.

2. Organize the Material. The procedures must be written in a logical and flowing manner so that the reader can understand the meaning. If the text is not properly planned, the possibility is great that the intended audience will not clearly understand what is expected of them. The procedure must be broken up into easily digestible bits of information. Do not expect the user to read a long and involved passage and then successfully execute the appropriate processes.

The television program *Friends* gave us a perfect example of what can go wrong if procedures are not properly followed or if they are designed incorrectly. The character Rachel was creating a dessert trifle from a recipe. She started with sponge cake, then custard, then fruit, then sponge cake, and then the pages of the cookbook stuck together. She finished the trifle with a layer of ground meat and potatoes. She had combined the trifle recipe with one for shepherd's pie. If the procedure is created in a convoluted manner, this could happen to your organization.

3. Read and Edit the Materials. Do not just run the spellchecker and assume that the editing is complete. Before handing over the material to the *editor*, proofread what has been written and see if it makes sense to you. If you are unable to understand what you have written, then it will probably be more difficult for others to understand. After the technical writer has developed the draft procedure, have the document proofed for grammar and spelling. Once that is complete, have someone in the group read through the procedure to see if it follows a logical sequence. Once these steps have been completed, the procedure is ready for the SME to review.

4. Find Subject Experts. The first step in any procedure development process is to either know the subject or find someone who does, and then use this knowledge to write the procedure. The subject expert may not understand the procedure writing process, so it may be necessary for you to sit with them and take notes on how the process works and then write the procedure. Make sure that one of the editors is the subject expert. However, the subject expert should not be the person to test the procedure. The expert knows the topic so well that he or she might assume information that is not present in the procedure.

5. Use Clear, Familiar Words. The procedure's intended audience will not be pleased if they are confronted with a document filled with words, expressions, and acronyms with which they are unfamiliar. It will be important to have a definition section in some procedures. This should be done up front and provide the reader with whatever is necessary to complete the process at hand.

Do not use big words; remember the reading and comprehension level of the intended audience. Multiple syllables may be imprecise, and avoid the use of the various "ese" languages (financialese, auditese, legalese, securityese, computerese, etc.).

I enjoy watching *Inside the Actor's Studio* on the Bravo network. The part I like best comes toward the end of the show when James Lipton asks the guest the ten questions created by Bernard Pivot:

1. What is your favorite word?
2. What is your least favorite word?
3. What turns you on creatively, spiritually, or emotionally?
4. What turns you off?
5. What is your favorite curse word?
6. What sound or noise do you love?
7. What sound or noise do you hate?
8. What profession other than your own would you like to attempt?
9. What profession would you not like to do?
10. If heaven exists, what would you like to hear God say when you arrive at the "Pearly Gates"?

It is fun to listen to each guest and hear how they answer these questions. I am always interested in the first, the favorite word. The actor/singer Will Smith said his favorite word is "antidisestablishmentarianism." My favorite word is "epistemology," the study of knowledge. These are not the types of words you should use when you are writing procedures. Do not use "in the near future;" use "soon." Instead of "at this point in time," use "now."

Make sure to define all acronyms. There is nothing more irritating than to be reading a text that contains a number of *TLAs* (a TLA is a Three-Letter Acronym for three-letter acronyms). The user will lose interest and comprehension if there are undefined terms in the text. I had the good fortune to work with nine other authors in the development of *The Total CISSP ® Exam Prep Book*. While we were developing the material, I began to put together a list of acronyms. At the conclusion we had uncovered over 400 acronyms used in the IT and information security profession. Watch out for overuse of acronyms.

6. Keep Sentences Short and Simple. Remember the KISS (Keep It Simple Sweetie) principle. Long sentences increase the level of user frustration and decrease the level of user understanding. An appropriate average sentence length for procedures is between ten and fifteen words. Unless you are a writer of the caliber of a James Joyce, it would be wise to keep the sentences to the 15-word maximum level. Typically, procedures are better if the sentences are brief and often they do not have to be correct syntax-wise. Phrases such as "Hit Enter" or "toggle switch" are sufficient when writing procedures.

7. Use Illustrations to Support the Topic. "A picture is worth a thousand words" may be a cliché, but it is true. Whenever applicable, break up the text with a graphic that depicts what is being discussed. These graphics can be pictures, charts (flow, pie, bar, etc.), tables, or diagrams. These will help the user visualize the subject and can provide the material necessary for a clear understanding of the process.

Illustrations include the use of screen prints. This will help users if they are interacting with a computer system. By providing a picture of the screen, users will be able to visualize what the process looks like and what is expected as a response.

8. Use the Active Voice. In the active voice, the sentences stress what must occur. It will identify who is responsible for what action. For example, a *passive voice* might read as follows: "All tape drives are to be cleaned by the tape operators." An *active voice* might read as follows: "The tape operators are responsible for cleaning the tape drives on each shift." The active voice identifies who is responsible and what they are responsible for.

9. Ensure Grammar and Punctuation are Correct. The number-one deadly sin is not taking care of this key element. Too many times, materials have been sent out for content review and the text is filled with errors of grammar and punctuation. It is hard enough to get a critique of the subject; by presenting reviewers with error-filled material, they will correct the form and forget to comment on the substance. If this is not your strong suit, find someone who can do these edits.

10. Use a Conversational Style. This does not mean that the text should be full of slang and idioms; it should just be presented in an informal style.

Most people communicate better when they are speaking than when they are writing. Many individuals write to impress the reader as opposed to writing to express an idea. One very easy way around this problem is to write as if you are talking to the intended audience. However, if you have a tendency to speak like William F. Buckley, Jr., then you might want to have someone else review the material. Although a conversational style is preferred, this form does not relieve you of the responsibility of being precise.

4   KEY ELEMENTS IN PROCEDURE WRITING

There are four key purposes for writing a procedure:

1. The first is to fulfill some need. If a task or process has to be performed in a specific manner, then there is a definite need for a procedure. If you happen to find a set of procedures, do not immediately assume that everything in the document needs to be recreated. First, perform an examination of the procedures and, with the SME, determine if each procedure is still required.
2. Once the need has been established, it will be necessary to identify the target audience.
3. Describe the task that the procedure will cover. It will be necessary to have opening remarks that present the scope of what the procedure is attempting to accomplish. Do not just start the procedure. Explain what the procedure is attempting to do and lay out any prerequisites that need to be done before beginning the procedure process.
4. The intent of the purpose should also be made known to the user. When the readers have completed the tasks set up in the procedure, identify what they should expect to occur.

5   PROCEDURE CHECKLIST

Not every procedure will require all the elements found in the procedure development checklist. Some may even require additional steps. As with any checklist, this is only a series of thought starters. The list that will be used by you may have additional items, or fewer.

1. *Title.* Establish what the topic of the procedure is going to be. Try to avoid being cute with your choice of words. Remember that you are writing for a business environment.
2. *Intent.* Discuss what the procedure is attempting to accomplish in general terms.
3. *Scope.* Briefly describe the process that the procedure is going to cover. (e.g., implementing a UNIX user ID request).
4. *Responsibilities.* Identify who is to perform what steps in the procedure. Use job functions rather than individual names.

5. *Sequence of events.* It is very important for the user to understand the timing and conditions for performing the tasks identified in the procedure. Some tasks are not executed at a specific time but must be performed when a specific condition is met.

6. *Approvals.* Identify any necessary approvals and when these approvals must be met. Approvals will be obtained prior to the execution of the procedure process.

7. *Prerequisites.* List any preconditions that must be met before starting the procedure process.

8. *Definitions.* Remember the audience. It will be beneficial to include a discussion of any terms and acronyms that are included in the body of the procedure.

9. *Equipment required.* Identify all equipment, tools, documents, and anything else the individual executing the procedure will need to perform the tasks.

10. *Warnings.* Some tasks, if operated in an improper sequence, could cause severe damage to the enterprise. Identify those key tasks and review the importance of understanding exactly when the task is to be executed and under what set of circumstances.

11. *Precautions.* Identify all steps to be taken to avoid problems or dangers (e.g., "Unplug before performing maintenance.")

12. *Procedure body.* These are the actual steps to be performed in the execution of the procedure.

6   GETTING STARTED

Now that you understand what the "do's and don'ts" of procedure writing are all about, it is time to get down to the actual task. A procedure is the step-by-step process that an employee will use to complete a specific task. Therefore, to write a procedure, it will be necessary to have a strong understanding of the task at hand. Very few of us have a sufficient level of knowledge for every subject. Thus, it will be necessary for us to seek out subject matter experts (SMEs) to help in the development of procedures.

The SMEs are usually those employees who handle a specific set of tasks daily and it will be their knowledge that must be turned into a procedure. Many organizations have requested that the SMEs write the procedures themselves. This method has met with limited success. What is currently recommended is that the organization hire documentation experts to interview the SMEs and then write the procedures.

Our employees are generally overworked. By asking them to perform a task that most do not want to do will cause lengthy delays in completing the process. By conducting an interview (not to last longer that 90 minutes) and having the documentation expert write the draft document, it may be possible to actually complete the procedure development process on time.

Once the draft is completed, it should be given to the SME and the SME's backup for review and critique. Allow this process to take five to ten workdays. Once the comments are incorporated, send the procedures out for a final review and include the SME's supervisor. After the procedures are returned, make any final adjustments and then publish them. Ensure that the SME reviews the procedures at least annually for changes.

7   PROCEDURE STYLES

There are, perhaps, as many as six different styles of procedures. Any one of them may meet the needs of your organization:

1. Headline
2. Caption
3. Matrix
4. Narrative
5. Flowchart
6. Playscript

Of these, the first one (headline) should be used very seldom. Others (especially caption and playscript) should be used very often.

The choice of layout will depend on the subject matter to be presented and the individuals using the material.

Each of them has its advantages and disadvantages. We examine eight of the most popular forms of procedures and will identify the positive side to each as well as any shortcomings.

The following general guidelines should be applied no matter what layout is used.

- *Every subject should have a summary.* A summary (Tier 2 policy) introduces the subject to the reader and outlines the scope and objectives of the procedure. It may present policy and background information, such as why a procedure is to be carried out and who is responsible for carrying it out.
- *Use brief paragraphs.* Keep your words and sentences brief and simple, as well as paragraphs.
- *Keep subjects brief.* Do only one procedure per procedure.
- *Write only to the audience concerned.* Know to whom you are writing and use them as a focus group.
- *Cross-reference only when necessary.* This will increase the need to monitor other sources to keep the procedures current.
- *Include detail.* The inclusion of detail does not contradict the requirement of being brief. One of the most consistent problems with procedures is the tendency to leave out details.

7.1 Headline

A headline style (Table 1) is a title line placed above the text. It is usually printed in bold and briefly summarizes or suggests the content of the text that follows (like a newspaper).

7.1.1 Headline Pros and Cons. Pros:

- The procedure is divided into organized blocks of data.

Cons:

- The procedure is meant to be read from beginning to end.
- The headline is used to grab the reader's eye and not as a means of retrieval.

7.2 Caption

Captions (Table 2) are key words that appear in the left margin of the page and highlight or describe the blocks of text opposite them.

7.2.1 Caption Pros and Cons. Pros:

- Layout is simple.
- Easy to read.
- Easy to retrieve information.
- Can be used for almost any subject.
- Can be mixed with other styles.

Cons:

- Writers tend to overuse.
- Should not be used for describing sequenced actions.

Sometimes Difficult to Organize Material Into Meaningful Order. The caption style is best used for descriptive text that answers all the writing questions: who, what, when, where, and why. Examples of subject matter that best lends itself to caption include:

- Policy statements
- Responsibility statements
- Descriptions of forms, reports, or equipment

7.3 Matrix

A matrix (see Table 3) is a chart that lists related constants and variables (or independent and dependent variables) on horizontal and vertical axes. At the intersection of lines drawn from each axis can be found such information as:

- Relationship between constants and variables

Table 1. Headline Procedure Example

Policies and Procedures Implemented Effectively

1. Project Initiation:
    1.1. Conduct project definition and confirmation meeting with customer.
    1.2. Develop documentation.
    1.3. Present findings and obtain approval of SOW.
    1.4. Develop Engagement Agreement.
    1.5. Develop Non-Disclosure Agreement.
2. Pre-Site Visit to Outline Expectations and Security Requirements:
    2.1. Determine project ownership.
    2.2. Determine client's expectations.
    2.3. Define project scope:
        2.3.1. Scope statement
        2.3.2. Scope verification
        2.3.3. Scope change control
    2.4. Define project approach:
        2.4.1. Define project milestones
        2.4.2. Define project schedule
        2.4.3. Define project deliverables
    2.5. Define project organization.
    2.6. Define project constraints.
    2.7. Define project assumptions.
    2.8. Define project risks.
    2.9. Define quantifiable project success criteria.
    2.10. Develop and submit Project Charter.
    2.11. Obtain client approval of Project Charter.
3. Facilitated Site Visit to Gather Data:
    3.1. Identify existing security policy and procedure documentation.
    3.2. Determine existing security policy hierarchy/definitions.
    3.3. Identify existing corporate policy development/maintenance process.
    3.4. Evaluate organizational security culture.
    3.5. Determine Requirements:
        3.5.1. Regulatory
        3.5.2. Legal requirements
        3.5.3. Contractual
        3.5.4. Business
    3.6. Identify policy responsibilities:
        3.6.1. Development
        3.6.2. Review
        3.6.3. Approval
        3.6.4. Communication
        3.6.5. Implementation
        3.6.6. Compliance monitoring
        3.6.7. Exception approval

(continued)

Table 1. Headline Procedure Example (Continued)

3.6.8. Maintenance
3.6.9. Awareness
3.7. Collect documentation:
3.7.1 Incident reports
3.7.2. Risk assessments
3.7.3. Audit reports
3.7.4. Organization charts
3.7.5. Security awareness materials
4. Planning for the Development of Policies and Procedures Documentation:
4.1. Analyze existing policies against identified policy requirements.
4.2. Conduct analysis of existing policies against leading practices (i.e., BS 7799).
4.3. Document and prioritize policy shortfalls and identify policy needs.
4.4. Present interim findings to client.
4.5. Obtain client approval of findings
4.6. Develop required documentation.
5. Documentation Review by Client:
5.1. Provide draft policy and procedure documentation to the client for review.
5.2. Establish review process:
5.2.1 Establish Review Panel composition
5.2.2. Validate review responsibilities
5.2.3. Validate review schedule
5.3. Assist client with review sessions.
5.4. Coordinate with client to keep review on schedule.
5.5. Address comments received from client reviewers.
6. Formal Presentation of Engagement Deliverables:
6.1. Prepare final deliverable by updating draft deliverable to incorporate validated reviewer comments.
6.2. Obtain client sign-off and approval.

Table 2. Caption Procedure Example

Hiring Responsibilities

Systems:	The Supervisor is responsible for:
	1. Recommending a candidate
	2. Obtaining approval to hire from the manager
	3. Notifying Human Resources
Human Resources:	The Hiring Officer is responsible for:
	1. Making the job offer, in accordance with company policy
	2. Induction and orientation interviews

Table 3. Matrix Procedure Example

	Confidential	Internal Use	Public
Labeling of documents	Document should identify **owner** and be marked **"CONFIDENTIAL"** on cover or title page	No special requirements	Document may be marked **"PUBLIC"** on cover or title page
Duplication of documents	Information **owner** to determine permissions	Duplication for business purposes only	No special requirements
Mailing of documents	No classification marking on external envelope; **"CONFIDENTIAL"** marking on cover sheet; confirmation of receipt at discretion of information **owner**	Mailing requirements determined by information **owner**	No special requirements
Disposal of documents	**Owner**-observed physical destruction beyond ability to recover	Controlled physical destruction	No special requirements
Storage of documents	Locked up when not in use	Master copy secured against destruction	Master copy secured against destruction
Read access to documents	**Owner** establishes **user** access rules; generally highly restricted	**Owner** establishes **user** access rules, generally widely available	No special requirements; generally available within and outside company
Review of document classification level	Information **owner** to establish specific review date (not to exceed one year)	Information **owner** to review at least annually	No special requirements

- Actions to be performed, depending on variables or condition answers

7.3.1 Matrix Pros and Cons. Pros:

- Data is presented in a simple and logical order
- Repetitive information is eliminated
- A one-page matrix may replace many pages of text
- Retrieval time and reading time are saved

Cons:

- Maintaining data can be time consuming
- Initial setup can also take time

7.4   Narrative

A narrative procedure style presents information in paragraph format. It presents the process in a conversational or narrative form. This method does not present the user with easy-to-follow steps; it requires the user to read the entire paragraph to find out what is expected. This method is recommended for such items as policy statements, company philosophy, or background material.

Table 4 shows an example of the narrative form of procedure writing. Note how all the information that the user will need is presented. The discussion flows through a logical transgression of the steps to be followed.

Pros:

- Written in the manner in which people speak
- Very thorough

Cons:

- Too difficult to use
- Reader cannot retrieve information quickly

The narrative style lets users know how to do something by telling them a story. For some, this is the method that is easiest to understand. However, for most, the narrative style is too long. Typically, the narrative form of procedures is used in the instructions portion of an assemble document.

7.5   Flowchart

A flowchart procedure is a pictorial representation in which symbols are used to depict persons, places, actions, functions, or equipment. It gives the user a diagram of the decision-making process and what is expected at each step when a decision is made.

It is best used when providing the user with an overview of what the process is going to be. The flowchart will help the users understand their portion of the procedure. They will be able to see where decisions are to be made and what direction to take based on the decision. It will be necessary to have a key to ensure that users understand what the flowchart symbols mean.

The flowchart procedure style is best used to present an overview for the user and should be considered as a supplement to the actual procedure text. This process of laying out the procedure in a flowchart is

Table 4. Narrative Procedure Example

Petty Cash Procedure

Purpose

To define the procedure for employee reimbursement via petty cash routine.

Policy

Petty cash transactions are for emergency use ranging in dollar value between $0.01 and $50.00 and do not require prior approval of the Purchasing Department.

Petty cash is available to all Rensselaer employees incurring authorized, non-travel expenses on behalf of Rensselaer.

If a receipt or request is greater than $50.00, this must be reimbursed using the Direct Payment Request Form. The check will be issued to the requesting individual. (Please see Direct Payment Request Policy 3.14.

Payment in full must be made at the time of purchase or at the time of delivery. No charges are allowed.

Items that cannot be purchased with petty cash include:
• Firearms, narcotics, syringes, needles, or radioactive material
• Publications or printing services that are subject to Library control
• Transactions involving exchanges or trade-ins
• Services involving an employer/employee relationship

Procedure

To request the establishment of a petty cash fund, it is necessary to submit a memorandum to the Accounts Payable section of the Controller's Office. The memorandum should include the following: location of the fund (campus address), reason a fund is needed, amount, custodian, date, and supervisor's name and signature.

If approved, a check will be made payable to the custodian. The check may be cashed at the Bursar's Office. The custodian must sign a statement, acknowledging the receipt and control of the cash. An authorized signature for the account should also be supplied to the Controller's Office.

Standard Petty Cash Receipt forms should be filled out for an employee to be reimbursed for related business expenses incurred. Receipts supporting the expenses must be submitted and include the following information: amount, date, vendor, description, business purpose, account to be charged, custodian signature and signature of individual incurring costs and requesting reimbursement.

When the amount of cash in the petty cash fund is low and needs to be replenished, a Petty Cash Summary is completed. The custodian must sign the form and then the supervisor must sign the form after he or she has approved the reconciliation.

The petty cash accounts should be reconciled monthly. A reconciliation procedure similar to the one necessary when requesting a replenishment of the fund is appropriate. A file should be maintained storing reconciliations and copies of reports submitted to the cashier for reimbursements.

actually beneficial to the writer of the procedure. By developing a decision flow process, the procedure writer will have a better chance of developing a logical and correct procedure.

Pros:

- Easy to read
- Technical types are familiar with the style

Cons:

- Nontechnical types do not like flowchart style

An example of a flowchart-type policy might include the narrative shown in Table 5 and then the actual flowchart (Figure 2).

7.6   Playscript

For anyone who has ever been in a play or has had the opportunity to read a play in a literature class, this style will be familiar. The process identifies each of the main participants, the actual commands to be entered, and any direction needed to complete the process.

Table 5. Flowchart Procedure Example

Levels of ROOT Exposure

An individual may obtain a ROOT (or systems administration) level account, depending upon the user's work assignment. Securing a ROOT account requires the approval of a level B Information Systems Manager, with subordinate approval as well.

If a user is part of the System Administration Staff, the user may be granted access via the System Administration or Root group, depending upon the platform being utilized. Users who are Department System Administrators may be granted department administrator access. Any user who is a Workgroup Administrator may be granted workgroup administrator access. Users who are Project Administrators may be granted access as necessary, depending upon the project. Any user-initiated root request will be denied root access.

Definitions (Levels of Root Access):

System Administrator or Root Access: Full access to all computer resources.

Department System Administrator Access: Full access to all computer resources available to the specific department.

Workgroup Administrator Access: Full access to all computer resources available to the specific workgroup.

Project Administrator Access: Access will be determined on a project-by-project basis and limited to only those areas necessary to satisfy the requirements of the project.

All user IDs with any ROOT level access will be added to the audit log functions and security will be notified to monitor all ROOT access IDs.

Any violations or abuses of a ROOT level access must be reported to Security Management (e-mail notification or security incident form) and to the MIS Department (security incident form).

Figure 2. Flowchart

The playscript identifies each individual involved in the procedure. Each step involved in the procedure is described in detail and when each step is to be executed. The playscript is easy to understand and the language used eliminates unnecessary words (adjectives and adverbs). Keep the sentences to the point; remember that you are writing procedure, not the great American novel. A typical statement might be "sign and date forms" or "forward form 1040A to supervisor."

In the Playscript style (Table 6) it is best to only describe one function in any one step. As part of the definition section of the procedure, define the key participants in the procedure and use a form of shorthand to call out that participant. For example, instead of having to identify the Corporate Information Officer, use CIO. For the Manager of Information Systems, Operation, and Quality Assurance, you may want to shorten this title to Manager. The key here is to keep it simple, but eliminate any confusion.

Table 6. Playscript Procedure Example 1

Submitting Papers for Public
Employee:
1.   Shall submit to their manager:
     A.   Information about the conference, journal, magazine, etc. where the information will be submitted for potential presentation.
     B.   The submission guidelines of the conference, journal, magazine, etc. where the information will be presented.
     C.   An abstract of the presentation, article, or white paper that will be published or presented.
     D.   A writing and research timeline.
The Manager will then:
1.   Approve the presentation, white paper, or article.
2.   Not approve the presentation, white paper, or article. →Stop.
The Employee will then:
1.   Submit the abstract to conference.
2.   Begin writing white paper or article.
3.   Begin any required research.
4.   Provide brief updates to manager when each part of timeline is completed.
5.   Ensure presentation, white paper, or article complies with the Information Protection policy.
6.   If submitting to a conference, receive presentation acceptance; if declined →Stop
7.   Submit final paper or presentation to manager for final approval.
Manager will then:
1.   Give final approval
2.   Decline →Stop
Employee:
1.   Submit article or white paper to journal or magazine, etc.
2.   Receive acceptance from magazine or journal or they decline →Stop.
3.   Give presentation at conference.
Stop

Another variation on the playscript style of procedure is the *tree style* (see Table 7). This uses the same basic layout of the playscript, but it allows the user to drill down to each of the steps identified.

8   PROCEDURE DEVELOPMENT REVIEW

Now that you understand what the do's and don'ts of procedure writing are all about, we must now get down to the actual task. A procedure is the step-by-step process that an employee will use to complete a specific task. To write a procedure, then, it will be necessary to have a strong understanding of the task at hand. Very few of us have a sufficient level of knowledge for every subject. Therefore, it will be necessary for us to seek out subject matter experts (SMEs) to help in the development of procedures.

The SMEs are usually those employees who handle a specific set of tasks daily and it will be their knowledge that must be turned into a procedure. Many organizations have requested that the SMEs write the procedures themselves. This method has met with limited success. What is currently recommended is that the organization hire documentation experts to interview the SMEs and then write the procedures.

After the SME has been interviewed, write the procedure and then send it to the SME and the SME's backup. Have them review and edit the procedure. Take the edits and incorporate them into the procedure and then publish the procedure. There is no need for additional rounds of reviews. When writing the procedure, remember the following:

- Establish a small, knowledgeable initial review panel.
- Do not create all the procedures by yourself. Seek out personnel in areas affected by the controls and gain their expertise and assistance in this process.
- Be certain that the procedures resemble the procedures currently being used in your organization.
- Try to get on the agenda of the IS Steering Committee to present your program and solicit that committee's support.
- Whenever possible, accept and implement the comments created by the reviewers. At the very least, contact the reviewer and explain why the comments could not be included.
- If there appears to be a conflict, set up a meeting, at the respondent's location if possible, to resolve the problem.
- Be persistent. You are going to have to keep after the reviewers to get their responses.

9   OBSERVATIONS

When I first began developing procedure manuals in 1977, I had to divide the material into major categories. I was part of the information processing

Table 7. Playscript Drill-Down Procedure Example

Employee Standards of Conduct

Intent:

The intent is to define standard procedures for employee conduct.

Scope:

The procedure will outline acceptable and unacceptable behavior for all employees of Microsoft Corporation.

Responsibilities:

It is the responsibility of management to ensure a just and fair environment for all employees. It is the responsibility of the employee to avoid conflicts of interest, report misconduct, and to follow all standards of conduct.

Sequence of Events:

A grievance, misconduct, or question regarding a conflict-of-interest situation must arise.

Approvals:

The termination of an employee must have final approval from senior management.

Prerequisites:

None.

Definitions:

Employee: Any person compensated for services rendered by The Company.

General Auditor: Person responsible for advising in and investigating all reported misconduct and violations of standards of conduct.

Immediate Family Member: As defined by the Internal Revenue Code of the United States.

Insider Information: Nonpublic information.

[Equipment Required:]

Information Protection policy

Conflict of Interest policy

Warnings:

None.

Precautions:

None.

Procedure Body:

Standards of Conduct

Employees

Shall act in an ethical manner, and shall avoid actions that have the appearance of being unethical.

Shall abide by applicable laws, regulations, and professional standards.

Shall avoid conflict of interest situations. (See Conflict of Interest policy for more information.)

Shall meet individual performance expectations.

Shall abide by company and organizational policies and practices.

Shall accurately and honestly record and report corporate information. Employees shall also maintain the confidentiality of corporate information. (See Information Protection policy.)

Shall treat co-workers and others with dignity and respect.

(continued)

Table 7. Playscript Drill-Down Procedure Example (Continued)

Employees

1. Are expected to use intelligence, common sense, and good judgment in applying these standards of conduct.

2. When in doubt, shall direct questions relating to the standards of conduct to their managers.

3. Those who observe conduct that does not appear consistent with these standards of conduct should discuss the matter with their managers. However, employees who feel uncomfortable reporting to their managers, or who are not satisfied with the action taken, rather than letting the matter drop, should seek the counsel of the General Auditor.

Any employee who feels that he or she has been the subject of a violation of the standards of conduct should immediately report the matter to his or her manager or to the Vice President of Human Resources.

Manager

1. Take reports of Standard of Conduct violations or suspected violations, from employees.

2. Report fraudulent activity to the General Auditor, in the Risk Management Office.

3. Investigate all complaints in as discreet a fashion as possible.

4. Take action where appropriate, once the investigation is complete.

5. Provide appropriate feedback to those who report misconduct.

General Auditor

1. Take reports of fraudulent activity from Managers.

2. Investigate all complaints in as discreet a fashion as possible.

3. Take action where appropriate, once investigation is complete

4. Provide appropriate feedback to those who report misconduct.

(continued)

Table 7. Playscript Drill-Down Procedure Example (Continued)

Vice President of Human Resources

1. Take reports of possible standards of conduct violations from employees.
2. Investigate all complaints in as discreet a fashion as possible.
3. Take action where appropriate, once investigation is complete.
4. Provide appropriate feedback to those who report misconduct.

The Corporation

1. Will not retaliate against any employee who reports suspected misconduct.
2. Shall provide or select legal counsel and indemnify any employee who becomes involved in a legal matter arising out of employment with Microsoft Corporation, if, in the opinion of the General Counsel, the employee was acting in good faith, within the scope of the job responsibilities, and legal counsel or indemnification is not otherwise available to the employee

---

organization and I had been charged with helping each area establish its daily procedures. The applications development group was assigned the Commercial Application Development (CAD) manual. The organization we were part of had a group of engineers that developed programs in Fortran and were not part of information systems. The use of CAD was acceptable back then because drafting was still being generated on drafting boards. This document contained all the information programmers would need to perform any of their job assignments.

The Applications department also had the Database Administration group reporting to them, but they were assigned the responsibility of developing their own manual, the Database Administrators Guide.

Computer Systems, the systems programmers, had their own set of procedures and they were divided by platform (TSO, IMS, CICS) or software package. The document was often "missing" or "out for updating" when the audit staff came through. However, I did see at least a few procedures in this document.

The area that had the most procedure documents was Operations. The operators had the Computer Operators Orientation manual (COOM) and it dealt with all the tasks the console operators had to perform, even IPL procedures. The Tape Library had its own procedures, as did the Production Control Group and Scheduling. The Help Desk was just being developed and procedures were being created for them.

In the information security area we had the Account Administration procedures and the Computer Technology Security Manual (CTSM). This contained every requirement I could find that affected the security role. I had access to the audit guide used by our audit teams and created a section entitled "Audit and Inventory." This section contained a calendar of tasks and functions that had to be performed on a regular basis. These included everything from ordering the annual inventory of all electronic media, down to the changing of the cipher lock combinations.

When you begin to create your procedure documents, it might be helpful to divide the organization into manageable portions. We even had a Computer Users Guide. It contained all the procedures the user community needed to use when working with information systems. This included how to request a new user ID, how to submit a request to applications programming, or who to contact with various questions. Anything that the user community might need was available in this document.

10 SUMMARY

When writing procedures, it is best to keep the language as simple as possible. Attempt to stay away from flowery phrases and multi-syllable words. Keep the sentences short and the terms crisp. Identify what each role is in the procedure and find the style that best meets your organization's needs.

This chapter reviewed the definitions of policy, procedure, standard, and guideline. The writing requirements were discussed and the material reinforced what was discussed in the sections on "Planning and Preparation" and "Developing Policies."

We then examined the procedure key elements:

1. Identify the procedure need.
2. Identify the target audience.
3. Establish the scope of the procedure.
4. Describe the intent of the procedure.

We then examined the procedure 12-point checklist and six styles of procedures:

1. Headline
2. Caption
3. Matrix
4. Narrative
5. Flowchart
6. Playscript

Chapter 8
Creating a Table of Contents

1   INTRODUCTION

A Table of Contents is really a checklist established by you to ensure that important topics are properly addressed. Today we can go to the National Institute of Standards and Technology (NIST) Special Publications Series 800 (csrc.nist.gov/publications/nistpubs/) to obtain copies of the special documents that are available and that we can use as a guideline for what to include. Some of the documents date to 1991, but the content of the older documents seems appropriate even with today's technology.

The two best sources for what might be considered for inclusion in your information security standards and procedures document are the ISO 17799 and the (ISC)² Common Body of Knowledge®. As we saw in the chapter on standards, the ISO 17799 provides a number of topics in ten very important areas of information systems and security:

1. Security Policy
2. Organizational Security
3. Asset Classification and Control
4. Personnel Security
5. Physical and Environmental Security
6. Communications and Operations Management
7. Access Control
8. Systems Development and Maintenance
9. Business Continuity Planning
10. Compliance

I believe that these ten topics are a good starting point for your security manual. There are additional topics that need to be addressed, and the ISO 17799 also brings up some items that are not appropriate for your specific organization. Your document probably will not include these ten topics exactly, but it does give you a good starting point.

In this chapter we examine how to establish a table of contents — not the mechanical process that your word processor package can do for you.

This will be how to determine what kinds of items belong in an information security standards and procedures document or any other business-related document.

2   DOCUMENT LAYOUT

There are mechanics involved in assembling any form of manual. The document layout has the same requirements, regardless of what type of text is created. These physical characteristics will remain fairly constant. There are three key elements that will make up the contents of the table of contents, and therefore the inner working of the manual. These three elements are the ways in which material is cataloged in the document. These elements are identified as *section, topic,* and *subject.*

1. *Section.* This is the broad heading under which similar material will be lumped. The ten areas identified in ISO 17799 could be considered the "sections" of an information security manual.
2. *Topic.* This is a finer breakdown of the material that fits under the section heading.
3. *Subject.* This is the actual material that will be covered.

A typical table of contents might look like the one in Table 1.

The item identified as "1. Telecommunications" is the *section* of that portion of the security manual. All of the material under this section heading has been included by this organization as items that must be discussed and established in order to have its employees understand what is expected of them when accessing telecommunications services provided by the organization. There would typically be a Tier 1 policy addressing management's goals and objectives for telecommunications.

Those items identified by the number scheme of 1.1, 1.2, 1.3, and 1.4 are the *topics* that will be addressed under the telecommunications section. Typically, each topic would contain a Tier 2 policy that would address the topic requirements for the user community. A Tier 2 policy has more leeway to add why the topic needs to be protected and how its improper use could impact the organization.

Finally, those items identified with three-digit numbers (1.1.1, etc.) are the *subjects* or applications that provide the detail of the topic headings. A Tier 3 policy might be used to identify who the owner is, who has authorization authority, and what is allowed for each of these subjects.

3   DOCUMENT FRAMEWORK

The first section of the procedure document usually contains those pages that are considered to be unnumbered; that is, they normally have some form of Roman numeral. These documents are typically as follows.

Table 1. Sample Table of Contents

3.1 Title Page

This is the first page of the document and it identifies exactly what the document is. Some experts recommend that Management Endorsement appear first. What will be required within one's organization depends on how procedure documents are prepared. Keep the title page as clean and simple as possible.

A suggestion: keep the title as brief as possible and choose the words as carefully as possible. The document will probably be known by a word or acronym derived from the full title. Something like Information Protection Policies and Procedures might be shortened to IP3; but something like Customer User Primer (CUP) may not generate the level of respect expected. Choose the title carefully.

When selecting a title, there are some words that one might want to consider avoiding. Among such words is the term "security." Security means different things to different people. The term is imprecise; it conjures up images of guards, dogs, fences, guns, and badges. This is not the image that many would want for the information protection document.

3.2   Management Endorsement Page

Of all the important pages to be found in the document, each document should have a message from someone in a position of authority to the document holders. This message ensures that the policies, standards, and procedures contained in the document are implemented by the organization. The endorsement page will provide visible evidence that the document and its contents have management's support. If at all possible, the signatory should be the CEO, President, Executive Vice President, or the CIO to provide maximum impact.

The Management Endorsement page should state briefly the aim of the document: the basis for the document (i.e., industry standards, internal controls, company policy, legislation, regulations, etc.).

3.3   Amendment Record

This is a historical record of all of the updates made to the document. It will identify what changes were made to the document, who submitted the changes, and when the changes were implemented. In many documents, the amendment record establishes that unauthorized revisions are not to be made.

The first of the numbered pages in the procedure document is the Table of Contents. This will list the materials found in the text and is divided into the categories of *section, topic,* and *subject,* and the place to find the document (page number). The Table of Contents provides a cover-to-cover review of the contents and the organization of the document.

4   PREPARING A DRAFT TABLE OF CONTENTS

I am an advocate of using facilitated processes to get input as quickly as possible from those individuals with a stake in the process or who have a vested interest. When I work with clients, I like to have them schedule a four-hour working meeting that will allow us to identify and categorize the items that should be included in the manual we are going to develop.

I know that I can use the material identified in a document such as ISO 17799, but that may not reflect the current working environment found at this organization. I will use the material in ISO 17799 as a checklist-type reminder to ensure that we have covered all the pertinent items.

Prior to the meeting, I like to prepare the conference room with flipchart paper posted around the room with section headings on each one. I will use a variation on the ISO 17799 main sections as a starting point. On each piece of chart paper I will identify the section, such as the ones below.

1. Physical Safeguards
2. Security Awareness and Training
3. Personnel Security
4. System Monitoring and Incident Response
5. Risk Assessment
6. Asset Classification
7. Cryptography
8. Malicious Code Protection
9. Identification, Authentication, and Authorization
10. Remote Access
11. Network Security
12. Systems Development

When the selected team arrives, remind them of the objective of the session — that they are there to help identify topics that need to be covered in an organization information security manual. It will be helpful if the attendees are given notice of what is expected of them in the meeting notice. Other material that will be needed to complete this process are Sharpie® Pens and Post-It® Notes (use the 3 by 5 size).

Everyone will be given a pen and a pad of Post-Its. Their initial assignment is to identify any issue that needs to be part of the security manual. There are no bad ideas or answers. The goal here is to capture as many ideas as possible. Once they have the concept of what is to be accomplished, then set them free to write and post. It may be necessary to go over each section heading with them to give them an understanding of what the heading means and give them an example or two of each. The results of this session might look like the one in Table 2.

Once the brainstorming session is complete, I like to give the team a coffee break and ask them to look over each section and combine any like issues and eliminate any duplicates. This process should take about 15 to 20 minutes and will speed up the process that is to follow.

Once the sections have been cleaned of duplicates and like items combined, it will be necessary to begin the final process for this session. This step will identify the topics and then the subjects that will support those topics. I recommend that each section have a champion assigned to facilitate this process. Divide the attendees into teams and have them complete the assigned task. This will take the bulk of the time reserved for this exercise. Some of the items that were identified under a specific section might not actually belong there. Have the team identify those that appear not to belong, and these items will have to be addressed after the meeting.

Table 2. Brainstorming Results Table

Telecommunications	Physical Security	Administration	Information Protection
Firewall administration	Whiteboards and sensitive material	Contractor controls (information access, personnel, hiring, discharge, etc.)	Password conventions
Firewall services and usage policy	Desktop protection	Cleaning crews	Protecting customer information
Mail and news usage	Line of sight	Change procedures	Information access and authorization controls
Telecommunications	Off-site storage	Communication with the press	Levels of ROOT exposure
Telephone eavesdropping	Company address and phone number usage	Spin teams	Audit logs maintenance and storage
Voice-mail directory for entire company	Asset marking	Investigations	Backups of information
Web access and download	Asset protection	Third-party requests for access	Posting employee lists in public areas
Internet access control (external)	Cabinet controls	Background checks	Information classification (secret, critical, confidential, internal use, restricted, public, private, etc.)
Read security of newsgroups	Clear (clean) desk policy	Credit backgrounds	Release of information to public
Access control	Critical incident procedures	Ethics policy	Marking classification levels
Token card usage	Network failures	Drug testing	Discussing classified information with third parties
Access authorization levels	Shredding documents	Company identification away from the campus	Approval process for release of confidential information
User authentication	Removal of trash	Reception area conversations	Non-disclosure agreements

(continued)

170

Table 2. Brainstorming Results Table (Continued)

Log-in banners	Off-site assessments	Hiring foreign nationals	Confidentiality agreements
Screen saver time-outs	Duress response	Hiring and termination policy	Employee discussion of company business (at work and off-site)
Workstation administration	Visitor procedures	Export regulations	Confidential information controls during travel
E-mail policy	Investigations	Monitoring for compliance	Whiteboards
E-mail privacy	Tailgating, piggybacking	Employee privacy	Meeting notes and Franklin® Planners
Standardized e-mail and news SIGs	After-hours access (employee, contractor, visitor)	Telephone log monitoring	Internal system auditing
Server administration	Physical access to building	Threat management	Audit responsibilities
Modem usage	Employee identification cards	Disaster planning	System monitoring
	Contractors' identification cards	State and federal law compliance	Protecting company intellectual properties
	Visitor badges	Intercom usage	Monitoring Web activities
	Hardware protection (on-site, off-site)	Phone usage	System alarms
	Mailbox access	Employee training	Intrusion detection
	Alarms	Employee standards of conduct	Trade secret controls
	Keys and lock controls	Workplace violence	Competitive advantage controls
	Security card and hardware token handling	Health and safety standards	Plans and strategic information
	Electronic defenses	Risk assessment practices	Information classification categories

It will be necessary to review what a topic is and then what a subject is. It is always best to give examples of what it is they are to accomplish (reference Table 1 of this chapter). The results of this process might look like the one in Table 3.

Once this is complete, it is necessary to identify a group or department that will be responsible for that specific section of the manual. It should be obvious for most sections. One can easily match operations, applications, systems programming, telecommunications, and information security to a specific organization. This assignment should take place in the meeting. Finally, once the department or group has been assigned, it will be necessary for that group to identify the subject matter expert (SME) who will be responsible for providing the information for the procedure.

This form of information gathering can be used or you can take existing documents such as ISO 17799 to get an idea of what should be included in your information security manual table of contents. Keep an open mind, regardless of what format you use. The objective is to include all the issues that reflect your organization, but not every issue in the industry.

5   SECTIONS TO CONSIDER

To add to your reference information, we examine some of the sections addressed in current industry standards.

- *Systems Development and Maintenance.* To ensure that security is built into IT systems, management identifies, justifies, agrees to, and documents security requirements during the requirements phase of an IT system development project. Security requirements are included in the requirements analysis stage of each system development project, and requirements for security controls are specified in statements of business requirements.
- *Anti-virus.* Precautions are applied to prevent and detect the introduction of malicious software, and safeguard the integrity of the software and data. Virus detection and prevention measures and appropriate user awareness procedures are implemented.
- *Business Continuity Plan.* Business continuity planning represents a broad scope of activities designed to sustain and recover critical services following an emergency. The IT disaster recovery plan (DRP) fits into the broader emergency preparedness environment that includes the enterprise business continuity plan. Ultimately, an organization would use a suite of plans to properly prepare response, recovery, and restoration activities for disruptions affecting the enterprise. Because there is an inherent relationship between information processing and the business process or mission of the enterprise, there should be coordination between the organization BCP and the IT DRP. This will ensure that recovery strategies and

Table 3. Brainstorming Results

1. Physical Security
    1.1. Office Area Controls
        1.1.1. Line of sight
        1.1.2. Cabinet controls
        1.1.3. Clear desk policy
        1.1.4. Shredding of documents
        1.1.5. Removal of trash
        1.1.6. Whiteboards and sensitive material
    1.2. Backups
        1.2.1. Off-site storage
        1.2.2. Off-site assessment
    1.3. Incident Response
        1.3.1. Critical incident procedures
        1.3.2. Network failures
        1.3.3. Duress response
        1.3.4. Investigations
        1.3.5. Alarms
        1.3.6. Emergency response plan
    1.4. Business Continuity Plan
        1.4.1. Business impact analysis
        1.4.2. Threat assessment (risk analysis)
        1.4.3. Disaster recovery plan
        1.4.4. Business continuity plan
    1.5. Physical Access
        1.5.1. Visitor procedures
        1.5.2. Tailgating and piggybacking
        1.5.3. After-hours access
        1.5.4. Physical access to buildings
        1.5.5. Identification cards
            1.5.5.1. Employees
            1.5.5.2. Contractors
            1.5.5.3. Visitors
            1.5.5.4. Security card and token handling
        1.5.6. Electronic defenses
        1.5.7. Physical access (false ceilings, plaster board, etc.)
        1.5.8. Access control (copiers, fax machines, printers)
    1.6. Property Controls
        1.6.1. Asset marking
        1.6.2. Asset protection

supporting resources neither negate each other nor duplicate efforts.

To provide a common basis of understanding regarding IT recovery plans, we take a moment to discuss several other types (see Table 4).

Table 4. Different Forms of Continuity Planning

Plan	Purpose	Scope
Business Continuity Plan (BCP)	Provide procedures for sustaining essential business operations while recovering from a significant disruption	Addresses business processes; IT addressed based only on its support for business process
Business Recovery (Resumption) Plan (BRP)	Provide procedures for recovering business operations immediately following a disaster	Addresses business processes; not IT focused; IT addressed based only on its support for business process
Continuity of Operations Plan (COOP)	Provide procedures and capabilities to sustain an organization's essential, strategic functions at an alternate site for up to 30 days	Addresses the subset of an organization's missions that are deemed most critical; usually written at headquarters level; not IT focused
Crisis Communications Plan (CCP)	Provide procedures for disseminating status reports to personnel and the public	Addresses communications with personnel and the public; not IT focused
Cyber Incident Response Plan (CIRP)	Provide strategies to detect, respond to, and limit consequences of malicious cyber-incident	Focuses on information security responses to incidents affecting systems or networks
Disaster Recovery Plan (DRP)	Provide detailed procedures to facilitate recovery of capabilities at an alternate site	Often IT-focused; limited to major disruptions with long-term effects
Emergency Response Plan (ERP)	Provide coordinated procedures for minimizing loss of life or injury and protecting property damage in response to a physical threat	Focuses on personnel and property particular to the specific facility; not business process or IT system functionality based

- *Physical Security.* This addresses the threats, vulnerabilities, and countermeasures that can be utilized to physically protect an enterprise's resources, to include sensitive information, people, facilities, data, equipment, support systems, media, and supplies.
- *Applications and Systems Development Security.* This refers to the controls included within systems and applications software, as well as the steps used in their development. *Applications* are agents, applets, software, databases, data warehouses, and knowledge-

based systems. These applications can be used in distributed or centralized environments.

- *Telecommunications and Network Security.* This encompasses the structures, transmission methods, transport formats, and security measures used to provide integrity, availability, authentication, and confidentiality for transmissions over private and public communications networks and media.
- *Information Security Program.* Security management entails the identification of an organization's information assets and the development, documentation, and implementation of policies, standards, procedures, and guidelines; and includes management tools such as asset or information classification and risk analysis and management that are used to identify threats, classify assets, and to rate their vulnerabilities so that effective security controls can be implemented.
- *Identification and Authentication.* Identification is the means by which an individual provides a claimed identity to the system. Authentication is the means of establishing the validity of this specific claim. Authentication includes one- and two-factor identification as well as biometrics.
- *Accountability.* This is the process that can connect an individual to an action. The document should inform employees of their responsibilities and that there are tools in place to monitor their activities. Included in these discussions will be retention periods for all system logs and who is responsible for reviewing these logs.
- *Auditability.* Audit trails maintain a record of system activity, both by system and application processes and by individual activity. They can assist in detecting security violations, performance problems, and flaws in applications. Employees must be made aware of what the audit trail is used for and that they are accountable for the actions found in the audit logs.
- *Remote Access.* This method of connecting to a network occurs when a shared, publicly accessible system is used as part of the process. All remote access connections to internal systems must be authorized and access control user ID authentication must occur.

Risk Management. Risk management is the process that allows business managers to balance operational and economic costs of protective measures and achieve gains in mission capability by protecting business processes that support the business objectives or mission of the enterprise. Senior management must ensure that the enterprise has the capabilities needed to accomplish its mission.

Most organizations have tight budgets for security. To get the best bang for the security buck, management needs a process to determine spending.

Table 5. Risk Management Overview

System Development Life-Cycle Phases	Risk Management Activities
Analysis. The need for a new system, application, or process and its scope are documented.	*Analysis.* Identified risks are used to support the development of system requirements, including security needs.
Design. The system or process is designed.	*Design.* Security needs lead to architecture and design trade-offs.
Development. The system or process is purchased, developed, or otherwise constructed.	*Development.* The security controls and safeguards are created or implemented as part of the development process.
Test. System security features should be configured, enabled, tested, and verified.	*Test.* Safeguards and controls are tested to ensure that decisions regarding risks identified are reduced to acceptable levels prior to movement to production.
Maintenance. When changes or updates are made to the system, the changes to hardware and software are noted and the risk analysis process is revisited.	*Maintenance.* Controls and safeguards are re-examined when changes or updates occur at regularly scheduled intervals.

Effective risk management must be totally integrated into the System Development Life Cycle (SDLC).

The typical SDLC has five phases (see Table 5):

1. Analysis
2. Design
3. Construction
4. Test
5. Maintenance

Telecommuting. Telecommuting has become a popular trend in the workplace. As employees and organizations employ remote connectivity to network systems, the security of these remote endpoints has become increasingly important to the overall information security program. Accompanying and contributing to this explosive growth is the ability of broadband connections for the remote user. These developments complicate the process of securing the organization's information resources and the network itself. It will be necessary to provide policies, standards, and procedures on the use of applications, protocols, and network architecture in your document.

Firewalls. Firewalls are vulnerable to misconfiguration and the failure to apply properly tested and applied patches or other security mechanisms. It will be necessary to establish standards to perform firewall configuration and administration requirements. While the firewall is considered the organization's first line of defense, it should be used in concert with layering of firewalls and other security systems throughout the network. An organization must strive to maintain all systems in a secure manner and not depend solely on the firewall to stop security threats. Your organization will need to establish a backup plan in case the firewall fails.

6   SUMMARY

The only limits to the sections and topics that can be part of the information security standards and procedures document, or for that matter any standards and procedures document, are what can be thought of by your team of experts. The key to an effective document is to include what is necessary for your specific enterprise. Do not include sections, topics, or subjects just because some international standard has identified it as an item. Remember that most international standards are actually only guidelines. They recommend that you do a risk analysis to determine if you need that specific control or not.

Do the research that is necessary to understand where your organization currently is, how it got where it is, and what will be needed to move it forward. Establish a compliance plan. Identify what elements are missing; identify an organization to champion that section; identify SMEs; interview the SMEs; write the standards and procedures; and review them annually.

Chapter 9
Understanding How to Sell Policies, Standards, and Procedures

1 INTRODUCTION

For years I have heard information security professionals discuss their jobs in terms of overhead, as if this is some evil thing. Nearly every employee within an enterprise is overhead. Even the CEO, CFO, CTO, and CIO are all overhead. However, they have learned what we need to learn, and that is that we all add value to the bottom line of the enterprise. Our task, just like the big "C's," is to ensure that the business objectives or mission of the enterprise are met. What the information security professional has failed to do is to sell the services of information security.

We must examine our services — such as risk analysis, policies, procedures, standards, vulnerability assessments, and business continuity planning — and determine how each of these services supports the business objectives. Before you can be effective, you will need to take stock of the services your team offers and prepare your own unique sales pitch for management. The remainder of this chapter offers some ideas on how to meet this goal.

2 BELIEVE IN WHAT YOU ARE DOING

Whenever I am teaching a class on information security issues, I always give the attendees a homework problem. The exercise is to come up with four things that you, as a security professional, do to help your enterprise meet its business objectives or mission. These four items should be expressed in non-security, non-technical, non-audit terms. Use the language of the business unit managers to express your four value-added statements.

When creating your value-added statements, do not state that you "add users to the system using ACF2." Instead, sell your services by stating that you ensure that authorized users are given access to information resources in a timely and efficient manner. Tell your audience what it is that you do that enables them to do their job.

3 RETURN ON INVESTMENT FOR SECURITY FUNCTIONS

Just as you have to prepare to sell your job and its duties to management and fellow employees, so must you be prepared to sell the services you provide. Again, these services must be presented to the user community in the language they understand. *Security requirements* or *audit requirements* are not part of the business process and they do not exist. There are only business or mission requirements. So when we present our services, we must use the terms that management uses.

Risk Analysis. Before any resources are spent on controls, safeguards, products, hardware, or software, a risk analysis should be conducted to see if these are necessary. A formal risk analysis process will provide management with the information it needs to make decisions about what resources must be spent to enable the enterprise to meet its obligations. Risk analysis is a cost control process.

Policies. Management establishes its goals and objectives for protecting the assets of the enterprise by implementing policies. Policies are used to introduce the concepts of what is expected of all employees when using enterprise assets and what noncompliance can lead to. The message of any policy is also included in the contract language so that third parties are aware of their responsibilities.

With policies implemented along with an awareness program, the enterprise can then seek relief in the courts, if necessary, to protect their assets. Policies establish the behavior expected of all personnel granted access to that asset.

Procedures. These are probably the easiest security measure to explain return on investment. Procedures are the step-by-step processes used to complete a task. They provide users with the information needed to complete a task and assure management that the tasks are being completed in a uniform and approved manner. Procedures improve efficiencies in employee workflow and assist in the prevention of misuse and fraud.

Standards. Remember Y2K, that historical event that caused many of us a lot of extra work? It was lack of standards or the ignoring of standards that made management spend so much money to retrofit the fixes. Standards are a way of ensuring that programs and systems will work together and that when there is a need to do error searching, the people looking through old code will be better able to understand what is out there.

By establishing standards, the enterprise limits rogue applications, systems, platforms, hardware, or software. There is less time spent in supporting non-standard activities or products. When a new application or system is moved into production, the existing systems and applications will not have to make modifications to handle non-standard information or data. Standards are a cost-savings process that support the efficient running of the enterprise.

Business Continuity Planning (BCP). Since the events of September 11, 2001, most organizations have seen the need to implement an enterprise-wide continuity plan. Management has always been charged with a fiduciary responsibility to protect the assets of the enterprise. BCP is a process that allows management to show that it has exercised due diligence with respect to the information processing resources and assets. By having a plan and testing the plan, the enterprise is showing employees, stakeholders, and interested third parties that the continued operation of the enterprise has been addressed and is taken seriously.

Although these are only examples of how to sell your information security services, they do provide an idea of how this can and should be done. To be successful, the information security professional must step into the role of the businessperson. Security is a portion of the entire business process and must use the words and objectives of the business units to be successful. Our goal is not just to have security endure, but we want it to prevail. To do this we must become an active voice in the business or mission of our organizations.

4   EFFECTIVE COMMUNICATION

An effective information security program will depend on how well the message is communicated to the audience. While many of us are confident in the importance of the message we will be presenting, the message is often missed because of other factors. To be as effective as possible, it might be helpful to identify potential barriers to effective communication.

- *Image.* Dress as the audience is dressed, only a little better. While many organizations have converted to the business casual dress, when you are presenting, it is important to exhibit the proper respect and professionalism to your audience. I once worked for a company that was headquartered in the Pacific Northwest. I had just finished 22 years with a global manufacturer located in the Midwest that had just begun business casual attire. I was shocked at the attire of my fellow employees. I believe it is known as "grunge-rock chic." When we went to do work at the client site, I required the salesperson to inform us as to how the clients dressed. I had to make sure we abandoned our avant-garde look and became more traditional. I went to a meeting one time and did not recognize my own employee; he had "cleaned up real nice."

- *Prepare.* Nothing will turn off an audience quicker than a presenter that stumbles around for materials or loses his or her place. Make certain that all audiovisual equipment is working properly (get there early and test everything).

- *Present.* Do not read your presentation. Use bullet points or brief phrases to speak from. With any luck, your audience will know how to read. Avoid reading verbatim the presentation slides. Speak to the audience as if you are having a conversation with them.

- *Jargon.* As information security professionals, we speak a very strange language. Many of us have also come from the Information Systems environment and this will compound the problem. I strongly recommend that you practice the presentation in front of a select focus group.

- *Audience.* Know your audience and speak to them in terms they will understand. Each and every department has its own language. Do your homework and learn what terms are important to them and use them correctly in your presentation.

- *TLAs.* A TLA is a Three-Letter Acronym (TLA) for a three-letter acronym. The next time you attend a meeting, keep a running score of the TLAs and FLAs (four-letter acronyms) that are bandied about. Say what you mean, keep the TLAs to a minimum, and define them before using them.

- *Idioms.* Be careful with language. Our organizations have many different ethnic groups and slang terms may be misunderstood or even offensive. Be mindful of those in your audience and select your terms wisely.

- *Priorities.* As security professionals, we feel that security is the organization's most important objective. However, Purchasing, Accounting, Payroll, Human Resources, etc. have other priorities.

- *Schedule.* Just as every department has unique language and priorities, they also have deadlines. Schedule your presentations around their busy periods. Try to become part of a regular staff meeting if possible.

- *Time.* Keep the awareness sessions brief and businesslike. At Gettysburg, Edward Everett was the featured speaker and spoke for nearly two hours. President Lincoln spoke second, his speech lasted less than five minutes, and the world remembers his "Gettysburg Address." Remember that it is quality not quantity that will make a successful presentation.

Information security is an important part of doing business today. The message of employee responsibilities must be presented to them on a regular basis. To have a chance for success, a good presenter will be clear, concise, and brief. Know your audience and play to their needs and concerns. By doing your homework, the audience will be more open to receiving the message. If they accept the message as being meaningful, then the objectives of information security will become incorporated into the business process.

5   KEEPING MANAGEMENT INTERESTED IN SECURITY

For the first time in nine years, the economy is facing a marked downturn. Half a working generation has never known the sting of a tight economy. What is going to happen to the E-business environment now that some of the whiz kids are going to be looking for work?

The complexion of the business environment has changed completely since 1990 and the safeguards that have been installed must now be tested to ensure that the enterprise is safe for an even more competitive atmosphere. This chapter discusses how to:

- Understand your enterprise's business needs
- Understand management's needs
- Sell your message to the enterprise
- Believe in the value you add to the enterprise
- Identify the changing environment

5.1   Enterprise Business Needs

For security professionals there are three key elements in any security program: integrity, confidentiality, and availability. Management is concerned that information reflects the real world and that they can have confidence in the information available to them so that they can make informed business decisions. One of the goals of an effective security program is to ensure that the organization's information and its information processing resources are properly protected.

The goal of confidentiality extends beyond just keeping the bad guys out; it also ensures that those with a business need have access to the resources they need to get their jobs done. Confidentiality ensures that controls and reporting mechanisms are in place to detect problems or possible intrusions with speed and accuracy. (See Table 1.)

In a pair of surveys, the Big X Accounting firms of Ernst & Young and Deloitte & Touche interviewed Fortune 500 managers and asked them to rank in importance to them information availability, confidentiality, and integrity. As can be seen from the results Table 1, the managers felt that

Table 1. Management Concerns Matrix

Fortune 500 Managers Rate the Importance of
Information:

Deloitte & Touche	Rate 1 – 3	Ernst & Young
1	Availability	2
3	Confidentiality	3
2	Integrity	1

information needed to be available when they needed to have access to it. Implementing access control packages that rendered access difficult or overly restrictive is a detriment to the business process. Additionally, other managers felt that the information must reflect the real world. That is, controls should be in place to ensure that the information was correct. Preventing or controlling access to information that was incorrect was of little value to the enterprise.

An effective information security program must review the business objectives and the mission of the organization and ensure that these goals are met. Meeting the business objectives of the organization and understanding the customers' needs are what the goal of a security program is all about. An awareness program will reinforce these goals and will make the information security program more acceptable to the employee base.

So how do you determine what the business objectives or mission of your enterprise are? Research the existing documents. For publicly held companies, check the annual earnings report. The goals and objectives of the company are outlined in this report. For other private-sector organizations, check with the Marketing staff to see what is given out to prospective clients and investors. For government agencies, check the agency charter statement. Keep this information posted in your work area.

The next thing to understand is that there is no such thing as audit requirements or security requirements. There are only business requirements or mission requirements. If a control mechanism or safeguard gets in the way of accomplishing the business or mission of the enterprise, then the security element will lose.

5.2   Management Needs

In the 1992 presidential campaign, the Clinton camp used the phrase "It's the economy, stupid." In our profession, we should keep the phrase "it's the business, sweetie" tacked up in our cubicles and offices. Never lose sight of the fact that the objective of information security is to support the business of the enterprise. Security for security's sake is of no value.

Telling the users that controls are being implemented to be "in compliance with audit requirements" is self-defeating. Find out what has to be done and then find a way to sell the product to your audience based on the business objectives or the mission of your organization.

5.3   Where We Are

"Ask today's information processing professionals to describe the changes that have strongly influenced their current work environment, and they will probably answer in terms of technologies, architectures, hardware, and software designs. This is hardly surprising, because intelligent workstations, distributed processing, and distributed data implementations all seem to be dominating and reshaping the marketplace." Sound familiar? Sound like where you are today? These were the thoughts of Harry B. DeMaio in September 1984. DeMaio saw that the "data security" group needed to shift its focus away from the hardware and system infrastructure and move toward involving the customer, the owner, in the safeguard implementation process. Moving the group away from "security" and into information protection.

5.4   Elements of Information Protection

Information protection should be based on eight major elements.

Information protection should support the business objectives or mission of the enterprise. This idea cannot be stressed enough. All too often, information security personnel lose track of their goals and responsibilities. The position of the ISSO (Information Systems Security Officer) has been created to support the enterprise, not the other way around.

Information protection is an integral element of due care. Senior management is charged with two basic responsibilities: a duty of loyalty — this means that whatever decisions they make must be made in the best interest of the enterprise. They are also charged with a duty of care — this means that senior management is required to protect the assets of the enterprise and make informed business decisions. An effective information protection program will assist senior management in meeting these duties.

Information protection must be cost effective. Implementing controls based on edicts is counter to the business climate. Before any control can be proposed, it will be necessary to confirm that a significant risk exists. Implementing a timely risk analysis process can complete this. By identifying risks and then proposing appropriate controls, the mission and business objectives of the enterprise will be better met.

Information protection responsibilities and accountabilities should be made explicit. For any program to be effective, it will be necessary to publish an information protection policy statement and a group mission statement. The policy should identify the roles and responsibilities of all employees. To be completely effective, the language of the policy must be incorporated into the purchase agreements for all contract personnel and consultants.

System owners have information protection responsibilities outside their own organization. Access to information will often extend beyond the business unit or even the enterprise. It is the responsibility of the information owner (normally the senior level manager in the business that created the information or the primary user of the information). One of the main responsibilities is to monitor usage to ensure that it complies with the level of authorization granted to the user.

Information protection requires a comprehensive and integrated approach. To be as effective as possible, it will be necessary for information protection issues to be part of the system development life cycle. During the initial or analysis phase, information protection should receive as its deliverables a risk analysis, a business impact analysis, and an information classification document. Additionally, because information is resident in all departments throughout the enterprise, each business unit should establish an individual responsible for implementing an information protection program to meet the specific business needs of the department.

Information protection should be periodically reassessed. As with anything, time changes the needs and objectives. A good information protection program will examine itself on a regular basis and make changes wherever and whenever necessary. This is a dynamic and changing process and therefore must be reassessed at least every 18 months.

Information protection is constrained by the culture of the organization. The ISSO must understand that the basic information protection program will be implemented throughout the enterprise. However, each business unit must be given the latitude to make modifications to meet their specific needs. If your organization is multinational, it will be necessary to make adjustments for each of the various countries. These adjustments will have to be examined throughout the United States. What might work in Des Moines, Iowa, may not fly in Berkley, California. Provide for the ability to find and implement alternatives.

Information protection is a means to an end and not the end in itself. In business, having an effective information protection program is usually secondary to the need to make a profit. In the public sector, information protection is secondary to the agency's services provided to its constituency. We, as security professionals, must not lose sight of these goals and objectives.

Computer systems and the information processed on them are often considered critical assets that support the mission of an organization.

Protecting them can be as important as protecting other organizational resources such as financial resources, physical assets, and employees. The cost and benefits of information protection should be carefully examined in both monetary and nonmonetary terms to ensure that the cost of controls does not exceed the expected benefits. Information protection controls should be appropriate and proportionate.

The responsibilities and accountabilities of the information owners, providers, and users of computer services and other parties concerned with the protection of information and computer assets should be explicit. If a system has external users, its owners have a responsibility to share appropriate knowledge about the existence and general extent of control measures so that other users can be confident that the system is adequately secure. As we expand the user base to include suppliers, vendors, clients, customers, shareholders, and the like, it is incumbent upon the enterprise to have clear and identifiable controls. For many organizations, the initial sign-on screen is the first indication that there are controls in place. The message screen should include three basic elements:

1. The system is for authorized users only.
2. Activities are monitored.
3. By completing the sign-on process, the user agrees to the monitoring.

5.5 Common Threats

Information processing systems are vulnerable to many threats that can inflict various types of damage that can result in significant losses. This damage can range from errors harming database integrity to fires destroying entire complexes. Losses can stem from the actions of supposedly trusted employees defrauding a system, from outside hackers, or from careless data entry. Precision in estimating information-protection-related losses is not possible because many losses are never discovered, and others are hidden to avoid unfavorable publicity.

The typical computer criminal is an authorized, nontechnical user of the system who has been around long enough to determine what actions would cause a "red flag" or an audit. The typical computer criminal is an employee. According to a recent survey in "Current and Future Danger: A CSI Primer on Computer Crime & Information Warfare," more than 80 percent of the respondents identified employees as a threat or potential threat to information security. Also included in this survey were the competition, contract personnel, public interest groups, suppliers, and foreign governments.

The chief threat to information protection is still errors and omissions. This concern continues to make up 65 percent of all information protection problems. Users, data entry personnel, system operators, programmers, and the like frequently make errors that contribute directly or indirectly to this problem.

Dishonest employees make up another 13 percent of information protection problems. Fraud and theft can be committed by insiders and outsiders, but is more likely to be done by one's own employees. In a related area, disgruntled employees make up another 10 percent of the problem. Employees are most familiar with the organization's information assets and processing systems, including knowing what actions might cause the most damage, mischief, or sabotage.

Common examples of information-protection-related employee sabotage include destroying hardware or facilities, planting malicious code (viruses, worms, Trojan horses, etc.) to destroy data or programs, entering data incorrectly, deleting data, altering data, and holding data "hostage."

The loss of the physical facility and/or the supporting infrastructure (power failures, telecommunications disruptions, water outage and leaks, sewer problems, lack of transportation, fire, flood, civil unrest, strikes, etc.) can lead to serious problems and constitute 8 percent of information-protection-related problems.

The final area is malicious hackers or crackers. These terms refer to those who break into computers without authorization or exceed the level of authorization granted to them. While these problems get the largest amount of press coverage and movies, they only account for 5 to 8 percent of the total picture. They are real and they can cause a great deal of damage. But when attempting to allocate limited information protection resources, it may be better to concentrate efforts in other areas. To be certain, conduct a risk analysis to see what your exposure might be.

5.6   You Add Value!

As discussed above, almost everyone of us is overhead. The key to being successful is to identify what value it is that you do that supports the business objectives or mission of your organization. In his book, *How to Get Your Point across in 30 Seconds or Less,* Milo O. Frank tells us that the attention span of the average individual is 30 seconds. To fulfill this limited timeframe of attention span, you will need to get the message out to management quickly.

This 30-second message is also known as the elevator message. That is, you get on the elevator at work and the CEO is standing there. The CEO sees your identification badge and asks you what you do for the organization. You need to be ready to tell this person, in business terms, what value you add to the bottom line.

Do not say that you add users to the system or that you write rules for ACF2. Let management know that you are responsible for ensuring that employees have access to the resources they need to do their job and that you assist information owners in protecting those corporate assets.

Information security is an important part of doing business today. The message of employee responsibilities must be presented to them on a regular basis. To have a chance for success, a good presenter will be clear, concise, and brief. Know your audience and play to their needs and concerns. By doing your homework, the audience will be more open to receiving the message. If they accept the message as being meaningful, then the objectives of information security will become incorporated into the business process.

6 WHY POLICIES, STANDARDS, AND PROCEDURES ARE NEEDED

The overall objective of an information security program is to protect the integrity, confidentiality, and availability of information. The primary threats that keep an organization from attaining this goal are unauthorized access, modification, destruction, and disclosure. These threats can be either accidental or deliberate.

An information protection program should be part of any organization's overall asset protection program. The goals and objectives that make up the information security program must be understandable by all employees.

As long as there have been Information Systems Security Officers (ISSOs), there has been a need to create and implement information security policies and procedures. The ISSO was usually brought in from one of the various groups within Information Technology and charged with the responsibility to create these documents. The background in IT often helped the ISSO in understanding technical issues, but it was sometimes a hindrance in grasping the business strategies and objectives. With this very vaguely defined charter, the ISSO would usually try to find a book on the subject or look to attend a seminar or workshop. The information gathered from these resources often provided the how-to, but usually failed in the "why-for."

6.1 Legal Requirements

Are there legal and business requirements for policies and procedures? The answer to that question is a resounding — yes. Not only are there requirements, but the laws and acts define who is responsible and what they must do to meet their obligations. Under the "Model Business Corporation Act," which has been adopted in whole or in part by a majority of states, the directors and officers of a corporation are required to perform specific duties: a duty of loyalty and a duty of care.

6.1.1   Duty of Loyalty. By assuming office, senior management commits allegiance to the enterprise and acknowledges that the interest of the enterprise must prevail over any personal or individual interest. The basic principle here is that senior management should not use its position to make a personal profit or gain other personal advantage. The duty of loyalty is evident in certain legal concepts:

- *Conflict of interest.* Individuals must divulge any interest in outside relationships that may conflict with the enterprise's interests.
- *Duty of fairness.* When presented with a conflict of interest, the individual has an obligation to act in the best interest of all parties.
- *Corporate opportunity.* When presented with "material inside information" (advanced notice on mergers, acquisitions, patents, etc.), the individual will not use this information for personal gain.
- *Confidentiality.* All matters involving the corporation should be kept in confidence until they are made public.

6.1.2   Duty of Care. In addition to owing a duty of loyalty to the enterprise, the officers and directors also assume a duty to act carefully in fulfilling the important tasks of monitoring and directing the activities of corporate management. The Model Business Corporation Act established legal standards for compliance. A director shall discharge his or her duties:

- In good faith
- With the care an ordinarily prudent person in a like position would exercise under similar circumstances
- In a manner he or she reasonably believes is in the best interest of the enterprise

6.1.3   Federal Sentencing Guidelines for Criminal Convictions. The Federal Sentencing Guidelines define executive responsibility for fraud, theft, and anti-trust violations, and establish a mandatory point system for federal judges to determine appropriate punishment. Because much fraud and falsifying corporate data involves access to computer-held data, liability established under the Guidelines extend to computer-related crime as well. What has caused many executives concern is that the mandatory punishment could apply even when intruders enter a computer system and perpetrate a crime.

While the Guidelines have a mandatory scoring system for punishment, they also have an incentive for proactive crime prevention. The requirement here is for management to show "due diligence" in establishing an effective compliance program. There are seven elements that capture the basic functions inherent in most compliance programs:

1. Establish policies, standards, and procedures to guide the work-force.
2. Appoint a high-level manager to oversee compliance with the policy, standards, and procedures.
3. Exercise due care when granting discretionary authority to employees.
4. Assure compliance policies are being carried out.
5. Communicate the standards and procedures to all employees and others.
6. Enforce the policies, standards, and procedures consistently through appropriate disciplinary measures.
7. Develop procedures for corrections and modifications in case of violations.

These guidelines reward those organizations that make a good-faith effort to prevent unethical activity. This is done by lowering potential fines if, despite the organization's best efforts, unethical or illegal activities are still committed by the organization or its employees. To be judged effective, a compliance program need not prevent all misconduct; however, it must show due diligence in seeking to prevent and detect inappropriate behavior.

6.1.4   The Economic Espionage Act of 1996. The Economic Espionage Act (EEA) of 1996 for the first time makes trade secret theft a federal crime, subject to penalties including fines, forfeiture, and imprisonment. The act reinforces the rules governing trade secrets in that businesses must show that they have taken reasonable measures to protect their proprietary trade secrets in order to seek relief under the EEA.

In "Counterintelligence and Law Enforcement: The Economic Espionage Act of 1996 versus Competitive Intelligence," author Peter F. Kalitka believes that given the penalties companies face under the EEA, that business hiring outside consultants to gather competitive intelligence should establish a policy on this activity. Included in the contract language with the outside consultant should be definitions of:

- What is hard-to-get information?
- How will the information be obtained?
- Do they adhere to the Society of Competitive Intelligence Professionals Code of Ethics?
- Do they have accounts with clients that may be questioned?

6.1.5   The Foreign Corrupt Practices Act (FCPA). For 20 years, regulators largely ignored the FCPA. This was due, in part, to an initial amnesty program under which nearly 500 companies admitted violations. Now the federal government has dramatically increased its attention on business activities and is looking to enforce the act with vigor. To avoid liability under the FCPA, companies must implement a due diligence program that includes a set of internal controls and enforcement. A set of policies and procedures that are implemented and audited for compliance are required to meet the test of due diligence.

6.2 Business Requirements

It is a well-accepted fact that it is important to protect the information essential to an organization, in the same way that it is important to protect the financial assets of the organization. Unlike protecting financial assets, which have regulations to support their protection, the protection of information is often left to the individual employee. As with protecting financial assets, we all know what the solutions are to protecting information resources. However, identifying these requirements is not good enough; to enforce controls, it is necessary to have a formal written policy that can be used as the basis for all standards and procedures (see Figure 1).

7 THE NEED FOR CONTROLS

With requirements to access information both within the campus environment and external through remote access, the need for an organization-wide information security policy with supporting standards and procedures is more important than ever. Ten years ago, the need for non-employees to access corporate information was less than it is today. There has been a decided change in the processing environment.

7.1 The Changing Environment

In 1974, the Computer Security Institute held its first annual conference and the issues of computer and information security were brought to the forefront (see Figure 2). Over the next ten years, the information

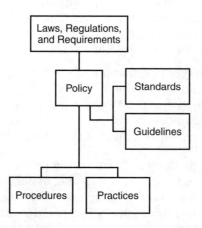

Figure 1. Policy Flow Diagram

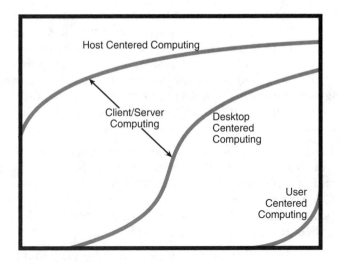

Figure 2. The Changing Environment

processing environment stayed fairly static. The world of computers was based around the mainframe. Policies and standards were developed to protect the information found on the mainframe computer systems. Products such as ACF2, RACF, TopSecret, and SAC were introduced to control access to the systems and the data they contained. Halon 1301 was touted as a safe way to protect computer rooms from fire. The Electronic Data Processing Auditors Association was founded and auditors were trained in how to conduct reviews of data processing facilities.

During the 1980s, the user community began to become disenchanted with IT due to its lack of responsiveness. A user needing a new application or an enhancement to an existing system might have to wait as long as six months before the request would be reviewed and then another couple of months before a decision on the merits of the request was debated. Once there was approval to begin the project, it might take as long as 18 months to deliver the finished product. Oftentimes, the finished product was not exactly what the client wanted.

By 1983 there were between six and ten million personal computers sold in the United States. Most of these early systems (Intel-based 286 processors) were found in corporations. Those departments that were dependent on IT for their new systems, were now turning to their processing capabilities. A shotgun marriage of sorts was created when the information users began to install personal computers and then found that they needed to access information still maintained in the mainframe. The offspring of this attempt at desktop computing is Client/Server Computing (CSC).

In some organizations, CSC meant that the controls seen now as restrictive in the mainframe environment were now taken away. Rapid Application Development (RAD) became the buzzword for cutting corners. Just when many more individuals were gaining access to corporate information, the controls that had been so hard-won in the mainframe environment were being chipped away. The ability to have a centralized control function and the increase of user IDs and passwords have required review of the security process.

In the mainframe environment, access control could be put on at the system level. In the client/server medium, the control had to be placed at the application level. That means that every new application will require the user to have a new user ID and password to gain access. Additionally, each application must maintain its own access control list. The ability to monitor and control access is greatly reduced.

The move to desktop computing is only the beginning in this changing environment. The trend of moving the processing has now extended to the need to take the information to the user, wherever the user may be. This user-based computing has seen a tremendous growth in such activities as telecommuting. Industry reports have identified telecommuting at 30 million workers, with growth projected at 18 percent per year.

The Internet and e-mail usage has been a leader in this move away from the controlled mainframe environment. According to Forrester Research Inc. (Cambridge, Massachusetts) back in 1992, only 2 percent of the U.S. population had access to e-mail. By 1997, that percentage had climbed to 15 percent of the total U.S. population; and by 2000, the level had reached 50 percent. These, along with other remote access requirements, have moved the security requirements into a totally different arena. The need for policies, standards, and procedures is greater than ever. The security professional must adapt to these changes and the controls must meet the needs of the mobile workforce.

7.2   Good Business Practices

Although there are legal and regulatory reasons why policies, standards, and procedures should be implemented, the bottom line is that good controls make good business sense. Failing to implement controls can lead to financial penalties in the form of fines and costs. Such activities can lead to loss of customer confidence, competitive advantage, and, ultimately, jobs. The avoidance of public criticism, and saving the time on the investigation and subsequent disciplinary process, are very effective benefits to the organization that can be obtained by implementation of proper controls.

Every organization is required to provide its services or products to its customers, either legally or contractually. To ensure that the business objectives are met in a timely and efficient manner, effective policies and standards must be in place. Protecting shareholder interests is a key component in the need to implement effective controls.

When preparing policies, standards, and procedures, tread lightly on the legal reasons (use them when needed) but learn to sell your product as any other product. To be accepted and implemented, the policies and standards will have to help managers meet their business objectives. When developing these documents, it will be necessary to understand what each business need is and then work to fulfill those requirements.

8   WHERE TO BEGIN?

To find out what the business objectives or the mission of the organization are, you can begin to search out documents that define the organization. Many organizations have published their goals and objectives in a document similar to that in Table 2.

For publicly held companies, search out the stockholders Annual Report. The business objectives and commitments to providing return-on-investment are presented and endorsed by the top executives of the organization. A key section of the Annual Report is the "Responsibility for Consolidated Financial Statements." The responsibility for the integrity rests with management and normally contains a statement similar to, "The Company maintains systems of internal controls supported by policies and procedures that are communicated throughout the Company."

Understanding the objectives or mission of the organization will help to ensure that the focus of the information security policies, standards, and procedures supports those objectives. Policies that hinder the completion of the business of the organization will be ignored or scrapped. When creating these documents, it will be necessary to keep this key element in mind.

Security for security's sake is of no value. The creation of policies, standards, and procedures must be beneficial to the organization. No policy should be created to ensure that the organization is in compliance with audit requirements. Policies, standards, and procedures are developed and implemented to ensure that the organization meets its legal and contractual obligations to its customers, clients, stockholders, and employees.

Table 2. Shared Beliefs Example

Shared Beliefs

The shareholders and customers of Company Corporation have entrusted the employees of Company Corporation with important responsibilities: to increase shareholder value by providing premier, world-class security solutions.

We have committed ourselves to fulfilling those responsibilities, recognizing that the commitment requires the personal dedication and leadership of each of us and the collective effort of all of us.

We are committed to teamwork and accountability.

We believe that unless we conduct ourselves as a team — and build team effort throughout the company — we cannot succeed. Further, we believe that a team succeeds only when all members understand the team goals, their individual roles, and how each person's performance and commitment contribute to achieving the goals. Our commitment to this concept is reflected in our willingness to accept accountability for results and to stake our personal success on those results.

We are committed to communication.

We practice open, honest, two-way communication and provide regular feedback. We believe that written communication cannot replace dialog between people; that effective communication is a prerequisite to effect action; and that trust, respect, and understanding are necessary for effective communication. We set examples through our behavior because our actions do, in fact, speak louder than our words.

We are committed to continuous improvement and benchmarking.

Continuous improvement in our skills, methods, and results is vital to our success in the highly competitive information security sector. We measure our success and our improvement by comparing our performance with that of our competitors and other companies that are world-class performers. We recognize that just as we strive for improved performance, so do our competitors. Benchmarking and continuous improvement, therefore, are ongoing processes that will ensure that our sights are constantly on target to become superior performers.

Our dedication to living these commitments will produce an environment in which employees are involved — involved in the goals of the company and their individual work groups — and sharing ideas and suggestions as valued contributors. In this way, we will provide value to customers, shareholders, and employees. Our goal is that every employee becomes committed to our shared beliefs.

9   SUMMARY

Every organization needs to implement policies, standards, and procedures. There are legal requirements for this:

- Model Business Corporation Act
- Duty of Loyalty
- Duty of Care
- Federal Guidelines for Sentencing
- Establish policies, standards, and procedures

- Appoint a manager responsible for compliance
- Ensure compliance to policies and standards
- Enforce the policies and standards
- Economic Espionage Act
- Trade secret theft is a federal crime
- Companies must take steps to protect their trade secrets
- Foreign Corrupt Practices Act

Companies must implement a due diligence program that includes internal controls and enforcement.

Business requirements have been dictated because of the changing environment. The move away from mainframe processing to desktop processing to user-based processing has changed the security requirements.

Good business practices require that policies, standards, and procedures are implemented to protect customer confidence, competitive advantage, and employee jobs.

Appendix 1A
Typical Tier 1 Policies

1   INTRODUCTION

Most organizations have a standard set of policies that govern the way they perform their business (see Figure 1). There are at least 11 Tier 1 policies; this means that a policy is implemented to support the entire business or mission of the enterprise. There are also Tier 2 policies; these are topic-specific policies and address issues related to specific subject matter. The Tier 3 policies address the requirements for using and supporting specific applications. Later in the book we present examples of a number each of these policies; for now, we present the Tier 1 policy title and a brief description of what the policy encompasses.

The remainder of this appendix presents Tier 1 organization-wide policies. These are examples of what a typical policy might look like. As discussed in Chapter 1, each policy has a direct bearing on the overall information security program. Make certain to review your organization's

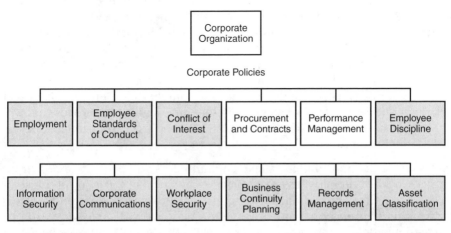

Figure 1. Sample Tier 1 Policies Included

policies and see that, wherever appropriate, the information security language is incorporated.

2   TIER 1 POLICIES

2.1   Shared Beliefs

The Company's customers have entrusted the employees of The Company with important responsibilities: to increase their value by providing premier, world-class information technology services and solutions.

We have committed ourselves to fulfilling those responsibilities, recognizing that the commitment requires the personal dedication and leadership of each of us and the collective effort of all of us.

- *We are committed to teamwork and accountability.* We believe that unless we conduct ourselves as a team — and build team effort throughout the company — we cannot succeed. Further, we believe that a team succeeds only when all members understand the team goals, their individual roles, and how each person's performance and commitment contribute to achieving the goals. Our commitment to this concept is reflected in our willingness to accept accountability for results and to stake our personal success on those results.
- *We are committed to communication.* We practice open, honest, two-way communication and provide regular feedback. We believe that written communication cannot replace dialogue between people; that effective communication is a prerequisite to effect action; and that trust, respect, and understanding are necessary for effective communication. We set examples through our behavior because our actions do, in fact, speak louder than our words.
- *We are committed to continuous improvement and benchmarking.* Continuous improvement in our skills, methods, and results is vital to our success in the highly competitive information security sector. We measure our success and our improvement by comparing our performance with that of our competitors and other companies that are world-class performers. We recognize that just as we strive for improved performance, so do our competitors. Benchmarking and continuous improvement, therefore, are ongoing processes that will ensure that our sights are constantly on target to become superior performers.

Our dedication to living these commitments will produce an environment in which employees are involved — involved in the goals of the company and their individual work groups — and sharing ideas and suggestions as valued contributors. In this way, we will provide value to customers and employees alike. Our goal is that every employee becomes committed to our shared beliefs.

3   EMPLOYEE STANDARDS OF CONDUCT

3.1   Policy

The Company employees are expected to conduct themselves in a professional and business-like manner at all times when on company property or
when representing the company.

3.2   Responsibilities

Employees:

- Shall act in an ethical manner, and shall avoid actions that have the
  appearance of being unethical.
- Shall abide by applicable laws, regulations, and professional
  standards.
- Shall avoid situations in which there may be a conflict of interest
  (see *Conflict of Interest* policy for more information).
- Shall meet individual performance expectations.
- Shall abide by company policies and practices.
- Shall accurately and honestly record and report corporate informa-
  tion in a timely manner.
- Shall also maintain the confidentiality of corporate information (see
  Information Classification policy).
- Shall treat co-workers and others with dignity and respect.
- Are expected to use intelligence, common sense, and good judgment
  in applying these standards of conduct.
- Shall direct questions relating to the standards of conduct to their
  supervisors.
- Who observe conduct that does not appear consistent with these
  standards of conduct should discuss the matter with their supervi-
  sor; the supervisor shall report fraudulent activity to the General
  Counsel.
- Who have suffered a violation of the standards of conduct should
  immediately report the matter to their supervisor or to the Vice
  President, Human Resources.

Managers and Supervisors:

- Shall be investigated in as discreet a fashion as possible. Once the
  investigation is complete, appropriate action will be taken.
- Shall provide appropriate feedback to those who report misconduct.
- Shall retaliate against employees who report suspected misconduct.
- Will manage corporate information, personnel, and physical properties relevant to their business operations, as well as monitor the
  actual utilization of all corporate assets.

3.3 Compliance

Employees who violate these standards of conduct are subject to disciplinary action up to and including discharge. In some cases, employees may also be subject to criminal charges.

The Company management has the responsibility to ensure that all employees are aware of their obligation to behave in an ethical manner and to note variances from established conduct standards and initiate appropriate corrective action.

3.4 Unacceptable Conduct

Supervisors shall follow appropriate disciplinary procedures, up to and including discharge, for employees whose work performance or behavior does not meet the standards of conduct. Some examples of unacceptable conduct are shown below. This list is not all-inclusive.

- Work performance:
  - Failure to meet job requirements
  - Unacceptable work performance
- Attendance and tardiness:
  - Absence without notice or permission
  - Failure to notify as required
  - Excessive tardiness or excessive absence
- General conduct:
  - Conflict of interest activities
  - Dishonesty
  - Failure to maintain acceptable appearance and hygiene standards
  - Gambling or operating a lottery while on the job
  - Possession of unauthorized weapons or cameras on company property
  - Sleeping on the job
  - Unauthorized use or possession of company property
  - Insubordination
  - Violation of a copyright or software licensing agreement, including the introduction of non-company-approved software or code into any company system

3.5 Harassment

Harassment can take many forms in words or actions that are either implied or clear and direct. It is not limited by position, sex, or race. Harassment includes, but is not limited to, sexual harassment, verbal abuse, or threatening others.

Sexual harassment refers to behavior of a sexual nature that is unwelcome and offensive and is a form of misconduct that undermines the integrity of the employment relationship. Sexual harassment includes unwelcome sexual advances, requests for sexual favors, and other verbal or physical conduct or communication of a sexual nature when:

- Such conduct or communication has the purpose or effect of substantially interfering with an individual's employment or creating an intimidating, hostile, or offensive work environment.
- Submission to such conduct or communication is made a term or condition, either explicitly or implicitly, to obtain employment
- Submission to, or rejection of, such conduct or communication by an individual is used as a factor in decisions affecting such individual's employment.

3.6   Fireable Offenses

Employees who commit any of the following will normally be subject to immediate discharge. This list is not all-inclusive. An employee may be discharged for serious offenses or for any reason management deems appropriate including:

- Absence without notice for **three** consecutive work days
- Defrauding the company
- Falsifying company records
- Physical assault
- Possessing, selling, distributing, dispensing, manufacturing, or using illegal drugs while on company premises or conducting company business
- Theft of company, employee, customer, or supplier information resources or other property
- Willfully destroying company, employee, customer, or vendor information resources or other property

4   CONFLICT OF INTEREST

4.1   Policy

The Company employees are expected to adhere to the highest standards of conduct. To assure adherence to these standards, employees must have a special sensitivity to conflict-of-interest situations or relationships, as well as the inappropriateness of personal involvement in them. Although not always covered by law, these situations can harm The Company or its reputation if improperly handled.

A conflict of interest occurs when an employee's personal interests conflict with the company's interests. Conflicts of interest may also involve relationships between members of the employee's immediate family and The Company. In conflict-of-interest situations, employees are expected to act in the best interests of the company.

4.2   Standards

The following standards for ethical behavior are established for all employees in dealing with conflict-of-interest situations:

- When actual or potential conflict-of-interest situations arise, or where there is an *appearance* of such conflict, employees shall remove themselves from involvement in the matter. In no case should employees become involved to the extent where they are or could be influenced to make decisions that are not in the company's best interest.
- Employees shall not solicit or accept personal gain, privileges, or other benefits through involvement in any matters on behalf of The Company.
- Employees shall direct their efforts to company business while at work, and shall use company resources only for management-approved activities. Resources include, but are not limited to, equipment, supplies, corporate information, and company-paid time.

4.3   Responsibilities

Employees:

- Whenever faced with an actual or potential business-related conflict-of-interest situation, employees shall seek guidance from their supervisors.
- When conflict-of-interest questions cannot be resolved within the organizational unit, employees may request advice from the General Auditor.
- When requested, employees shall also disclose actual and potential conflict-of-interest situations to the General Auditor.

Management

- The General Auditor shall review each situation and advise the organizational unit of any recommended action the employee should take.

4.4   Common Conflict-of-Interest Situations

The specific situations described in this section are common, but are not all-inclusive of business-related conflict-of-interest situations that may arise for The Company employees.

- **Gifts, expenses, and products.** Giving gifts, providing meals and entertainment, company travel, and offering site tours and product samples are common business practices. Because the intent of these practices is to build relationships and influence business decisions, such practices can result in a conflict of interest. The Company expenses incurred in any of the following situations are subject to organizational approval.
    - *Gifts.* Gifts generally benefit the employee, but not the company. In dealing with suppliers, customers, or others outside the company, employees shall not accept or give money or gifts, except an occasional unsolicited, nonmonetary item of a token nature, such as an advertising novelty of nominal value.
    - *Meals and entertainment.* In dealing with suppliers, customers, or others outside the company, employees shall not accept or provide meals or entertainment, except when there is a business purpose. The provider of the meal or entertainment should be present at the occasion. Frequent or repeated acceptance of meals and entertainment may be an indicator of the employee's personal gain, and could raise questions about the legitimacy of the business purpose for such occasions. When there is a business purpose for frequent meals or entertainment, The Company encourages reciprocation.
    - *Travel.* When there is a business purpose for travel, The Company should reimburse all travel expenses. Employees should not accept air transportation offered by vendors or others outside the company when convenient commercial transportation is available. Generally, The Company should pay for lodging expenses.
    - *Product samples.* If business dictates that a sample product or service of more than nominal value is needed, The Company should pay for it.
- **Outside work.** Employees who have another job outside of The Company shall not represent themselves as performing work for The Company when working in such jobs. Furthermore, they may not use The Company resources in performing the other job. Employees shall not be employed by competitors of The Company.
- **Interest in outside business organizations.** Employees shall avoid significant financial or management interest in any business that does or seeks to do business with The Company if such involvement could cause employees to make business decisions that are not in The Company's best interest.
- **Use of confidential or proprietary information.** Employees entrusted with such information shall restrict access and use to authorized individuals inside and outside the company who have a clear business need to know this information.

- **Insider trading.** No employee who has material nonpublic ("insider") information relating to The Company or one of its customers may use that information in buying and selling related securities, either directly or indirectly. Furthermore, employees may not engage in other actions to take personal advantage of that information or pass it on to others. Even the appearance of an improper transaction must be avoided to preserve The Company's reputation for adhering to the highest standards of conduct.

5 EMPLOYMENT PRACTICES

5.1 Policy

The Company is an Equal Opportunity Employer. Organizational units are responsible for selecting and maintaining a competent workforce. For hiring, transfers, and promotions, supervisors will document, as appropriate, the basis for decisions and actions. The organizational unit shall retain this documentation for seven years.

5.2 Filling Job Vacancies

- When an organizational unit identifies a need to establish a new position, they shall consult with Human Resources to establish the position and post the job vacancy.
- The Vice President of the hiring organization shall approve any decision to hire.
- Organizational units may contact Recruiting Selection Staffing (RSS) for assistance in filing job vacancies. RSS can assist the organizational unit by providing:
  - Company-wide posting of opening
  - Screening applications for minimum requirement qualifications
  - Coordinating medical examinations or skill aptitude tests
  - Scheduling background checks where appropriate

5.3 Termination of Employment

Termination of employment may be either involuntary or voluntary. All paperwork for employee termination must be maintained for seven years. For information regarding discharge, refer to the Employee Discipline Policy.

5.4 Responsibilities

When terminating employment, employees have the responsibility to:

- Notify management in writing at least two weeks prior to resignation date.
- Notify management 90 days prior to retirement date.

- Return all Company property, including intellectual property, hardware, and software.

The Company Management has the responsibility to:

- Check all outstanding payroll deduction balances before authorizing release of employee's final payroll check.
- Obtain all Company property, including such items as identification badges, keys, parking tags, access cards, and computer equipment.
- Give approval all employee personal property being removed from the premises.
- Contact RSS to conduct an Employee Exit Interview.

6   RECORDS MANAGEMENT

6.1   Policy

It is the policy of the Company to accommodate the timely storage, retrieval, and disposition of records created, utilized, and maintained by the various departments. The period of time that records are maintained is based on the minimum requirements set forth in state and federal retention schedules.

6.2   Role of Retention Center

The role of the Retention Center is to receive, maintain, destroy, and service inactive records that have not met their disposition date. Each business unit is to establish schedules to comply with the minimum amount of time records should be maintained in compliance with state and federal guidelines. Retention requirements apply whether or not the records are transferred to the Retention Center. Copies of the schedules must be maintained by the business unit and available for inspection.

6.3   Role of Records Manager

The role of the Records Manager is to administer the Records Management program. The Records Manager is well acquainted with all records and record groups within an agency and has expertise in all aspects of records management. The duties of the Records Manager include planning, development, and administration of records management policies. These duties also include the annual organizationwide inventory of all information assets to be conducted by the business unit manager with reports sent to the Records Manager.

6.4   Role of Management Personnel

Management Personnel are responsible for records under their control.

6.5 Role of Departmental Records Coordinator

The Departmental Records Coordinator is a liaison between the department and the Retention Center. It is recommended that each department appoint a Records Coordinator in writing. The letter of appointment should include the Records Coordinator's full name, department, and telephone extension. The letter should be forwarded to the Retention Center and maintained on file.

6.6 Type of Documents Maintained in Retention Center

- Record Retention accepts only public records that are referenced in the State Retention Schedule, except student transcripts. Copies of student transcripts may be obtained from Records and Admissions located at the Student Service Center.
- Record Retention does not accept personal, active, or non-records.
- Record Retention stores only inactive and permanent records until final disposition according to state and federal retention schedules. Examples include personnel files, purchase orders, grade books, or surveys.
- Record Retention receives and stores inactive permanent records from TVI departments until final disposition according to state and federal retention guidelines.
- Record Retention ensures records are classified according to state and retention guidelines.
- Record Retention ensures records are tracked and entered into an electronic records management software system that tracks record boxes, and assigns retention schedules, permanent box numbers, destruction dates, and shelf locations.

6.7 Services

- If a department has obsolete records that are deemed confidential or sensitive, or copies of non-records, a special request for shredding may be sent to the Record Retention Center. The records can be shredded by the Record Retention Center staff or transferred to the State Record Center for destruction.
- Departments must complete a Request for Destruction form for confidential or non-records to be shredded. Departments are required to purchase forms from Central Stores at Shipping & Receiving.
- The Record Retention Center provides consulting services to departments on filing systems and maintenance of records.

6.8 Transferring Records

- Departments should transfer records to Record Retention for storage in January, July, and October.

- Records with a retention period of two years or more should be transferred to Record Retention.

6.9 Record Retrieval

- Records are retrieved and delivered to customers by request, given 24-hour notice.
- Records can be retrieved for customers on an emergency basis as requested.
- Management personnel, the records coordinator, or the requester will sign for receipt of records. Records are to be checked out for no longer than 30 days. If a longer period is required, a written request should be sent to the Retention Center. If records are checked out for more than a year, the records will be permanently withdrawn from inventory.
- Permanent Withdrawal: If a department wishes to withdraw a record permanently from storage, forward a request to the Record Retention Center by phone, fax, or inter-office mail. The department will complete a Withdrawal Request form and the records will be deleted from inventory.
- Second-Party Withdrawal: If a department requests a record originating from another department, then the requesting department must contact the department of origin to obtain authorization. The department of origin will contact the Record Retention Center for records withdrawal. The department requester must view the requested records at the Record Retention Center.
- Records should not be returned via inter-office mail, due to the confidential nature of the documents.

6.10 Record Destruction

- Record Retention destroys records according to state guidelines in January, July, and October.
- Records are destroyed by the Record Retention Center according to state and federal guidelines when legal requirements are met. A Destruction Request form will be sent to the originating department for review and signature by the Departmental Records Coordinator and by management personnel. Only when the Destruction Request has been reviewed, signed, and returned to Record Retention will the expired records be destroyed. Authorized personnel will shred confidential records. If departments wish to keep the records past their assigned destruction date, management personnel can extend the date no longer than one year unless a litigation, audit, or investigation is pending. Records kept by the department past the retention date of destruction will be permanently withdrawn from inventory.

- All records scheduled for destruction are reviewed by the Institute's Records Manager and by State Records Analysts for approval.

7   CORPORATE COMMUNICATIONS

7.1   Policy

Correspondence, in whatever format, represents the Company to the outside world. It is vital that all communications reflect ethical and legal behavior. As an employee of the Company, you are responsible for ensuring that all correspondence, regardless of the format (letter format, e-mail, voice-mail, Internet, presentations, etc.), meets these standards.

7.2   Standards

All Company communications shall be:

- Truthful, credible, and consistent with the company's performance and actions
- In accordance with applicable Company policies, state and federal laws, and regulatory requirements

7.3   Responsibilities

Employees who fail to comply with this policy will be considered in violation of the Company's *Employee Standards of Conduct* and will be subject to appropriate corrective action.

The Company Management has the responsibility to:

- Ensure that all employees are aware of their rights and obligations relating to Company correspondence.
- Implement security practices and procedures that are consistent with Company policies in all forms of communication.
- Note variances from established security practices and for initiating appropriate corrective action.

8   ELECTRONIC COMMUNICATIONS

8.1   Policy

The Company maintains electronic communication systems (e-mail, voice-mail, video mail, etc.) to assist in company business both internally and externally. These systems, including the equipment and the data stored in the system, are and remain the property of the Company.

- The Company reserves the right to retrieve and review any messages composed, sent, or received.
- Company-provided electronic communication systems are only to be used for management-approved activities.

8.2   Responsibilities

- Employees should be aware that even when messages are deleted or erased, it may still be possible to recreate the message; therefore, the ultimate privacy of message control may not be assured.
- While electronic communication systems may accommodate the use of passwords for security, this control does not ensure message confidentiality.
- Electronic communication messages are not to be created or sent which may constitute intimidating, hostile, or offensive material on the basis of race, color, creed, religion, national origin, age, sex, martial status, lawful alien status, non-job-related physical or mental disability, veteran status, sexual orientation, or other basis prohibited by law (refer to *Employee Standards of Conduct*).

8.3   Compliance

The Company management will:

- Manage corporate information, personnel, and physical property relevant to business operations, as well as the right to monitor the actual utilization of all corporate assets.
- Ensure that all employees are aware of their obligation to use electronic communication systems in an ethical and proper manner.
- Note variances from established security practices and for initiating corrective action.

Employees who fail to comply with this policy will be considered to be in violation of the Company's *Employee Standards of Conduct* and will be subject to appropriate corrective action. The sharing of passwords with unauthorized personnel violates this policy

9   INTERNET SECURITY

9.1   Policy

The Company, through the Internet, provides computing resources to its staff to access information, communicate, and retrieve and disseminate organization- and business-related information. Use of the public Internet by Company employees is permitted and encouraged where such use is suitable for business purposes in a manner that is consistent with the *Employee Standards of Conduct* and as part of the normal execution of an employee's job responsibilities.

9.2   Provisions

- The use of company-provided access to the Internet is intended exclusively for management-approved activities.

- All access to the Internet by employees must be accomplished through the Company-provided method.
- The Company Chief Information Officer (CIO) must approve all publications/content files not classified as Public in accordance with the *Information Classification* policy.
- The Company's policies regarding Employee Standards of Conduct, Conflict of Interest, Information Protection, and Information Classification also apply to the use of the Internet.

9.3   Responsibilities

The Company management will:

- Ensure that all employees are aware of this policy.
- Report all security-related incidents to appropriate management upon discovery.
- Ensure that employees review and sign the Internet Usage and Responsibility Statement.

Employees who fail to comply with this policy will be considered in violation of the Company's *Employee Standards of Conduct* and will be subject to appropriate corrective action.

10   INTERNET USAGE AND RESPONSIBILITY STATEMENT

I, _____, acknowledge and understand that access to the Internet, as provided by The Company, is for management-approved use only. This supports the Company policies on *Employee Standards of Conduct* and *Information Classification*, and among other things, prohibits the downloading of games, viruses, inappropriate materials or picture files, and unlicensed software from the Internet.

I recognize and accept that while accessing the Internet, I am responsible for maintaining the highest professional and ethical standards, as outlined in the Company policy on *Employee Standards of Conduct*.

I have read and understand the policies mentioned above and accept my responsibility to protect the Company's information and reputation.

Name _____ Date _____

11   EMPLOYEE DISCIPLINE

11.1   Policy

Employees found to be in violation of Company policies are subject to appropriate disciplinary procedures. The Employee Discipline process is a system of performance management that ensures that individual responsibility for actions by employees is addressed.

11.2   Positive Recognition

- Coaching to improve performance is an effective tool for management to communicate with employees and informally discuss work performance, attendance, or conduct.
- Company management will coach to help an employee who performs well in a job to reach higher levels of performance or to correct an emerging employee performance problem.

11.3   Formal Discipline

Formal discipline is a series of corrective steps taken to improve performance and change behavior. Formal discipline is issued when an employee does not respond to coaching or a performance is serious enough to warrant formal discipline.

The decision to issue discipline and the level of discipline issued depend on the seriousness of the offense and the employee's record, and it is within the sole exclusive discretion of management.

There are three formal discipline levels: oral reminder, written reminder, and decision-making leave (DML).

- *Oral reminder.* This is the first level of formal discipline. Employees may have a maximum of three active oral reminders at any time, and they must each be in separate categories. An oral reminder remains active for six months.
- *Written reminder.* This is issued when an employee's commitment to improve is not met within the six-month oral reminder active period. Only two written reminders may be active at any one time, and they must be in different categories. A written reminder must be reviewed with Human Resources and, if appropriate, Labor Relations prior to issuance. A written reminder remains active for 12 months.
- *Decision-making leave (DML).* This is the final level of formal discipline. When a DML is issued, the employee is directed to take the following workday off, with pay, to decide if a commitment to overall satisfactory performance improvement can be made. A DML must be reviewed prior to issuance with Human Resources and, if appropriate, Labor Relations. There may be only one active DML and it remains in effect for 18 months.

Any of the three levels of formal discipline may be issued without following the above sequence when a single incident is deemed sufficiently serious.

11.4   Deactivation

Once the time period prescribed for the formal levels of discipline is deactivated, the discipline shall be disregarded for purposes of further discipline. The expired formal documentation is to be removed from the employee's organizational unit personnel record. All records of formal discipline will remain part of the Company's permanent records.

11.5   Discharge

A discharge is normally issued when, in management's judgment, other levels of discipline are unsuccessful in getting the employee to correct unacceptable performance or the offense is serious enough to warrant immediate discharge. However, an employee may be discharged for any reason management deems appropriate.

Management's judgment is final and exclusive, subject to limited review only under the Employee Review System or applicable labor agreement grievance procedure.

An employee may be discharged if a performance problem that warrants formal discipline occurs during a period when a DML is active.

Immediate discharge without following the normal Employee Discipline process may also occur. Dischargeable offenses are listed in the *Employee Standards of Conduct.*

12   GENERAL SECURITY

12.1   Policy

It is the responsibility of Company management to provide a safe and secure workplace for all employees.

12.2   Standards

- The Company offices will be protected from unauthorized access.
- Areas within buildings that house sensitive or high-risk equipment will be protected against fire, water, and other hazards.
- Devices that are critical to the operation of company business processes will be protected against power failure.

12.3   Responsibilities

- Senior management and the officers of the Company are required to maintain accurate records and to employ internal controls designed to safeguard company assets and property against unauthorized use or disposition.
- The Company assets include but are not limited to physical property, intellectual property, patents, trade secrets, copyrights, and trademarks.

- Additionally, it is the responsibility of Company line management to ensure that staff is aware of, and fully complies with, the Company's security guidelines and all relevant laws and regulations.

12.4 Compliance

- Management is responsible for conducting periodic reviews and audits to assure compliance with all policies, procedures, practices, standards, and guidelines.
- Employees who fail to comply with the policies will be treated as being in violation of the *Employee Standards of Conduct* and will be subject to appropriate corrective action.

13 BUSINESS CONTINUITY PLANNING

13.1 Policy

The continued operations of Company business activities in the event of an emergency must be addressed by each business unit in a Business Continuity Plan (BCP). The business unit BCPs must be coordinated with the Company BCP and the Company Emergency Response Plan.

13.2 Standards

- Every business unit will have a documented and tested BCP.
- Each business unit will conduct a Business Impact Analysis (BIA) to determine its critical business processes, applications, systems, and platforms. The BIA results will be presented to the Information Security Steering Committee (ISSC) for review and approval.
- The BIAs will be reviewed annually by the business unit to ensure the results are still appropriate.
- The business unit BCPs must be coordinated with the Company-wide BCP.

13.3 Responsibilities

- Senior management and the officers of the Company are required to review and approve business unit BCPs as well as the Company BCP.
- Additionally, it is the responsibility of company line management to ensure that the business unit BCP is current.

13.4 Compliance

- Management is responsible for conducting periodic tests of the BCP to ensure that the continued processing requirements of the Company are met.

14   INFORMATION PROTECTION

14.1   Policy

Information is a Company asset and is the property of the Company. The Company information includes information that is electronically generated, printed, filmed, typed, stored, or verbally communicated. Information must be protected according to its sensitivity, criticality, and value, regardless of the media on which it is stored, the manual or automated systems that process it, or the methods by which it is distributed. Customer information that has been entrusted to the Company will also be safeguarded in accordance with this policy.

To ensure that business objectives and customer confidence are maintained, all employees have a responsibility to protect information from unauthorized access, modification, disclosure, and destruction, whether accidental or intentional.

14.2   Responsibilities

- Senior management and the Officers of the Company are required to employ internal controls designed to safeguard company assets, including business information.
- It is a line management obligation to ensure that all employees understand and comply with the Company's security policies and standards, as well as all applicable laws and regulations.
- Employee responsibilities for protecting Company information are detailed in the *Information Classification* policy.

14.3   Compliance

- Company management has the responsibility to manage corporate information, personnel, and physical property relevant to business operations, as well as the right to monitor the actual utilization of all corporate assets.
- Employees who fail to comply with the policies will be considered in violation of the Company's *Employee Standards of Conduct* and will be subject to appropriate corrective action.

15   INFORMATION CLASSIFICATION

15.1   Policy

Information is a company asset and is the property of the Company. Company information includes information that is electronically generated, printed, filmed, typed, stored, or verbally communicated. Information must be protected according to its sensitivity, criticality, and value, regardless of the media on which it is stored, the manual or automated systems that process it, or the methods by which it is distributed.

15.2   Classification Levels

To ensure the proper protection of corporate information, the Owner (defined below) shall use a formal review process to classify information into one of the following three classifications: Public, Confidential, and Internal Use.

Public. Public information is information that has been made available for public distribution through authorized Company channels. (Refer to *Corporate Communications* policy for more information.) This information is available to anyone inside or outside the Company. Access to Public information is unrestricted. Examples include items such as company brochures, marketing presentations, and news releases.

Confidential. Confidential information is information that, if disclosed, could violate the privacy of individuals, reduce the Company's competitive advantage, or cause significant damage to the Company. The unauthorized disclosure, modification, or destruction of this information would adversely impact the Company or could subject it to legal action and penalties. Generally, this information is intended for use only within the Company. Access is restricted to authorized individuals and entities (see below).

Company Confidential information may also include:

- *All proprietary information that also is a trade secret.* Not all proprietary information, however, is a trade secret, and therefore confidential. For example, a company-wide broadcast is proprietary but not confidential. Such information will be classified as Public or Internal Use, but should be labeled with a copyright notice, if appropriate;
- *Contracts* that the Company considers confidential or that contain nondisclosure provisions;
- *Employee information,* such as personal information, medical information, compensation and benefits information, performance appraisals, records of disciplinary action, and other similar information.
- *Information from an outside entity that is in the Company's possession* and is confidential because of a contract provision or other legal obligation to treat the information confidentially; or
- Information related to outside entities, market conditions and strategies, or other expertise independently developed by The Company personnel, which is a the Company trade secret.

An employee of the Company may access and use the Company Confidential information only if:

- The employee needs the information to carry out his or her job duties, or the Company must provide the information to comply with a legal obligation; and
- The officer responsible for protecting the information, or his or her designee (i.e., Information Sponsor), approves the access in compliance with applicable policies, standards, and procedures.

An outside entity may access and use the Company Confidential information only if:

- There is a legitimate business need or legal requirement to permit the access and use.
- The officer responsible for protecting the information, or his or her designee, approves the access and it is in compliance with applicable policies, standard practices, and procedures.
- *Prior* to receiving access, the outside entity signs a standard Company nondisclosure agreement provided by the Law department or is bound by a general nondisclosure agreement as a condition of its work for the Company.

Requests by regulatory agencies or other outside entities that are related to ongoing or potential legal proceedings must be referred to the General Counsel, which will provide guidance based on the specific situation.

Internal Use. This information is intended for use only within the Company. The unauthorized disclosure, modification, or destruction of the information might adversely impact the Company. Internal Use information is information that is intended for use by employees when conducting Company business. Most information used in the Company will be in this category.

Access to Internal Use information is restricted to Company personnel. The information requires reasonable protection measures that will prevent unintended disclosure. Such information may be released to outside entities, including outside consultants or contractors, only in two circumstances: for legitimate business reasons, and in compliance with policies, standards, and procedures governing the release and protection of information.

Examples of Internal Use information include nonconfidential interoffice memos, corporate policies, standards, procedures, telephone directories, and organizational charts.

Declassification. The Owner is to establish a review process for all information classified as **Confidential**, and reclassify it when it no longer meets the criteria established for such information.

Reclassification. The information Owner may change the classification as the impact of its unauthorized disclosure, modification, or destruction changes. Upon changing the classification, the Owner will increase, decrease, or remove the classification as appropriate and will notify affected information users.

15.3 Responsibilities

Employees are responsible for protecting corporate information from unauthorized access, modification, destruction, or disclosure, whether accidental or intentional. To facilitate the protection of corporate information, employee responsibilities have been established at three levels: **Owner, Custodian,** and **User.**

- **Owner:** a Company manager of a business unit or office where the information is created, or who is the primary user of the information. **Owners** are responsible for:
  - Identifying the classification level of all corporate information within their organizational unit
  - Defining and implementing appropriate safeguards to ensure the confidentiality, integrity, and availability of the information resource
  - Monitoring safeguards to ensure their compliance and report situations of noncompliance
  - Authorizing access to those who have a business need for the information
  - Removing access from those who no longer have a business need for the information
- **Custodian:** employees designated by the Owner to be responsible for protecting information by maintaining safeguards established by the Owner.
- **User:** employees authorized by the Owner to access information and use the safeguards established by the Owner.

15.4 Compliance

- Company management has the responsibility to:
  - Manage corporate information, personnel, and physical property relevant to business operations, as well as the right to monitor the actual utilization of all corporate assets.
  - Ensure that all employees understand their obligation to protect company information.
  - Implement security practices and procedures that are consistent with the Company policies and the value of the asset.
  - Note variance from established security practice and for initiating corrective action.
- Employees who fail to comply with the policies will be considered to be in violation of the Company's *Employee Standards of Conduct*

and will be subject to corrective action up to and including loss of computer network access, discharge from the Company, and legal action.

- Non-Company employees who violate protection standards are subject to business actions, including loss of access to information systems/information, termination of contracts or other business relationships with the Company, and legal action.

These policies are provided to you as examples of what you might do in your own organization. Use them as guidelines — not standards — and alter them to meet your specific needs.

Appendix 1B
Typical Tier 2 Policies

1   INTRODUCTION

Where the Global Policy (Tier 1) is intended to address the broad organizationwide issues, the Topic-Specific Policy is developed to focus on areas of current relevance and concern to the organization. Management may find it appropriate to issue a policy on how an organization will approach Internet usage or the use of the company-provided e-mail system. Topic-specific policies may also be appropriate when new issues arise, such as when implementing a recently enacted law requiring protection of particular information (GLBA, HIPAA, etc.). The global (Tier 1) policy is usually broad enough that it does not require modification over time, whereas the topic-specific (Tier 2) policy is likely to require more frequent revisions as changes in technology and other factors dictate.

Topic-specific policies will be created most often by an organization. We examine the key elements in the topic-specific policy. When creating an *Information Security Policies and Standards* document, each section in the document normally begins with a topic-specific policy. The topic-specific policy will narrow the focus to one issue at a time. This will allow the writer to focus on one area and then develop a set of standards to support this particular subject.

Where the Tier 1 policies are approved by the Information Security Steering Committee, the topic-specific (Tier 2) policy may be issued by a single senior manager or director (see Figure 1).

The remainder of this appendix provides examples of Tier 2 topic-specific policies. These are examples of what a typical policy might look like. As discussed in Chapter 4, each policy has a direct bearing on the overall information security program. Make certain to review your organization's policies and see that, wherever appropriate, the information security language is incorporated.

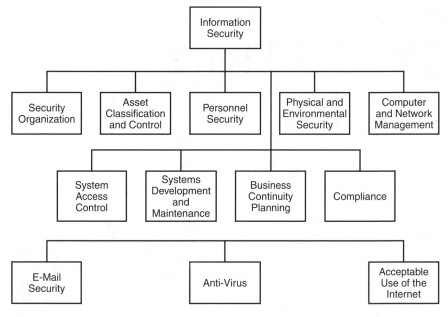

Figure 1. Typical Tier 2 Policies

2 ELECTRONIC COMMUNICATIONS

2.1 Policy

The Company maintains electronic communication systems (e-mail, voice-mail, video mail, etc.) to assist in company business both internally and externally. These systems, including the equipment and the data stored in the system, are and remain the property of The Company.

- The Company reserves the right to retrieve and review any messages composed, sent, or received.
- The Company-provided electronic communication systems are only to be used for management-approved activities.

2.2 Responsibilities

- Employees should be aware that even when messages are deleted or erased, it may still be possible to recreate the message; therefore, the ultimate privacy of message control may not be assured.
- While electronic communication systems may accommodate the use of passwords for security, this control does not ensure message confidentiality.
- Electronic communication messages are not to be created or sent that may constitute intimidating, hostile, or offensive material on

the basis of race, color, creed, religion, national origin, age, sex, martial status, lawful alien status, non-job-related physical or mental disability, veteran status, sexual orientation, or other basis prohibited by law (refer to *Employee Standards of Conduct*).

2.3 Compliance

The Company management will:

- Manage corporate information, personnel, and physical property relevant to business operations, as well as the right to monitor the actual utilization of all corporate assets.
- Ensure that all employees are aware of their obligation to use electronic communication systems in an ethical and proper manner.
- Note variances from established security practices and for initiating corrective action.

Employees who fail to comply with this policy will be considered in violation of The Company's *Employee Standards of Conduct* and will be subject to appropriate corrective action. The sharing of passwords with unauthorized personnel violates this policy.

3 INTERNET SECURITY

3.1 Policy

The Company, through the Internet, provides computing resources to its staff to access information, communicate, retrieve, and disseminate organization- and business-related information. Use of the public Internet by The Company employees is permitted and encouraged where such use is suitable for business purposes in a manner that is consistent with the *Employee Standards of Conduct* and as part of the normal execution of an employee's job responsibilities.

3.2 Standards

1. The use of company-provided access to the Internet is intended exclusively for management-approved activities.
2. All access to the Internet by employees must be accomplished through the Company-provided method.
3. The Company Chief Information Officer (CIO) must approve all publications/content files not classified as Public in accordance with the *Information Classification* policy.
4. The Company's policies regarding Employee Standards of Conduct, Conflict of Interest, Information Protection, and Information Classification also apply to use of the Internet.

3.3 Responsibilities

The Company management will:

- Ensure that all employees are aware of this policy.
- Report all security-related incidents to appropriate management upon discovery.
- Ensure that employees review and sign the Internet Usage and Responsibility Statement.

3.4 Compliance

Employees who fail to comply with this policy will be considered to be in violation of The Company's *Employee Standards of Conduct* and will be subject to appropriate corrective action.

4 INTERNET USAGE AND RESPONSIBILITY STATEMENT

I, _____, acknowledge and understand that access to the Internet, as provided by The Company, is for management-approved use only. This supports The Company policies on *Employee Standards of Conduct* and *Information Classification*, and among other things, prohibits the downloading of games, viruses, inappropriate materials or picture files, and unlicensed software from the Internet.

I recognize and accept that while accessing the Internet, I am responsible for maintaining the highest professional and ethical standards, as outlined in the Company policy on *Employee Standards of Conduct.*

I have read and understand the policies mentioned above and accept my responsibility to protect The Company's information and reputation.

Name _____ Date _____

5 COMPUTER AND NETWORK MANAGEMENT

5.1 Policy

Responsibilities and procedures for the management and operation of all computers and networks are assigned in the following manner:

- Clear, documented operating procedures are prepared for all operational computer systems to ensure their correct, secure operation.
- Incident management responsibilities and procedures are established to ensure quick, effective, and orderly response to security incidents.
- Management and execution of certain duties and areas of responsibility are kept separate in order to reduce opportunities for unauthorized modification or misuse of data or services.

- Development and operational facilities are segregated to reduce the risk of accidental changes or unauthorized access to operational software and business data.
- The risks posed by the use of an external contractor in the management of computer or network facilities are identified and appropriate security measures are incorporated into contracts.

Advance planning and preparation are conducted to ensure the availability of adequate capacity and resources. Measures to ensure this are:

- Capacity requirements are monitored and projections of future capacity requirements are made to reduce the risk of system overload.
- Acceptance criteria for new systems are established and tested prior to acceptance.
- Appropriate fallback arrangements for each IT service are established to provide an alternative, temporary means of continuing processing in the event of any damage to or failure of equipment.
- Processes are established to control changes to IT facilities and systems to ensure satisfactory control of all changes to equipment, software, or procedures.

Routine procedures are followed to take backup copies of data, log events and faults, and where appropriate, monitor the equipment environment. To achieve this, The Company has:

- A process to take regular backup copies of essential business data and software and to ensure that it can be recovered following a computer disaster or media failure.
- A mechanism to log all work carried out by computer operators.
- Procedures to log faults reported by users regarding problems with computer or communications systems, and to report and take corrective action.
- A process to monitor computer environments, including temperature, humidity, and power supply quality to identify conditions that might adversely affect the operation of computer equipment, and to facilitate corrective action.

The security of computer networks that span organizational boundaries is managed to safeguard information and to protect the supporting infrastructure. This is accomplished by controls to ensure the security of data in networks, and to protect connected services from unauthorized access.

Computer media are controlled and protected to prevent damage to assets and interruptions to business activities. To accomplish this The Company has:

- Established procedures for the management of removable computer media such as tapes, disks, cassettes, and printed reports
- Established procedures for handling sensitive data to protect such data from unauthorized disclosure or misuse
- Established controls to protect system documentation from unauthorized access
- Established a process to ensure that computer media are disposed of securely and safely when no longer required

Exchanges of data and software between The Company and other organizations are controlled to prevent loss, modification, or misuse of data. To implement this control, The Company has:

- Established formal agreements, to include software escrow agreements when appropriate, for exchanging data and software (whether electronic or manual) between organizations
- Applied controls to safeguard computer media being transported between sites to minimize its vulnerability to unauthorized access, misuse, or corruption during transportation between sites
- Applied, where necessary, special security controls to safeguard electronic data interchange against unauthorized interception or modification
- Established clear policies and guidelines to control business and security risks associated with electronic office systems

5.2 Responsibilities

- Company IT line management has the responsibility to ensure that the measures listed above are put in place and carried out effectively.
- The Company information security organization has the responsibility to provide services that will assist IT line management in implementing and monitoring compliance with these measures.
- All employees who install, operate, or maintain computer and network equipment and systems are required to comply with this policy.

5.3 Scope

The *Computer and Network Management Security* policy applies to all computer and network equipment and systems owned and operated by The Company.

5.4 Compliance

Company officers and senior management are required to ensure that internal audit mechanisms exist to monitor and measure compliance with this policy.

Company IT and, where appropriate, business unit line management have the responsibility to enforce compliance with this policy.

6   ANTI-VIRUS POLICY

6.1   Policy

Precautions are applied to prevent and detect the introduction of malicious software, and safeguard the integrity of the software and data. Virus detection and prevention measures and appropriate user awareness procedures are implemented.

6.2   Scope

The *Anti-Virus* policy applies to all Company IT systems and networks.

6.3   Responsibilities

- Company line management has the responsibility to ensure that the measures listed above are implemented effectively.
- Company information security organization has the responsibility to provide assistance to line management in the implementation of this policy.
- All users of Company IT systems and networks are to comply with this policy.

6.4   Compliance

Company officers and senior management are required to ensure that internal audit mechanisms exist to monitor and measure compliance with this policy.

Company line management has the responsibility to enforce compliance with this policy.

7   COMPUTER AND NETWORK MANAGEMENT

7.1   Policy

To conduct the business of The Company requires that computer systems and networks be operated in a safe and secure manner. The primary responsibility for this requirement is assigned to Information Systems. However, every employee is charged with the responsibility to use the provided services for the purposes intended and to comply with all security requirements.

7.2   Standards

Responsibilities and procedures for the management and operation of all computers and networks are assigned in the following manner:

- Clear, documented operating procedures are prepared for all operational computer systems to ensure their correct, secure operation.
- Incident management responsibilities and procedures are established to ensure quick, effective, and orderly response to security incidents.
- Management and execution of certain duties and areas of responsibility are kept separate in order to reduce opportunities for unauthorized modification or misuse of data or services.
- Development and operational facilities are segregated to reduce the risk of accidental changes or unauthorized access to operational software and business data.
- The risks posed by the use of an external contractor in the management of computer or network facilities are identified and appropriate security measures are incorporated into contracts.

Advance planning and preparation are conducted to ensure the availability of adequate capacity and resources. Measures to ensure this include:

- Capacity requirements are monitored and projections of future capacity requirements are made to reduce the risk of system overload.
- Acceptance criteria for new systems are established and tested prior to acceptance.
- Appropriate fallback arrangements for each IT service are established to provide an alternative, temporary means of continuing processing in the event of any damage to or failure of equipment.
- Processes are established to control changes to IT facilities and systems to ensure satisfactory control of all changes to equipment, software, or procedures.

Routine procedures are followed to take backup copies of data, log events and faults, and where appropriate, monitor the equipment environment. To achieve this, The Company has:

- A process to take regular backup copies of essential business data and software and to ensure that it can be recovered following a computer disaster or media failure
- A mechanism to log all work carried out by computer operators
- Procedures to log faults reported by users regarding problems with computer or communications systems, and to report and take corrective action
- A process to monitor computer environments, including temperature, humidity, and power supply quality to identify conditions that might adversely affect the operation of computer equipment, and to facilitate corrective action

The security of computer networks that span organizational boundaries is managed to safeguard information and to protect the supporting infrastructure. This is accomplished by controls to ensure the security of data in networks, and to protect connected services from unauthorized access.

Computer media are controlled and protected to prevent damage to assets and interruptions to business activities. To accomplish this, The Company has:

- Established procedures for the management of removable computer media such as tapes, disks, cassettes, and printed reports
- Established procedures for handling sensitive data to protect such data from unauthorized disclosure or misuse
- Established controls to protect system documentation from unauthorized access
- Established a process to ensure that computer media is disposed of securely and safely when no longer required

Exchanges of data and software between The Company and other organizations are controlled to prevent loss, modification, or misuse of data. To implement this control, The Company has:

- Established formal agreements, to include software escrow agreements when appropriate, for exchanging data and software (whether electronic or manual) between organizations
- Applied controls to safeguard computer media being transported between sites to minimize its vulnerability to unauthorized access, misuse, or corruption during transportation between sites
- Applied, where necessary, special security controls to safeguard electronic data interchange against unauthorized interception or modification
- Established clear policies and guidelines to control business and security risks associated with electronic office systems

7.3 Responsibilities

- Company IT line management has the responsibility to ensure that the measures listed above are put in place and carried out effectively.
- The Company information security organization has the responsibility to provide services that will assist IT line management in implementing and monitoring compliance with these measures.
- All employees who install, operate, or maintain computer and network equipment and systems are required to comply with this policy.

7.4 Scope

The *Computer and Network Management Security* policy applies to all computer and network equipment and systems owned and operated by The Company.

7.5 Compliance

Company officers and senior management are required to ensure that internal audit mechanisms exist to monitor and measure compliance with this policy.

Company IT and, where appropriate, business unit line management has the responsibility to enforce compliance with this policy.

8 PERSONNEL SECURITY

8.1 Policy

Information security is addressed at the recruitment stage, included in job descriptions and contracts, and monitored during an individual's employment. To ensure compliance with policy objectives:

- Security responsibilities are stated in employee job descriptions.
- Employment applications for jobs that require access to sensitive information are screened.
- Employees are required to sign nondisclosure agreements.
- Users are trained in security procedures and the correct use of IT facilities before they are granted access to IT facilities. Users are trained in information security policies and procedures, security requirements, business controls, and the correct use of IT facilities.
- Incidents affecting security are reported through management channels as quickly as possible. This is accomplished by:
  - Formal reporting and incident response procedures that identify action to be taken on receipt of an incident report.
  - Users who are aware that they are required to note and report all observed or suspected security weaknesses in or threats to systems or services.
  - Users who know to note and report to IT support any software that does not function correctly.

8.2 Scope

The *Personnel Security* policy applies to all staff hired by The Company after the implementation of this policy.

8.3 Responsibilities

- Company line management has the responsibility to ensure that security responsibilities are stated in employee job descriptions.
- The Human Resources department has the responsibility to ensure that the other measures in this policy are in place and properly carried out.
- The Information Security department has the responsibility to implement the educational material called for in this policy.

8.4 Compliance

Company officers and senior management are required to ensure that internal audit mechanisms exist to monitor and measure compliance with this policy.

Company line managers have the responsibility to enforce compliance with this policy.

Violations of security policy reflected in The Company's *Employee Discipline* policy.

9 SYSTEMS DEVELOPMENT AND MAINTENANCE POLICY

9.1 Policy

To ensure that security is built into IT systems, management identified, justified, agrees to, and documents security requirements during the requirements phase of an IT system development project. Security requirements are included in the requirements analysis stage of each system development project, and requirements for security controls are specified in statements of business requirements.

Security controls are designed into applications systems to prevent loss, modification, or misuse of user data. These controls are:

- Validation of data input to applications systems to ensure that it is correct and appropriate
- Incorporation of validation checks into systems to detect corruption caused by processing errors or through deliberate acts
- Consideration of the use of encryption to safeguard the confidentiality and integrity of highly sensitive data during transmission or in storage
- Consideration of the use of message authentication for applications where it is vital to protect the integrity of message content from unauthorized changes or corruption

To ensure that IT projects and support activities are conducted in a secure manner, the responsibility for controlling access to application system files is assigned to and carried out by the owning user function or development group. That responsibility takes the form of:

- Ensuring that strict control is exercised over the implementation of software on operational systems
- Ensuring that all application system test data is protected and controlled

Project and support environments are strictly controlled to maintain the security of application system software and data. This control takes the form of:

- Strict control over the implementation of changes to minimize the potential for corruption of information systems
- When changes to the operating system occur, review of application systems to ensure that there is no adverse impact on security
- Discouraging the modification of vendor-supplied software packages

9.2 Responsibilities

- Company system development and maintenance management has responsibility to ensure that the measures listed above are put in place and carried out effectively.
- Company information security organization has the responsibility to provide assistance to system development and maintenance management in the implementation of this policy.
- All employees engaged in systems development and maintenance are required to comply with this policy.

9.3 Scope

The *Systems Development and Maintenance Security* policy applies to all systems development and maintenance activities carried out by Company activities.

9.4 Compliance

Company officers and senior management are required to ensure that internal audit mechanisms exist to monitor and measure compliance with this policy.

Company IT line management has the responsibility to enforce compliance with this policy.

10   APPLICATION ACCESS CONTROL POLICY

10.1   Policy

To prevent unauthorized access to information held in information systems. Users of application systems, including support staff, should be provided with access to information and application systems and that access should be based on individual business application requirements.

10.2   Standards

Security tools will be used to control access within application systems. Access to software and information will be allowed only for authorized users. Only the least amount of access to software and information — necessary to carry out the tasks for which the access is needed — will be granted. Application systems will:

- Make sure only the information owner and those people and processes authorized by the information owner have access to the application system.
- Provide protection against using software utilities that bypass the system or application controls.
- Control the use of other systems with which our information is shared, to change or delete the information.

10.3   Responsibilities

Application owners must ensure compliance with this policy.

All employees of The Company or any other organization who access The Company's applications, plus information owners and those who maintain and administer security tools are responsible for complying with this policy.

10.4   Scope

This policy applies to all Company employees — full-time, part-time, or contract — and anyone doing business with The Company who has access to The Company's applications.

10.5   Compliance

Failure to comply with this policy may result in disciplinary action, which may include termination of employment.

10.6   Supporting Standards

To be able to enforce this policy, the Company has established standards that include but are not limited to:

- Information access restriction

- Use of system utilities
- Access control to source libraries
- Sensitive system isolation
- Data classification
- Outside application access restriction
- External user access request (e.g., Energy WAVES)
- Vendor support of applications
- Third-party support

11   DATA AND SOFTWARE EXCHANGE POLICY

11.1   Policy

Exchanges of information and software between The Company and any other organization will be controlled in accordance with its classification. The exchange of information will comply with any regulatory policies and legal agreements. Exchanges will be carried out only by prior agreement. Management approval and/or legal contract will be acquired and documented before information and software exchanges take place.

11.2   Responsibilities

Company senior management is responsible for enforcement of compliance with this policy.

All employees of The Company or any other organization — plus information owners and those who maintain and administer security tools — who access The Company's applications are responsible for complying with this policy.

11.3   Scope

This policy applies to all Company employees — full-time, part-time, or contract — or anyone doing business with The Company who needs electronic access to The Company's information and software.

11.4   Compliance

Failure to comply with this policy may result in disciplinary action, which may include termination of employment.

11.5   Supporting Standards

To be able to enforce this policy, The Company has established standards that include but are not limited to:

- Encryption
- Digital certificates
- E-mail security

- E-business transactions
- FTP
- Instant messaging
- EDI data exchange
- Message digest
- Information and software exchange agreements
- Security of media in transit
- Security of electronic office systems
- Publicly available systems
- Other forms of information exchange

12   NETWORK ACCESS CONTROL

12.1   Policy

Connection to The Company's network — and services we can access — will be granted when a comparison of the business need versus the security impact to the entire network says it is prudent to do so. Network connections to sensitive or critical business applications or users in high-risk locations must have the prior approval of the owners of the business applications. Approval for network connections and services will be given only for the minimal access needed to meet business requirements.

12.2   Responsibilities

The Information Protection Manager is responsible for the enforcement of this policy.

All employees of The Company or any other organization, plus information owners and those who maintain and administer security tools, who access The Company's network are responsible for complying with this policy.

12.3   Scope

This policy applies to all Company business units, plus anyone who is doing business with The Company and who needs access to The Company's network to do business.

12.4   Compliance

Failure to comply with this policy may result in disciplinary action, which may include termination of employment.

12.5   Supporting Standards

To be able to enforce this policy, the Company has established standards that include but are not limited to:

- Remote access
- Third-party access
- Limited services
- Enforced path
- User authentication
- Node authentication
- Remote diagnostic port protection
- Network segregation
- Network connection control
- Network routing control
- Security in network services
- Protection from malicious software

13 NETWORK MANAGEMENT POLICY

13.1 Policy

Network security standards, procedures, and tools will be established to protect the network and preserve the confidentiality of the information on every part of the network. Network monitoring tools and processes will be put in place to detect and react to network failures, external network probes, and unauthorized network access attempts. Remote network management capabilities will be authorized where an assessment of the business need versus the security impact to the entire network warrants that they are both necessary and prudent to use.

13.2 Responsibilities

The Network Manager in each business unit is responsible for the enforcement of this policy. Where a business unit does not have a Network Manager, the person (or unit) who has been assigned responsibility for network management for that business unit has this responsibility.

All employees of The Company or any other organization — plus information owners and those who maintain and administer security tools — who access the Company's network are responsible for complying with this policy.

13.3 Scope

This policy applies to all Company business units, plus anyone who is doing business with The Company and who needs access to The Company's network to do business.

13.4 Compliance

Failure to comply with this policy may result in disciplinary action, which may include termination of employment.

13.5   Supporting Standards

To be able to enforce this policy, The Company has established standards that include but are not limited to:

- Firewalls and routers
- Monitoring and IDSs
- 24/7 all-component monitoring
- Remote management capability for key network components

14   INFORMATION SYSTEMS' OPERATIONS POLICY

14.1   Policy

The Company will decide and document — in standards — who has responsibility for the management and operation of all information-processing systems. The Company will also document the procedures necessary for operating all information processing systems and those procedures will include specific requirements for segregation of duties — that will not allow any single person to control multiple critical systems.

14.2   Responsibilities

The senior management of The Company is responsible for the enforcement of this policy.

Employees who operate The Company's computing equipment are responsible for complying with this policy.

14.3   Scope

This policy applies to all business units, plus anyone who is doing business with the company and who needs access to Mega Energy's information processing systems to do business.

14.4   Compliance

Failure to comply with this policy may result in disciplinary action, which may include termination of employment.

14.5   Supporting Standards

To be able to enforce this policy, The Company has established standards that include but are not limited to:

- Documented operating procedures
- Operational change control
- Incident management procedures
- Segregation of duties
- Separation of development and operational systems
- External facilities management

15 PHYSICAL AND ENVIRONMENTAL SECURITY

15.1 Policy

Information processing facilities that are critical to The Company's business will be housed in secure areas, protected by a defined security perimeter, with security barriers and entry controls. These controls will be adequate to restrict access to the facilities to authorized people and to provide control over the disruption of normal business activities.

15.2 Responsibilities

The senior management of The Company is responsible for the enforcement of this policy.

All employees of The Company or any other organization who access the Company's information processing facilities, plus information owners and those who maintain and administer security tools, are responsible for complying with this policy.

15.3 Scope

This policy applies to all business units, plus anyone who is doing business with The Company and who needs access to The Company's information processing facilities to do business.

15.4 Compliance

Failure to comply with this policy may result in disciplinary action, which may include termination of employment.

15.5 Supporting Standards

To be able to enforce this policy, The Company has established standards that include but are not limited to:

- Physical security perimeter
- Physical entry controls
- Securing offices, rooms, and facilities
- Working in secure areas
- Isolated delivery and loading areas
- Equipment sitting and protection
- Power supplies
- Cabling security
- Equipment maintenance
- Security of equipment off-premises
- Secure disposal or re-use of equipment
- Clear desk and clear screen policy
- Removal of property

16 USER ACCESS POLICY

16.1 Policy

Access rights to information and services will be based on the principle of least privilege and consistent with regulatory guidelines, (e.g., affiliate compliance rules). Access to information will be granted only in accordance with established standards for the initial registration, maintenance, and deletion of users' access.

The establishment of the ability to override any of the above will require the approval of a department manager or a department manager's documented designee.

16.2 Responsibilities

In each business unit, the people who manage computer resources (but no lower than department manager level) are responsible for ensuring compliance with this policy.

All employees of The Company or any other organization — plus information owners and those who maintain and administer security tools — who access the Company's network are responsible for complying with this policy.

16.3 Scope

This policy applies to all business units, plus anyone who is doing business with The Company and who needs access to The Company's network to do business.

16.4 Compliance

Failure to comply with this policy may result in disciplinary action, which may include termination of employment.

16.5 Supporting Standards

To be able to enforce this policy, The Company has established standards that include but are not limited to:

- Intrusion detection
- Audit standards for user access rights
- Management of access privileges related to job changes
- Administrator access
- Backup and recovery of user access control files
- User registration
- Privilege management
- User password management
- Review of user access rights

17   EMPLOYMENT AGREEMENT

This Employment Agreement, between _____ (the "Company") and _____ (the "Employee").

1. For good consideration, the Company employs the Employee on the following terms and conditions.
2. **Term of Employment.** Subject to the provisions for termination set forth below, this agreement will begin on _____, 20___, unless sooner terminated.
3. **Salary.** The Company shall pay Employee a salary of $_____ per year, for the services of the Employee, payable at regular payroll periods.
4. **Duties and Position.** The Company hires the Employee in the capacity of _____. The Employee's duties may be reasonably modified at the Company's discretion from time to time.
5. **Employee to Devote Full Time to Company.** The Employee will devote full time, attention, and energies to the business of the Company, and, during this employment, will not engage in any other business activity, regardless of whether such activity is pursued for profit, gain, or other pecuniary advantage. Employee is not prohibited from making personal investments in any other businesses, provided those investments do not require active involvement in the operation of said companies.
6. **Confidentiality of Proprietary Information.** Employee agrees, during or after the term of this employment, not to reveal confidential information or trade secrets to any person, firm, corporation, or entity. Should Employee reveal or threaten to reveal this information, the Company shall be entitled to an injunction restraining the Employee from disclosing same, or from rendering any services to any entity to whom said information has been or is threatened to be disclosed, the right to secure an injunction is not exclusive, and the Company may pursue any other remedies it has against the Employee for a breach or threatened breach of this condition, including the recovery of damages from the Employee.
7. **Reimbursement of Expenses.** The Employee may incur reasonable expenses for furthering the Company's business, including expenses for entertainment, travel, and similar items. The Company shall reimburse Employee for all business expenses after the Employee presents an itemized account of expenditures, pursuant to Company policy.
8. **Vacation.** The Employee shall be entitled to a yearly vacation of _____ weeks at full pay.
9. **Disability.** If Employee cannot perform the duties because of illness or incapacity for a period of more than _____ weeks, the compensation otherwise due during said illness or incapacity will be reduced

by _____ (___ percent). The Employee's full compensation will be reinstated upon return to work. However, if the Employee is absent from work for any reason for a continuous period of over _____ months, the Company may terminate the Employee's employment, and the Company's obligations under this agreement will cease on that date.

10. **Termination of Agreement**. Without cause, the Company may terminate this agreement at any time upon ____ days' written notice to the Employee. If the Company requests, the Employee will continue to perform his or her duties and may be paid his or her regular salary up to the date of termination. In addition, the Company will pay the Employee on the date of the termination a severance allowance of $_____ less taxes and Social Security required to be withheld. Without cause, the Employee may terminate employment upon _____ days' written notice to the Company. Employee may be required to perform his or her duties and will be paid the regular salary to date of termination but shall not receive severance allowance. Notwithstanding anything to the contrary contained in this agreement, the Company may terminate the Employee's employment upon _____ days' notice to the Employee should any of the following events occur:

    a. The sale of substantially all of the Company's assets to a single purchaser or group of associated purchasers
    b. The sale, exchange, or other disposition in one transaction of the majority of the Company's outstanding corporate shares
    c. The Company's decision to terminate its business and liquidate its assets
    d. The merger or consolidation of the Company with another company
    e. Bankruptcy or Chapter 11 reorganization

11. **Death Benefit**. Should Employee die during the term of employment, the Company shall pay to Employee's estate any compensation due through the end of the month in which death occurred.

12. **Restriction on Post Employment Compensation**. For a period of _____ (___) years after the end of employment, the Employee shall not control, consult to, or be employed by any business similar to that conducted by the company, either by soliciting any of its accounts or by operating within Employer's general trading area.

13. **Assistance in Litigation**. Employee shall, upon reasonable notice, furnish such information and proper assistance to the Company as it may reasonably require in connection with any litigation in which it is, or may become, a party either during or after employment.

14. **Effect of Prior Agreements**. This Agreement supersedes any prior agreement between the Company or any predecessor of the

Company and the Employee, except that this agreement shall not affect or operate to reduce any benefit or compensation due to the Employee of a kind elsewhere provided and not expressly provided in this agreement.

15. **Settlement by Arbitration**. Any claim or controversy that arises out of or relates to this agreement, or the breach of it, shall be settled by arbitration in accordance with the rules of the American Arbitration Association. Judgment upon the award rendered may be entered in any court with jurisdiction.

16. **Limited Effect of Waiver by Company**. Should Company waive breach of any provision of this agreement by the Employee, that waiver will not operate or be construed as a waiver of further breach by the Employee.

17. **Severability**. If, for any reason, any provision of this agreement is held invalid, all other provisions of this agreement shall remain in effect. If this agreement is held invalid or cannot be enforced, then to the full extent permitted by law any prior agreement between the Company (or any predecessor thereof) and the Employee shall be deemed reinstated as if this agreement had not been executed.

18. **Assumption of Agreement by Company's Successors and Assignees**. The Company's rights and obligations under this agreement will inure to the benefit and be binding upon the Company's successors and assignees.

19. **Oral Modifications Not Binding**. This instrument is the entire agreement of the Company and the Employee. Oral changes have no effect. It may be altered only by a written agreement signed by the party against whom enforcement of any waiver, change, modification, extension, or discharge is sought.

Signed this_____ day of _____ 20____.

_____   _____
Company   Employee

These policies are provided to you as examples of what you might do in your own organization. Use them as guidelines, not standards, and alter them to meet your specific needs.

Appendix 1C
Sample Standards Manual

INTRODUCTION

You will use standards to flesh out supporting documents such as an Information Security Handbook or a Network Standards document or Application Programming Standards and Practices. You will use the standards to identify what is expected of the reader. There will also be a place for the guidelines in these documents.

Standards for each phase or section of an information security handbook need to be developed. Almost everyone in the enterprise recognizes the need for standards. However, developing them, adhering to them, and monitoring them is a logistical problem.

The following is a sample standards manual you can use to get ideas on how you might create your own document.

THE COMPANY INFORMATION SECURITY STANDARDS MANUAL

Version 0.2 Version Control Information

Version	Issued By	Date	Comment
Draft	Homer B. Simpson	31 Oct 03	Draft for review of style only
0.1	Justin A. Peltier	30 Nov 03	Input to workshop
0.2	John A. Blackley	15 Dec 03	Incorporates workshop comments

TABLE OF CONTENTS

INFORMATION SECURITY POLICIES AND PROCEDURES

PREFACE

Background

It is vitally important to the reputation, operation, and financial well-being of The Company (THE COMPANY) that its information is provided with mechanisms to ensure its availability, integrity, and confidentiality. In addition, legislative requirements governing the misuse of computers and the protection of personal, healthcare, and financial data require a commitment to ensuring the security of those resources.

About This Manual

This manual contains a series of information security standards that are common across THE COMPANY. They form a baseline against which external and internal auditors will measure Divisions during the course of their normal work.

Compliance with the contents is mandatory.

The manual is the responsibility of the Information Security Manager who, with the assistance of Information Security Administration, will ensure that the statements within it reflect changing business and technological needs. Further detail on responsibilities and the process of change control are given later.

Using the Standards

The manual is intended as a reference document to permit local procedures to be implemented in a consistent framework. The manual will be supported by local, individual staff practices, local briefings, managers' guidelines, and supporting awareness material.

In implementing the standards, the following process will be followed:

- Review existing procedures and practice against the standard.
- Document position against the standard.
- Perform a "gap analysis" to identify deficiencies.
- Document deficiencies.
- Plan to close gaps as identified.
- Document divisional and local practices/procedures.

Where a local practice requires a higher level of security than is defined in THE COMPANY's standards, then the higher level practice will be adhered to locally.

Change Control

The manual is intended to be a "live" document. It will be managed by THE COMPANY Information Security. All requests for amendments/additions must be made to the Information Security Manager.

The manual will be subject to version control and where sufficient changes have been received, a full reissue will occur. All amendments will be circulated to appropriate members of staff who will ensure that copies held (in whatever format) within THE COMPANY are updated and the amendment record noted.

CORPORATE INFORMATION SECURITY POLICY

Introduction

THE COMPANY views its information assets as a significant and valuable resource. It recognizes the threats to its business through the loss of any aspects of confidentiality, integrity, or availability. Its aim therefore is to limit the threats to those information assets.

Policy Statement

The purpose of the policy is to protect the company's information assets whether stored on computers, transmitted across networks, printed out or written on paper, sent by fax, stored on electronic and optical media, or spoken from all threats, whether internal or external, deliberate or accidental.

The Chief Executive has approved the Information Security Policy.

It is the policy of the company to ensure that:

- Information will be protected against accidental unauthorized access.

- **Confidentiality** must ensure the protection of valuable or sensitive information from unauthorized disclosure or intelligible interruption.
- **Integrity** of information will maintain the accuracy and completeness of information by protecting against unauthorized modification.
- **Regulatory** and **legislative** requirements will be met and this includes proper record keeping.
- **Business Continuity plans** will be produced, maintained, and tested to ensure that information and vital services are available to users when they need them.
- **Information security training** will be available to all staff.

All breaches of information security, actual or suspected, will be reported to and investigated by the Information Security Manager.

Standards will be produced to support the policy. These may include virus control, passwords, encryption — or any other measure deemed necessary to protect the company's information assets.

Business requirements for the availability of information and information systems will be met.

The Information Security Manager has **direct responsibility** for maintaining the Policy and providing advice and guidance on its implementation.

All managers are **directly responsible** for implementing the Policy within their business areas, and for adherence by their staff.

It is the responsibility of **each** employee to adhere to the Policy.

RESPONSIBILITIES

Overall responsibility for ensuring the satisfactory implementation of Information Security is that of the Chief Executive of a Division or the executive responsible for an equivalent unit. To permit that responsibility to be discharged, the following roles and responsibilities must be defined:

Manager

Managers must:

- Be aware of legislative and regulatory requirements, threats, protective measures, and practices that are relevant to their area of responsibility.
- Ensure that they and their staff are familiar with these and their corresponding duties and obligations.
- Appoint appropriate information or system owners.
- Ensure that agreed protective measures and practices are in place and operating effectively and efficiently.

- Report incidents that violate protective measures or threaten to cause an unacceptable risk.
- Investigate these occurrences.

Information Systems Manager/Team Leader

Managers with responsibility for Information Systems must carry out all the appropriate responsibilities as a Manager for their area. In addition, they will act as **Custodian** of information used by those systems but owned by other managers. They must ensure that these owners are identified, appointed, and made aware of their responsibilities.

All managers, supervisors, directors, and other management-level people also have an advisory and assisting role to IS and non-IS managers with respect to:

- Identifying and assessing threats
- Identifying and implementing protective measures (including compliance with these practices)
- Maintaining a satisfactory level of security awareness
- Monitoring the proper operation of security measures within the unit
- Investigating weaknesses and occurrences
- Raising any new issues or circumstances of which they become aware through their specialist role
- Liaising with internal and external audit

Information and System Owner

Any permanent employee of THE COMPANY can be appointed as "owner" for information or a system that processes information.

The owner must:

- Define appropriate requirements for the availability, confidentiality, and integrity of the information.
- Establish the exact nature and extent of authorized access to and use of information.
- Specifically authorize individuals for access to information.
- Ensure that accurate, up-to-date records are kept on authorities given.
- Regularly check the continuing validity and proper operation of the protective measures and authorities.
- Report occurrences that violate protective measures or threaten to cause unacceptable threats.
- Classify information in accordance with THE COMPANY's Information Classification standard.

Information and System User

Every individual using information or system processing information must:

- Be personally aware of the standards and of the threats and protective measures that concern them.
- Ensure that authority to access information is properly acquired.
- Comply with relevant laws, regulations, and rules with regard to information access and the operation of protective measures.
- Act safely, sensibly, and responsibly with respect to unexpected eventualities and ask when something is unclear.
- Draw to the attention of management any relevant issues, circumstances, or weaknesses in security arrangements.

Information Security Manager (ISM)

The ISM has a coordinating role across THE COMPANY to ensure that Information Security standards are kept current and consistently applied.

The ISM will:

- Provide a reference center for technical solutions.
- Provide central guidance and advice on legislation issues.
- Act as a clearing point for maximizing THE COMPANY's benefits in information-security-related purchasing solutions.
- Maintain an information source/library of current IS security practices and technology.
- Manage changes to this manual.
- Hold a central record of exceptions and plans for the implementation of Information Security.
- Provide a compliance view across THE COMPANY.
- Manage THE COMPANY wide initiatives relating to Information Security.

Information Security Administration

The ISMs are responsible for the practical implementation of standards and overall application of Information Security within the Division.

They will:

- Ensure that security procedures within THE COMPANY's Information Security Manual are adhered to.
- Facilitate THE COMPANY's information security awareness program.
- Monitor the applicability and effectiveness of the Security standards, practices, and procedures at a local level, and recommend changes.
- Ensure that THE COMPANY's Information Security Manual is current, properly controlled, and distributed.

- Implement the awareness program at a local level, from initiation to ongoing reinforcement seminars, and ensure resources and budget are available for this purpose.
- Be knowledgeable and current on legislative issues and be able to provide advice on legislative issues directly relevant to Information Security.

STANDARDS

Risk Management

Risk Analysis.

1. Threats must be analyzed:
   - During the analysis phase of the system development life cycle (SDLC)
   - During the development phase of the SDLC for new systems or applications
   - When changes to existing systems are required
   - When business processes change
   - When specific areas of concern are identified
2. Threats must be identified and risk levels established at various intervals during the life of a business process.
3. Any analysis of threats must include consideration of the following:
   - *Asset valuation:* identified assets and a valuation in terms of the possible impact of disclosure, modification, unavailability, destruction, or loss of integrity. Must include physical (hardware) and logical (software and information) elements.
   - *Threat assessment:* identification and risk level established based on probability of occurrence and impact to the business objectives or mission statement.
   - *Vulnerability assessment:* identify weaknesses in a system or control that can be exploited to violate the system's intended behavior.
4. All risk analysis and vulnerability assessments must be documented.

Protection of Information.

1. All systems must display, at initial sign-on to the system, a warning message conveying the fact that misuse of the system is an offense under relevant national legislation.
2. Screens displayed before user validation has succeeded must not contain welcome or identification messages.
3. Personal information held must only be held in accordance with specific national legislation or regulations.

4. Any users in doubt as to whether information they hold is covered by such legislation must seek advice from the Information Security Manager.
5. All users must comply with the terms of THE COMPANY's Information Classification procedures.

Use of Computing Resources.

1. Computer resources may only be used by authorized persons and for authorized purposes.
2. Authorization is to be granted by Managers (**owners**).
3. Managers maintain a record of authorizations granted to their staff or cause them to be maintained by a third party (**custodian**). In either case, managers will review these records at least semi-annually and affirm that the access granted is still appropriate.
4. The playing of games and use of other forms of personal entertainment on computer resources is strictly forbidden unless for authorized training purposes.
5. Other personal use of systems is allowable at the discretion of Managers.
6. Consult Information Security Administration regarding any requests for exceptions to policy and standards that may have a detrimental effect on THE COMPANY.

Outsourcing Controls.

1. All outsourcing agreement and contracts must include Information Security Policies, standards and procedures, confidentiality agreements, recovery and backup arrangements, security and system administration details, activity monitoring, and reporting.

Systems Development Conformance With Information Security Standards.

1. Systems development must comply with Information Security policies and standards.
2. Application and overall system security must be considered at each stage of development as an integral requirement.

Database Administration.

1. Database Administration must comply with Information Security policies and standards.
2. Access to databases must require the same authorization as access to data held in other systems
3. All databases shall be subject to regular integrity checks.

4. Access to information must be prevented unless the information is under the control of the DBMS software.
5. All shared information must be defined within THE COMPANY's data dictionary and be assigned a recognized data owner.

Transaction Logs.

1. Where applications have their own security, then the application must also maintain its own logs of authorized access privileges and unauthorized attempts at access.

Software Installation.

1. All PC software must be virus checked, on a stand-alone machine set aside for that purpose, prior to installation.
2. All PC software must be tested to ensure compatibility with current company client/server applications before being made available for installation.
3. The introduction of software into company computer systems by persons other than those authorized to do so by the Information Systems function is strictly forbidden.
4. Only licensed copies of software can be installed.
5. Anyone who suspects that any suspicious code is present within a system must immediately inform the appointed local contact point. Upon notification, Information Security Administration will ensure that:
   – The incident is logged.
   – Appropriate follow-up action is carried out to remove the code.
   – An attempt to identify its origin is carried out.
6. Any introduction of illegal code will be treated as a breach of employment contract.

Note: Where the decision to install software causes a significant change of use (e.g., from LAN workstation to LAN server), then this fact must be recorded on the inventory and an appropriate level of security implemented to reflect the change in environment.

Copyright and Software Piracy.

1. Regular reviews are to be carried out by the Information Systems Function to ensure that the terms of software licenses are being complied with. Managers, as stated in THE COMPANY corporate policy on copyright compliance, have a responsibility to ensure compliance in their area.
2. Any unauthorized software is to be isolated and access disabled.
3. All contracts with external Information Systems service providers (including facilities management arrangements) must make clear the

responsibility for ensuring that appropriate licenses are held by the provider for any products provided as part of the service.

4. The copying of software other than for legitimate backup purposes is strictly forbidden and may lead to disciplinary procedures.

Internet Access.

1. All connections must be made via a firewall protected, managed gateway. Where this is not possible, then the connections must be via a permanently isolated machine containing no significant company information and which does not run any Internet server services.

2. Certain Internet services (such as ftp, etc.) are restricted use. Requests for restricted use services must be authorized by the Information Security Manager.

3. All proposed firewall configurations and types must be approved by the Information Security Manager before being deployed.

4. All connections must comply fully with THE COMPANY's business policy for Internet usage.

5. Information Security Administration will ensure that a record giving details of the types of connection and users of that connection is maintained.

6. All activity is subject to logging; this must record the source and destination of any traffic across the Internet gateway, together with details of the date, time, and protocol.

7. Any misuse of a connection is a breach of the Employee Standards of Conduct. It is the authorized user's responsibility to ensure that no misuse takes place.

8. Use of encryption and digital signature techniques for external e-mail is required for information classified as **Confidential**. (*Note:* The tools and services to enforce this standard are currently in test. This standard will be enforced when those tools and services are deployed.)

9. All compressed software and attachments MUST be decompressed before virus checking.

E-Mail.

1. Users must not participate in, encourage, or forward any e-mail chain letters or advertising of non-company goods or services.

2. Users must not forward or further distribute company confidential information, inside or outside THE COMPANY, without authorization of the originator or appropriate management.

3. Any electronic messages that contain confidential information must be labeled as such.

4. Any personal or non-THE COMPANY business messages sent out of THE COMPANY must contain the following disclaimer statement: "The statements (opinions) herein are my personal statements (opinions) and are not statements (opinions) made by or on behalf of my employer, The Company (THE COMPANY)."
5. Employees and other authorized users must not use offensive or inappropriate language or statements, profanity, obscenities, derogatory, or slanderous remarks in any electronic mail messages including those discussing employees, customers, competitors, or others.
6. THE COMPANY is responsible for servicing and protecting its electronic communications networks. To accomplish this, it is occasionally necessary, as authorized by management, to intercept or disclose, or assist in intercepting or disclosing, electronic communications.
7. All official THE COMPANY electronic mail messages, including those containing formal management approval, authorization, delegation, or handing over of responsibility, or similar transactions, must be provided to the Records Management Control Center according to records retention policies and standards.

Remote Computing.

1. All usage of workstations away from the office must be authorized by line management and a record kept.
2. The user must be made aware of any THE COMPANY or legal requirements.
3. When a computer is transferred between employees, it must be checked to ensure that the software and data content are appropriate for the new owner.
4. All workstations, including laptops, for regular use away from the office must include anti-virus measures preventing the loading of infected electronic media. This includes employees' own workstations.
5. Additionally, all THE COMPANY's supplied workstations must include the following measures:
   - User ID and password combination or token controlled access
   - Encryption mechanism if the sensitivity of the information warrants it
   - Supplied backup software will be used
   - Marked with an anti-theft, indelible mark
   - Only have authorized software installed

(Note: The tools and services to enforce this standard are currently in test. This standard will be enforced when those tools and services are deployed.)

6. All workstations connecting remotely to THE COMPANY's resources must, in addition, include authentication of remote dial-up user before connection to a LAN or other THE COMPANY computing resource.
7. Full asset registration procedures must be followed.
8. Workstations used away from the office must be physically secured as individual property. Laptops, in particular, must not be left visible to passersby.
9. No information classified as "Internal Use" or above can be stored on the hard disk of a PC, which does not have user ID and password controlled access measures installed.

E-Commerce Security.

1. All proposals must be subject to risk analysis considering the types of transaction and the measures needed to protect them. Information Security Administration will take account of a business impact analysis in deciding on the level of security to be applied and may recommend encryption to preserve the confidentiality and integrity of messages. All business impact and risk analyses must be documented.
2. Segregation of duties is critically important in preventing abuse of privilege and must be demonstrated in any electronic transaction processing system.
3. A written contract setting out the acceptability of electronic transactions and covering liabilities in the event of error must be agreed upon with the trading partner.
4. Internationally accepted protocols must be followed.
5. The transactions must be supported by a log allowing establishment of receipt, acceptance, and validation of messages received, together with details of the individual handling the transaction.
6. A sender of THE COMPANY's information must ensure that the recipient's security arrangements at least match those employed within THE COMPANY. Where necessary, this must be enforced through contractual arrangements.
7. The security of any transaction process must be coordinated with the Information Security Administration, who may recommend processes to ensure non-repudiation, proof of delivery, and security of the transaction.
8. All E-commerce transactions must be encrypted to a standard acceptable to Information Security.

Virus Prevention.

1. Processes for preventing the introduction of viruses into THE COMPANY's equipment must be in place.

2. All virus scanning software must be current and updated at least monthly.
3. Managers are responsible for ensuring that virus scanning is carried out in their areas of responsibility.
4. All workstations must be scanned automatically at boot time, in real-time, and at other intervals as required by Information Security.
5. All software code must be checked for viruses before introduction to THE COMPANY's computer resources.
6. All virus occurrences must be logged and treated as security incidents.
7. All users will be made aware of procedures for dealing with virus incidents.

Access Control

Controlling Access Rights.

1. Users must obtain authorization before attempting to access computer resources.
2. The granting of access must be authorized by the appropriate Business Manager or System Owner, taking into account:
   - The requesting individuals need for such access
   - Potential conflict with segregation of duties or incompatible job functions
   - The level of access required (e.g., read, update, delete)
3. Formal documented procedures must be followed for requesting, authorizing, granting, and enabling access to computer resources.
4. Emergency access rights to systems for support purposes must be documented and approved by the System Owner or designee.
5. Application developers, and technical and operational staff must not be granted access to production systems and information unless specifically required to do so.
6. Enhanced monitoring must be put in place where application developers and technical and operational staff have access to production systems.
7. Business users must not be given access to development and test systems except where specifically required to do so for user testing.
8. The use of system utilities and devices capable of bypassing system access controls must be strictly limited and monitored. Security Administration must maintain a detailed log of the usage of such tools.
9. Security Administration must maintain records of all current access rights where they administer those access rights. This log is to be reviewed with System Owners or business managers at least annually.

10. Where business functions are accessed from locations outside of company controlled premises, the range of functions available to the user must be defined by the user's access.

User Identification.

1. All user IDs must be allocated by Information Security Administration where Information Security has been given that responsibility.
2. Each user ID must be assigned to one individual only.
3. Information Security Administration must keep records of all user IDs issued, who they were issued to, who authorized the issue, when it was issued, and whether it is current.
4. Unauthorized use of user IDs is to be considered a breach of the Employee Standards of Conduct.
5. Access control systems must maintain the identity of all current users allowed access. No "generic" or "ownerless" user IDs are permitted.

Passwords.

1. Passwords must:
   - Not be displayed by the system on entry
   - Be stored by systems securely and in encrypted form
   - Not be recorded in audit trails
   - Not be disclosed to others
   - Not be written down
   - Be changed at least every 90 days — more frequently for sensitive applications
   - Not be one of the last ten passwords used previously
   - Be a minimum of eight characters long
   - Not be system generated
   - Contain a mixture of alpha and numeric characters
   - Not be commonly used words
   - Not be names, common acronyms, initials, birthdays, calendar days or months, or phone numbers
   - Not be the same as the user ID
   - Not be manufacturer supplied
   - Be reset by the Information Services function following approved authorized procedures
   - Be changed immediately if it is thought that someone else may have discovered it and upon notification by security administration
2. Password rules must be enforced by the system wherever possible.

Note: The practice on Passwords includes more detail than other guidelines. This reflects the existing practices of THE COMPANY and also mirrors the ISO 17799 (International Standard for Information Security) —

commonly accepted as a "best practice" — and other industry standards for passwords.

User Validation.

1. All multi-user systems must, as a minimum, be password-protected although the requirement for a password, coupled with a user ID, will be enforced only wherever that capability exists.
2. The system must validate the user ID and password combination as a pair and reject the log-on attempt if it is invalid.
3. The system must not inform the user of which is wrong.
4. For sensitive systems, or where a log-on is being performed from a remote location, consideration must be given to the use of more rigorous authentication techniques such as smart cards/PINs, bio-metrics, or trusted techniques.
5. Repeated unsuccessful user validation must result in the user ID being disabled or suspended and generate an exception report.
6. Suspended or disabled user IDs must not be reset without following approved authorization procedures.

Access Timeout.

1. Where a facility is available, unattended terminals must enforce a timeout not exceeding 15 minutes.
2. Resumption of access must require the revalidation of the user's identity either through the entry of a valid user ID or password.
3. Access timeout facilities must restrict access to those aspects of screen blanking and keyboard locking required, permitting entry of the user details for revalidation.
4. Users must have the ability to switch on screen locking without the need to wait for timeout.
5. Messages displayed on the screen must not indicate who is logged on to the system.

Remote System Access.

1. Remote system access can only be obtained via access methods approved by Information Security.
2. Any remote access method used must employ at least the same level of controls as direct access methods — including the process for requesting and authorizing such access.

Other Access Methods.

1. The use of modems attached to any permanently network-connected device is not allowed.

Personnel Security Issues

Contractors and Temporary Staff.

1. User IDs for contract and temporary staff will be created with an automatic expiration date equal to the length of the contract. Where no length of contract is specified, the user ID will have an expiration date of three months from the date of creation. Extensions of this access must be requested by the contract or temporary employee's manager or supervisor.

Termination of Employment.

1. When it becomes known that permanent, contract, or temporary staff are to leave the organization, the relevant Manager must immediately inform Information Security Administration of that fact, providing the expected date of leaving.
2. Information Security Administration, upon receipt of this notification, must initiate an immediate review of the current access rights held by the individual in conjunction with the Manager, and must, if necessary, change or withdraw these rights.
3. Unless withdrawn earlier, the user's access rights must be withdrawn on the date of leaving.

Physical and Environmental Security Controls

Computer Rooms.

1. Computer rooms must have access control via a physical token or PIN, which must not be disclosed to unauthorized persons.
2. All computer rooms must display a notice stating that unauthorized access is not permitted.
3. All visitors must be supervised by authorized personnel at all times while within controlled areas.
4. All contractors, third-party engineers, etc. must not be left alone in computer rooms or other sensitive locations.
5. Details of all access by visitors must be recorded in the computer room visitor's book.
6. Smoking and the consumption of food and drink are not allowed in computer rooms.
7. Enhanced levels of environmental and fire protection must be installed in computer rooms, taking account of the value of the systems installed and their specific environmental needs as specified by the manufacturer(s) and local conditions.
8. Computer rooms containing business-critical systems must be provided with a UPS system, together with standby power capable of supporting the room for an extended period.

9. All authorized staff must be made aware of the specialized control systems installed; in particular, emergency procedures must be documented and regularly tested.
10. Procedures must ensure that visitors are made aware of evacuation procedures and the alarm signals used.
11. Operations Management is responsible for reviewing the logs from the physical access control system. Any unauthorized access attempts or unexpected out-of-hours access must be reported as a security incident.
12. Mobile phones must not be used in computer rooms.

Protection against Computer Theft.

1. Take reasonable steps to physically secure areas where workstations are located.
2. Maintain an asset register of hardware configurations to allow easy replacement of any stolen systems.
3. Never give details of hardware and software to unauthorized people.
4. Always make full backups of data and store them securely.

Network Security.

1. All central cabling and associated facilities must be kept either in a computer room environment or, where this is not feasible, in a locked room or riser.
2. Access to this equipment must be restricted to specific personnel.
3. Only properly authorized persons are allowed to connect devices to the network.
4. Network analyzers and data scopes must be stored securely and their use strictly controlled.
5. Network configuration information must be maintained and the network logs compared to this to identify unrecognized devices. Any devices so identified must be reported as a security incident.
6. When a new network connection is about to be installed on THE COMPANY's premises, the person or department ordering the service must be contacted to verify that this is, indeed, an authorized connection.
7. Adequate schematics of network cabling and server locations must be maintained. Schematics must include physical location and the person(s) responsible for any servers.
8. Any changes to network or server configurations must be processed in accordance with change control procedures.
9. Network operating software must ensure that when user sessions terminate, either normally or abnormally, all related network sessions are also terminated.

Retention, Storage, and Destruction of Information.

1. Information Security Administration, unless notified otherwise in a timely manner, will destroy information associated with a user ID when that user ID is deleted.
2. System support and data owners must ensure adequate backups and retention copies of systems and information held centrally on servers or host machines are maintained.
3. Users holding information locally must ensure that appropriate backups are taken and that regulatory, commercial, and fiscal requirements for retention of information are met.
4. All mission-critical backups and retention copies maintained by the centralized Information Systems function, or created locally, containing sensitive information must be stored in a secure off-site location, with suitable environmental and other controls.
5. Where sensitive information is no longer required, appropriate measures must be taken to ensure that the information is securely erased or rendered unreadable through physical destruction.

Media Handling.

1. Where media is held in off-site storage facilities, the process of retrieving that information must be tested regularly.
2. Access to designated storage areas must be restricted to authorized personnel by the use of physical access controls.
3. Staff must be made aware of media storage best practice as defined in THE COMPANY's practices and procedures.
4. Procedures must ensure that proper authorizations exist for all media movements to and from off-site stores or third parties. Secure methods of transport must be employed.
5. Details of the transport of media must be recorded.
6. Regular inventory checks must be carried out on all media stores and this log reconciled with the movement logs. Any unexplained discrepancies must be reported to Information Security Administration as a security incident.
7. Portable media containing company information may not be removed from company premises without the permission of the appropriate Manager.
8. All media must be securely erased or rendered unreadable before disposal.
9. Storage media must be subjected to low-level formatting or securely erased before reuse at change of ownership.
10. The measures described in THE COMPANY's Information Classification standards must be followed.

LAN Servers.

1. All significant business information must be stored on production system LAN servers, where it may be afforded the appropriate level of access control.
2. Production system LAN servers must either be kept in a secure computer room environment or the server itself must have enhanced physical access controls and other security features, such as cable locks and an uninterruptible power supply (UPS).

Data Transmission.

1. Appropriate measures must be employed to protect information during transmission. For example:
   - Data encryption
   - Use of Message Authentication Code (MAC) or Message Detection Code (MDC) algorithms
   - Use of transmission headers, checksums, and control totals
2. No information classified as "Confidential" must be transmitted across a network unless it is encrypted.
3. All scheduled THE COMPANY information transmissions must be included within the scope of the business continuity planning process.

Security Management

Logging of Security Events.

1. System Owners must ensure that, where suitable facilities can be provided, system logs:
   - Must include the individual user ID involved in the event, the date and time the event occurred, and details of the event
   - Must be reviewed on a regular and timely basis, making use of an exception reporting process to ensure that the most important events are seen and acted upon
2. Any unusual or suspicious events must be reported to Information Security Administration as a security incident.
3. Security systems must record all security-related events in a secured audit log. Typically, these events must include:
   - Invalid user authentication attempts
   - Log-on and activity of privileged users
   - Successful access to security system details
   - Access to resources outside normal hours
   - Changes to user security profiles
   - Changes to access rights of resources
   - Changes to system security configuration.
4. Audit logs must be securely managed

5. No access to amend the logs (other than by the system) must be allowed.
6. The security of audit logs must be reviewed regularly by Information Security Administration.
7. Retention periods for audit logs must be based on consideration of legal, regulatory, and business needs.

Information Security Monitoring.

1. Information Security Administration must use security analysis tools for the production of exception reports and other monitoring output.
2. Information Security Administration must be notified when thresholds of specific security-related events are reached.
3. Where a notified occurrence is felt to constitute a security incident, then escalation to Information Security Administration must occur.
4. Audit logging analysis tools, systems, and outputs must be subject to enhanced security.

Review of Access Rights.

1. Information Security Administration will carry out a review of each individual's access rights in conjunction with the relevant System Owner and Manager at least annually.
2. Information Security Administration will carry out an immediate review of an individual's capabilities should they be notified that the individual has changed roles within the company.
3. Managers must ensure that access granted to staff is appropriate to the role of that individual.

Encryption Management.

1. The company-approved encryption package must be used.
2. Consideration must be given to national restrictions on, and requirements for, the use of encryption. Contact Information Security Administration for information.
3. The management of encryption keys and mechanisms must be planned, and conform to standards of management agreed on with Information Security Administration.
4. Proprietary algorithms are not allowed.
5. All keys to encryption mechanisms used by THE COMPANY must be deposited with the Document Control Center.

Information Classification Process

The information classification process is set out below. It is intended to be as simple as possible, to allow clear decisions about the security needs of information, whether on paper or within systems.

INFORMATION SECURITY POLICIES AND PROCEDURES

Information Classifications.

1. The following classification terms will be used:
   - **Public:** Information that has been made available for public distribution through authorized company channels. (Refer to Communication policy for more information.)
   - **Internal use:** Information that is intended for use by employees when conducting company business. Most information used in THE COMPANY would be classified Internal Use.
   - **Confidential:** Information that, if disclosed, could violate the privacy of individuals, reduces the company's competitive advantage, or could cause significant damage to THE COMPANY. "Proprietary" is an equivalent to "Confidential."
2. Where no classification is apparent, information will be assumed to be "Internal Use."
3. It is permissible to mark (not classify) documents to indicate additional attributes. Examples of markings include:
   - **Addressee only:** information of a business nature that is only to be opened by the addressee.
   - **Private**: information of a business nature that is only to be opened by the addressee or nominated deputy.
   - **Personal**: self-explanatory.

Responsibilities.

1. Employees are responsible for protecting corporate information from unauthorized access, modification, destruction, or disclosure, whether accidental or intentional. To facilitate the protection of corporate information, employee responsibilities have been established at three levels: **Owner, Custodian,** and **User.**
   - **Owner:** The Company management of an organizational unit, department, etc. where the information is created, or that is the primary user of the information. **Owners** are responsible for:
     - Identifying the classification level of all corporate information within their organizational unit
     - Defining and implementing appropriate safeguards to ensure the confidentiality, integrity, and availability of the information resource
     - Monitoring safeguards to ensure their compliance and reporting situations of noncompliance
     - Authorizing access to those who have a business need for the information
     - Removing access from those who no longer have a business need for the information
   - **Custodian:** Employees designated by the Owner to be responsible for maintaining the safeguards established by the Owner.

   – **User:** Employees authorized by the Owner to access information and use the safeguards established by the Owner.

Classification Criteria.

1. In many instances, information will be "pre-classified" by its owner (for instance, all customer-related information will be classified "Internal Use"). However, all decisions about the level of classification of a document must comply with Figure 1.

Distribution

Measures.

1. The measures for handling distribution of the varying classes of information are detailed in Table 1. Note that the measures described for a classification include all those laid down for preceding levels of classification (except for general release).

Review and Compliance Monitoring

Review of Security Policies.

1. Information Security Administration will carry out a review, at least annually, of THE COMPANY's Information Security Standards to ensure their continuing validity.
2. Whenever significant change is to take place (e.g., the introduction of new technology or a major system change), Information Security Administration must be involved at the planning stage to ensure adequate provisions are made for any necessary change to security standards.

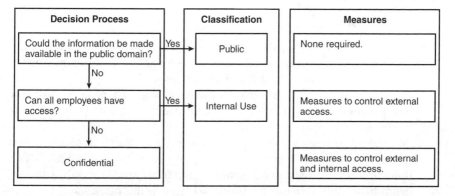

Figure 1. Classification Criteria. All references to employees include both temporary and permanent staff; however, decisions will need to be made locally about distribution of information to non-permanent staff.

Table 1. Measures

Classification	Distribution Mechanisms	Measures
Public	Any	None.
Internal Use	Any	None, but take reasonable steps to ensure non-corporate employees or agents do not see or hear information.
Confidential	Paper	Seal in double envelope, the inner one being clearly marked "Confidential."
		Clearly mark the outer envelope with the recipient's name and address.
		Do not mark classification on outside of envelope.
	Voice	Take steps to ensure that conversations cannot be overheard by those with no right to be aware of the information.
		Ensure that phone conversations are with who you think it is.
	Fax — transmission	Ensure correct number is dialed.
		Ring intended recipient to warn of arrival and request they confirm receipt.
		Do not leave fax unattended during transmission.
		Do not leave originals on fax machine.
	Fax — receipt	Always pick up faxes you know are arriving.
		Do not leave faxes on the fax machine.
	E-mail	Ensure the correct address is used.

3. Proposed amendments to THE COMPANY's Information Security Standards must be advised to the Information Security Manager for approval.

Compliance Monitoring.

1. Information Security Administration will ensure that procedures are developed to support standards in relevant departments and to maintain a checklist of the status of these.
2. Information Security Administration and/or Internal Audit will carry out planned reviews of compliance across the company and provide local management with feedback.
3. Managers are responsible for ensuring that staff members under their control are aware of and comply with all THE COMPANY's Information Security policies and standards. Advice may be sought from Information Security Administration when necessary.

4. Information Security Administration must receive a copy of all internal and external audit control/review reports relating to IT resources or processes with potential Information Security implications.

Appendix 1D
Sample Information Security Manual

THE COMPANY INFORMATION SECURITY POLICY MANUAL

Version Control Information

Version	Issued By	Date	Comment
Draft	Rich O'Hanley	31 Oct 03	Draft for review of style only
0.1	Justin A. Peltier	30 Nov 03	Input to workshop
0.2	John A. Blackley	15 Dec 03	Incorporates workshop comments

GENERAL

Definition

This Security Policy is a formal set of rules by which those people who are given access to the Company's technology and information assets must abide.

The Security Policy serves several purposes. The main purpose is to inform department users, Information Systems Services (ISS) staff, managers, and contractors of their obligatory requirements for protecting the technology and information assets of the Company.

The Security Policy describes the technology and information assets that we must protect and also identifies the threats to those assets. This is the first step in a risk analysis that must balance the cost of protection against the value of our assets.

The Security Policy also describes the user's responsibilities and privileges. What is considered acceptable use? What are the rules regarding Internet access? The Security Policy answers these questions, describes user limitations, and also outlines the penalties for violation of the Security Policy.

INFORMATION SECURITY POLICIES AND PROCEDURES

This document also contains selected procedures for responding to incidents that threaten the security of the Company's computer systems and network.

The Security Policy Committee

The Security Policy Committee shall be involved in the creation and review of all security policies included in this document. For a policy to be effective, it needs to be accepted at all levels in every department of the Company's office. That is why the Security Policy Committee should be composed of individuals who represent a cross section of the different departments within the Company. A list of individuals who should be members of the Security Policy Committee is as follows:

- The Security Administrator
- The Chief Information Officer
- Information Systems Services Technology Staff
- Representatives of User Departments
- Representative of the Inspector General
- Representatives of the Personnel Department
- Legal Counsel of the Company
- Auditors

The members of the Security Policy Committee are asked to serve for a period of at least one year. They will meet quarterly to review new security policies and amendments to existing policies. The duties of the Security Policy Committee include:

- Implement a Security Awareness Program to make all employees aware of the official Security Policy of the Company.
- Review and approve proposed new security policies.
- Review and approve changes to existing security policies.

WHAT ARE WE PROTECTING?

The first step in creating this security policy is to identify what we are protecting. It is our obligation to protect the technology and information assets of the Company. The computer systems and network of the Company are of valuable service to the shareholders and contain confidential information about the employees, clients, and Company business. This information must be protected from unauthorized access, theft, and destruction.

The technology and information assets of the Company are made up of the following components:

- *Computer hardware,* including computer equipment and operating systems, applications, files, servers and data

- *System software,* including operating systems, database management systems, TP monitors, backup and restore software, communications protocols, etc.
- *Application software* used by the various departments, including custom written software application and commercial off-the-shelf software packages
- *User department information* stored on various database systems (e.g., Oracle® and Sybase®), including information stored off-line on magnetic tape media as well as information available from online disk systems.
- *Communications network hardware and software,* including routers, routing tables, hubs, modems, multiplexers, switches, firewalls, private lines, and associated network management software and tools.

Classification of Information

User department information found in computer system files and databases shall be classified as either confidential or non-confidential.

The Department Directors shall classify the information controlled by them. The Chief Information Officer is required to review and approve the classification of the information and determine the appropriate level of security to best protect it. Furthermore, the CIO shall classify information controlled by units not administered by a Department Director.

Classification of Computer Systems

Security Level	Description	Example
RED	This system contains confidential information — information that cannot be revealed to personnel outside the Company. Even within the Company, access to this information is provided on a "need-to-know" basis. The system provides mission-critical services vital to the operation of the business. Failure of this system may have life-threatening consequences or an adverse financial impact on the business of the Company.	IBM mainframe system containing confidential Drivers, Vehicles, and other department information on DB2 databases. Novell and Windows NT/2000 Servers. UNIX servers containing confidential Drivers information on Oracle, Sybase, or other RDBMS databases. Network routers and firewalls containing confidential routing tables and security information.

(continued)

Security Level	Description	Example
GREEN	This system does not contain confidential information or perform critical services, but it provides the ability to access RED systems through the network.	User department PCs used to access mainframe and UNIX-based application. Management workstations used by systems and network administrators.
WHITE	This system is not externally accessible. It is on an isolated LAN segment, unable to access RED or GREEN systems. It does not contain sensitive information or perform critical services.	A test system used by system designers and programmers to develop new computer systems.
BLACK	This system is externally accessible. It is isolated from RED or GREEN systems by a firewall. While it performs important services, it does not contain confidential information.	A public Web server with nonsensitive information.

Local Area Network Classifications

A LAN will be classified by the systems directly connected to it. For example, if a LAN contains just one RED system, it shall be classified as a RED LAN, and all network users will be subject to the same restrictions as RED systems users. A LAN will assume the Security Classification of the highest level systems attached to it.

Definitions:

- **Externally accessible to the public:** The system may be accessed via the Internet by persons outside the Company without a log-on id or password. The system may be accessed via dial-up connection without providing a logon id or password. It is possible to "ping" the system from the Internet. The system may or may not be behind a firewall. A public Web server is an example of this type of system.
- **Non-public, externally accessible:** Users of the system must have a valid log-on id and password. The system must have at least one level of firewall protection between its network and the Internet. The system may be accessed via the Internet or the private intranet. An example would be a private FTP server that is used to exchange files with business partners.
- **Internally accessible only:** Users of the system must have a valid log-on id and password. The system must have at least two levels of firewall protection between its network and the Internet. The

system is not visible to Internet users. It may have a private Internet (non-translated) address and it does not respond to a "ping" from the Internet such as a private intranet Web server.

- **Threats to Security:** Identifying the technology and information assets of the Company is the first step in establishing our security policy. The next step is to identify potential threats that may adversely impact the operation of our network and systems or the integrity of our information. When deciding how to protect the assets of the organization, it is helpful to know what threats pose the greatest danger.

Amateur Hackers and Vandals

These people are the most common type of attackers on the Internet. The probability of attack is extremely high and there is also likely to be a large number of attacks.

These are usually crimes of opportunity. These amateur hackers are scanning the Internet and looking for well-known security holes that have not been plugged. Web servers and electronic mail are their favorite targets. Once they find a weakness, they will exploit it to plant viruses, Trojan horses, or use the resources of your systems for their own means. If they do not find an obvious weakness, they are likely to move on to an easier target.

The best way to reduce this type of threat is to reduce the number of public resources that are available. Public Web sites must be on a DMZ LAN protected by a filtering router that denies access to well-known vandals. Public Web sites must be backed up frequently and also have at least passive intrusion detection software (e.g., Tripwire) installed. They must be scanned daily to ensure that they have not been compromised.

Criminal Hackers and Saboteurs

The probability of this type of attack is low but not entirely unlikely, given the amount of sensitive information contained in the Company's databases. The skill of these attackers is medium to high as they are likely to be trained in the use of the latest hacker tools. The attacks are well planned and are based on any weaknesses discovered that will allow a foothold into the network.

It is difficult to stop this type of attack. The best defense is to eliminate the well-know means of attack and to limit what is publicly known of our network internals. Known bugs in Web servers, e-mail servers, firewalls, and other network components must be eliminated as soon as possible. The security team must keep up with the latest attack methodologies that are publicized on bugtraq reports, CERT (Computer Emergency Response Team) advisories, SANS (System Administration,

Networking, and Security) Institute newsletters, and other security organization publications.

Disgruntled Employees and Ex-Employees

These are the most dangerous types of attackers because they are motivated by some perceived grievance against the Company. They are likely to be skilled, very knowledgeable, and worst of all, trusted by management. The most successful attacks come from within the organization. A potentially dangerous situation can arise when a trusted employee quits or, worse yet, is fired under circumstances that cause hard feelings.

The Security Policy is designed to take account of this situation. Employees who are terminated or fired must return to their supervisor all computer equipment, modems, key cards, and security-related materials owned by the Company. System administrators must immediately disable their accounts on all systems to which they have access and change the root or system administrator passwords to all other systems to which they may have been privy. This means that the Personnel Department must notify the ISS Department of all terminations within 24 hours.

USER RESPONSIBILITIES

This section establishes usage policy for the computer systems, networks, and information resources of the Company. It pertains to all employees and contractors who must use the computer systems, networks, and information resources in the course of their job duties. It also pertains to Company business partners and individuals who are granted access to the network for the business purposes of the Company.

Acceptable Use Policy

User accounts on Company computer systems are to be used only for business of the Company and are not to be used for personal activities. Unauthorized use of a Company system is in violation of the law, constitutes theft, and is punishable by law. Therefore, unauthorized use of Company Information Systems Services computing systems and facilities may constitute grounds for either civil or criminal prosecution.

Users are responsible for protecting all confidential information used or stored on their accounts. This includes their log-on ids, passwords, and dial-up or dial-back modem phone numbers. Furthermore, they are prohibited from making unauthorized copies of such confidential information or distributing it to persons outside the Company.

Users shall not purposely engage in activity with the intent to harass other users, degrade the performance of the system, divert system resources to their own use, or gain access to Company systems for which they do not have authorization.

Users shall not attempt to access any data, scripts, or programs contained on Company computer systems for which they do not have authorization or the explicit consent of the owner of the data, scripts, or programs.

Users shall not attach unauthorized modems to their PCs or workstations for the purpose of remote access through a dial-up phone line. Furthermore, users may not install remote access software, such as pcAnywhere™, on their PCs or workstations. Such remote access requires the authorization of the employee's manager and the Security Administrator.

Users are required to report any weaknesses in the Company's computer security, and any incidents of misuse or violation of this policy to the Security Administrator.

Use of the Internet

The Company provides Internet access to employees who have a business need for access. Employees must obtain authorization from their Department Director and file a request with the Security Administrator.

The Internet is a business tool for the Company. It is to be used for management-approved activities only. Internet use for personal, non-business purposes is understandable and acceptable; however, employees must demonstrate a sense of responsibility and must comply with all appropriate Company policies as well as state and federal laws and regulations.

The Internet service may not be used for transmitting, retrieving, or storing any communications of a discriminatory or harassing nature or that are derogatory to an individual or group; pornography; defamatory or threatening communications; chain letters; gambling; or for any purpose that is illegal or for personal gain.

Electronic information created or communicated by an employee using the Internet will generally not be monitored by Company management. However, the following conditions must be noted:

1. Company Management reserves the right to monitor usage patterns for capacity planning.
2. Company Management reserves the right to review employee use of company-provided resources, including Internet activities.
3. Employees should have no expectation of privacy for any Internet usage or e-mail usage.

INFORMATION SECURITY POLICIES AND PROCEDURES

User Classification

There are many different types of users who have access to the computer systems and information resources of the Company. The needs of each type of user will vary, and not all users will need the same level of access to information. All users are expected to have knowledge of these security policies and are required to report violations to the security administrator. Furthermore, all users must conform to the Acceptable Use Policy defined in this document. The Company has established the following user groups and defined the access privileges and responsibilities:

User Category	Privileges and Responsibilities
Employees	Access to application and databases as required for job function. (RED or GREEN cleared)
System administrators	Access to computer systems, routers, hubs, and other infrastructure technology required for job function
	Access to confidential information on a "need-to-know" basis only
Security administrator	Highest level of security clearance
	Allowed access to all computer systems, databases, firewalls, and network devices as required for job function
Systems analyst /programmer	Access to applications and databases as required for specific job function
	Not authorized to access routers, firewalls, or other network devices
Contractors/ consultants	Access to applications and databases as required for specific job functions
	Access to routers and firewall only if required for job function; knowledge of security policies
	Access to Company information and systems must be approved by the appropriate Department Director
Government agencies and business partners	Access allowed to selected applications only when contract or access agreement is in place or required by applicable laws
General public	Access is limited to applications running on public Web servers
	The general public will not be allowed access to confidential information

ACCESS CONTROL POLICY

A fundamental component of our Security Policy is controlling access to the critical information resources that require protection from unauthorized disclosure or modification. The fundamental meaning of access control is that permissions are assigned to individuals or systems that are authorized to access specific resources.

Access controls exist at various layers of a system, including the network, UNIX® hosts, mainframe computers, databases, and user applications. At the system and network level, access control is implemented by logon id and password. At the application and database level, other access control methods can be implemented to further restrict access. The application and database systems can limit the number of applications and database tables available to users based on their job requirements.

Departmental User System and Network Access

Normal User Identification. All users will be required to have a unique log-on id and password for access to the mainframe computer, UNIX-based client/server systems, and the LAN operating system. The log-on id and password cannot be shared with other employees.

All users must follow the following rules regarding the creation and maintenance of passwords:

- Passwords must be a minimum of eight (8) characters long.
- Passwords must not be found in any English or foreign dictionary. That is, they do not use any common name, noun, verb, adverb, or adjective. These can be easily cracked using standard "hacker tools."
- Passwords must be changed every 35 days.
- User accounts will be frozen after three (3) failed log-on attempts.
- Log-on IDs and passwords will be suspended after 31 days without use.

Users are not allowed to access password files on the mainframe computer, UNIX systems, Windows NT® servers, routers, firewalls, or any network infrastructure component. Password files on servers will be monitored for access by unauthorized users. Copying, reading, deleting, or modifying a password file on any computer system is prohibited.

Users will not be allowed to log on as "root" on production UNIX systems or "system administrator" on production Windows NT/2000 systems. Users who need this level of access to production systems must request a Special Access account as outlined elsewhere in this document.

Employee user IDs and passwords will be deactivated if the employee is terminated, fired, suspended, placed on a leave of absence, or otherwise leaves the employment of the Company.

Departments must contact ISS immediately to report changes in employee status.

System Administrator Access

System administrators, network administrators, and security administrators will have root or system administrator level access to host systems, routers, hubs, and firewalls as required to complete the duties of their job.

The root password for UNIX systems and the system administrator password will be shared by a small group of systems administrators. The same rules for password creation apply to the root and system administrator passwords. The passwords should be chosen so that they are not easily cracked by hacker tools designed to decrypt passwords. These passwords should also be changed every 35 days.

All root and system administrator passwords will be changed immediately after any employee who has access to such passwords is terminated, fired, or otherwise leaves the employment of the Company.

Special Access

Special access accounts are provided to individuals requiring temporary root or system administrator privileges in order to perform their job. These accounts are monitored by the Security Administrator and require the permission of the user's Department Director. Monitoring of the special access accounts is done by entering the users into a Special Access Database and periodically generating reports to management. The reports will show who currently has a special access account, for what reason, and when it will expire. Special access accounts will expire in 35 days and will not be automatically renewed without written permission. The Special Access Database contains the following information:

Field Name	Field Name
User Name	Special Access Computer System
User Company Address	Special Access Logon ID
User Company Phone	Special Access Issue Date
User Department/Manager	Special Access Expiration Date
Reason for Special Access	Special Access Type

In cases where an individual has special access accounts on multiple systems, there will be a separate entry in the database for each account.

UNIX accounts requiring UID 0 must be approved by the Department Director and the Security Administrator and are monitored by the Operations Manager using the Special Access Database.

Connecting to Third-Party Networks

This policy is established to ensure a secure method of connectivity provided between the Company and all third-party companies and other government agencies required to electronically exchange information with the Company. Third parties refers to other government agencies, vendors, and consultants doing business with the Company, and other business partners that have a need to exchange information with the Company.

Third-party network connections are to be used only by the employees of the third party for the business purposes of the Company. The third-party company will ensure that only authorized users will be allowed to access information on the Company's network. The third party will not allow Internet traffic or other private network traffic to flow into the Company network.

A third-party network connection is defined as one of the following connectivity options:

- *Leased line.* Leased lines (e.g., T1) will terminate at a Company router on a third-party subnet.
- *VPN encrypted tunnel.* A VPN network connection will terminate on a Company firewall, and the third party will be subject to standard Company authentication rules.
- *Dial-up connection.* Dial-up connection to third-party networks will be permitted with a secure one-time password system.

A third-party subnet on the Company LAN will be isolated from RED and GREEN subnets by a filtering firewall designed to allow only traffic from authorized third-party subnets. The firewall will also conform to Company standards for firewall configuration.

Third-party network connections will be configured for TCP/IP and SNA/LLC protocols.

This policy applies to all new third-party connection requests and any existing third-party connections. In cases where the existing third-party network connections do not meet the requirements outlined in this document, they will be re-designed as needed.

All requests for third-party connections must be made by submitting a "Third-Party Connection Document" to the Security Administrator with approval of the CIO and the appropriate Department Director.

Connecting Devices to the Network

Only authorized devices may be connected to the Company network. Authorized devices include PCs and workstations owned by the Company that comply with the configuration standards of the Company. Other authorized devices include network file and print servers, UNIX hosts used as application and database servers, and network routers, hubs, firewalls, and other authorized network infrastructure devices used for network management and monitoring.

Users shall not attach to the network any Windows PCs, workstations, or UNIX-based (including Linux) host computers that are not owned or controlled by the Company. Users are specifically prohibited from attaching PCs or workstations running host port scanning, "sniffers," or TCP/IP filtering programs to the Company network.

Users are not authorized to attach any device that would alter the routing or bridging characteristics of the Company's network. These devices include routers, bridges, and host computers equipped with two or more network interface cards running a routing protocol. Installation and maintenance of bridges and routers are restricted to the Company Information Systems Services Department.

Remote Access Policy

Only authorized persons may remotely access the Company network over dial-up facilities. Remote access is provided to those employees, contractors, and business partners of the Company who have a legitimate business need to exchange information, copy files or programs, or access computer applications. Authorized connection can be remote PC to the SOS network or a remote network to SOS network connection.

The only acceptable method of remotely dialing in to the internal Company network is through the use of a secure one-time password.

Dial in with a Secure One-Time Password. One-time passwords are a highly secure method of authenticating remote access users. The Company's office uses the SecurID® system from RSA Security. It is based on a two-factor authentication scheme. The user is provided with a personal identification number (PIN) or password that must be committed to memory and a device that has a varying token number. The device is synchronized with the SecurID server located in the data center and changes the key number every 60 seconds. Remote users must enter their PIN and the key number when dialing into the remote access server.

Unauthorized Remote Access. The attachment of modems and dial-up lines to a user's PC or workstation that are connected to the Company's LAN is not allowed without the written permission of the Security Administrator. Additionally, users may not install personal software designed to provide remote control of the PC or workstation (e.g., pcAnywhere). This type of remote access bypasses the authorized, highly secure methods of remote access and poses a threat to the security of the entire network.

PENALTY FOR SECURITY VIOLATION

The Company takes the issue of security seriously. Employees who use the technology and information resources of the Company must be aware that they can be disciplined if they violate this policy. Upon confirmation of a violation of this policy, the Security Administrator will notify the offending employee's Department Director and the Human Resources department. Discipline that may be imposed on the employee shall be administered in accordance with the Company policy on Employee Discipline.

SECURITY INCIDENT HANDLING PROCEDURES

This section provides some policy guidelines and procedures for handling security incidents. The term "security incident" is defined as any irregular or adverse event that threatens the security, integrity, or availability of the information resources on any part of the Company's network. Some examples of security incidents include:

- Illegal access of a Company computer system. For example, a hacker logs on to a production UNIX server and copies the password file.
- Damage to a Company computer system or network caused by illegal access. Releasing a virus or worm would be an example.
- Denial-of-service attack against a Company Web server. For example, a hacker initiates a flood of packets against a Web server designed to cause the system to crash.
- Malicious use of system resources to launch an attack against other computers outside the Company's network. For example, the UNIX system administrator notices a connection to an unknown network and a strange process accumulating a lot of CPU time.

Create a Security Log

All security incidents will be recorded in a Security Log. The Security Log is a book that is kept by the Security Administrator to record all events that occur during a security incident. Any member of the security team may make an entry in the log. Entries in the log will be signed and dated by the person making the entry. The Security Log may be used by law enforcement officials during a criminal investigation. The log should report only known facts and refrain from speculation. Examples of information to be logged include:

- Dates and times that incident-related events were discovered
- Dates and times of incident-related phone calls

INFORMATION SECURITY POLICIES AND PROCEDURES

- People you have contacted or people who have contacted you
- Amount of time spent on incident-related tasks
- Names of systems, programs, files, or networks affected
- Patches or upgrades applied, including date and time applied

Five-Step Procedure

There are five steps to handling a security incident.

1. Protect the Systems. This step occurs before there is a security incident. Virus protection software will be installed on all PC and UNIX systems and updated regularly. All UNIX systems will have the Tripwire product installed to ensure the integrity of system and other important files. An active intrusion detection system will be installed on all secure computer systems containing confidential information.

2. Identify the Problem. There are several ways the Security Monitoring Team (SMT) can be made aware that a security incident is in progress. Security administrators routinely log on to secure systems to monitor user activities. They are trained to notice any unusual processes running or unusual user activity. Additionally, the intrusion detection systems are designed to alert the SMT when unusual activity is in progress on a computer system or the LAN.

All systems should be scanned for viruses and worms at least daily.

Run Tripwire and other intrusion monitors daily to detect changes to systems files.

Notify management after verification of a security incident.

3. Isolate the Problem. Once a security incident is discovered, it must not be allowed to spread to other systems. The infected systems must be removed from the network

4. Remove the Problem. Once the security incident has been isolated to one or more systems, the Security Incident Response Team (SIRT) will be in charge of removing the threat, whether it is a destructive virus or a malicious hacker.

5. Forensics and Recovery. After the problem has been removed, the SIRT will perform a damage assessment. Care must be taken not to access or modify any system files that may provide evidence to law enforcement authorities. The first task is to determine if any information was lost or modified. Then we must determine what information may have been stolen or compromised. Restore lost or destroyed information only after system files and other affected files have been copied.

Virus and Worm Incidents

Identify the Problem. Virus and worm incidents are somewhat similar. Worms are more dangerous in that they are self-replicating and can spread to hundreds of machines in a very short period of time. Viruses are not self-replicating but can spread quickly via e-mail or other means.

Once the problem has been identified as either a virus or a worm, the Security Administrator will notify the Chief Information Officer, who will then notify user Department Directors.

Isolate the Problem. It is important to isolate the infected system from the rest of the network as soon as possible. In the case where a worm is suspected, a decision must be made whether or not to disconnect the Company's network from the Internet and all other third-party networks. The Chief Information Officer or the Emergency Incident Response Team (EIRT) must authorize the isolation of the Company's network from the outside world.

Remove the Problem. Carefully remove the infected files from your system, saving them offline for later analysis.

Forensics and Recovery. Do not power off or reboot systems that may be infected without first removing the infected files. There are some viruses that will destroy disk data if the system is power-cycled or rebooted. Rebooting a system could also destroy needed information or evidence.

Restore any system files that may be infected from tape backups.

Send infected files to the FBI or CERT for analysis.

Malicious Hacker Incidents

Hacker incidents can vary in seriousness. Some amateur hackers are not destructive — the thrill and challenge of breaking into a system draws them. Other hackers are malicious and intent on stealing information or destroying valuable resources. Regardless, both activities are illegal and must be addressed by our procedures. Any hacker incident must be assumed to be a real threat to the Company's network.

There are three types of hacker incidents:

1. *An attempt to break into a system.* The hacker has not been able to break in. The System Administrator notices repeated probes and attempts to guess passwords or penetrate the firewall defenses. This type of incident is quite common, and the System Administrator must be able to distinguish between casual probes and pings, and serious attempts to break into a system.

2. *An active session on a system.* A hacker has been able to penetrate the system defenses and has managed to gain access to a system. A decision must be made whether to allow the activity to continue while we gather evidence or to knock the hacker off the system and lock him out. If the Security Administrator has any reason to believe that the hacker may be about to copy or destroy confidential information, he should kill the hacker's session immediately. If it is not possible to kill the hacker's session, then the Security Administrator or EIRT may disconnect the system from the Internet.

3. *Attack discovered after the fact.* Evidence of a hacker attack is discovered but the attacker is gone. The Security Administrator must decide if it is necessary to isolate the system from the rest of the network. Special care must be taken to not disturb evidence that may help law enforcement officials identify the offender.

Identify the Problem. Attempt to identify the identity of the hacker from the IP address and other protocol information. If the source of the attacks can be identified, the Security Administrator will attempt to contact the IT manager for that site in an effort to identify the offender. Note that a skilled hacker can hide his identity and true location and it may not be possible to identify him.

Isolate and Remove the Problem. If the attack is still in progress, the EIRT can deactivate the hacker's session or remove the system from the Internet as needed.

A malicious hacker incident should be reported to the Chief Information Officer as soon as possible. For an incident where an attack is in progress or an attack is discovered after the fact, the Chief Information Officer may notify local law enforcement officials, the FBI, and CERT in an effort to track down the offenders.

The EIRT should run Tripwire and/or other intrusion detection software in an attempt to identify any virus, worm, or Trojan horse left by the attacker. The EIRT will remove any malicious code or software found after the attack.

Forensics and Recovery. Before restoring the system, make copies of all system logs, process status information and suspicious files, and store them in a safe place.

Restore any files that the hacker may have modified by using clean backup tapes. Install patches or fixes to close any security vulnerabilities that the hacker may have used to gain access. Log all actions taken to restore the system in the Security Log Book.

Part 2
Information Security Reference Guide

Employees and contractors must work together to protect one of the company's most important assets — its information. As competitive pressures increase, the importance of protecting the company's confidential and critical information becomes even more important. The company must ensure that information is protected from unauthorized access, disclosure, modification, and destruction. Without the proper *security* of company assets, the company could suffer loss of customer confidence, market share, competitive advantage, and, ultimately, jobs. Working together, the company can prevent such losses as it strives to reach its goals more efficiently.

The purpose of this guide is to provide the Information Security Coordinator in each organizational unit with a reference document to support the development and implementation of a local Information Security program tailored to the organization's unique needs. The information presented is intended to be appropriate for the general company population. The guide is a working reference tool that will be updated and refined as a result of technological, business, or cultural environmental changes, and recommendations by the corporate Information Security coordination team.

The majority of the policies, standards, and guidelines recommended in this guide will fit without change into your organization. Others may need some modification to fit comfortably within your organization's environment. After analyzing an organization's needs, one may find that gaps exist and one needs to develop policies, standards, and guidelines unique to the organization. The guide has been formatted to permit easy extraction of definitions, policies, standards, and guidelines for inclusion into one's own organization program document. Additionally, corporate policy is repeated here to provide a complete reference. Corporate policies can only be modified with the approval of the Corporate Secretary. The policies, standards, procedures, and guidelines shown fit the definitions presented in Chapter 4.

For convenience, an electronic copy of this document is available in Microsoft Word format on the CD-ROM included. For questions concerning the application or interpretation of the instructions in this document, call the Information Security group. If you have Information Security concerns in your organization that cannot be resolved by immediate management, you are encouraged to contact the Corporate Information Security Coordinator or the General Auditor for investigation and appropriate action.

Chapter 10
Introduction to Information Security

1 DEFINITION OF INFORMATION

Corporate information is defined as any information relating to the company business that becomes known to an employee or contractor during the course of employment. Broadly, corporate information is that information used by the company in its business and is the result of some effort, expense, or investment that provides the company with a competitive advantage, and that the company wishes to protect from disclosure to third parties.

2 WHAT IS INFORMATION SECURITY?

Information security is the prevention of, and recovery from, unauthorized or undesirable destruction, modification, disclosure, or use of information and information resources, whether accidental or intentional.

3 WHY DO WE NEED TO PROTECT INFORMATION?

Publicly held companies are required to keep accurate records and to maintain internal controls to safeguard corporate assets against unauthorized use or disposition. In addition to the more traditional list of assets such as plant, land, equipment, money, and people, the list of corporate assets also includes information used to support the business. A company's physical assets are protected because lost or damaged assets damage the company's chances of success. In the same manner, protecting the company's information assets enhances its chance of success. Prudent asset security yields improved value for stockholders, better competitive position in the industry, and improved customer service. The following discussions provide some additional bases for safeguarding information.

3.1 Corporate Policies — Information Management

Management recognizes the increasing value of information to the efficient and effective operation of the company. Information has not only become critical to company success, but strategic to its long-term survival. Recognizing these facts, the corporate policy on information management was established in June 1991.

This policy identifies information as company property and a corporate asset. This includes all information, regardless of the medium on which it is transmitted or stored. Specifically, the policy includes information that is typed, handwritten, printed, filmed, or electronically generated or stored. Voice-mail is also corporate information. Additionally, the policy charges:

- Organization management with the responsibility to (create and) retain information necessary to conduct company business
- Managers with the responsibility to develop and administer information security programs that appropriately classify and protect corporate information
- Employees with the responsibility to protect corporate information from unauthorized access, modification, duplication, destruction, or disclosure
- Information providers with the responsibility to authorize access to those with a genuine business need

The policy also establishes that all information must fall into one of three information classifications (Confidential, Internal Use, or Public) and that each employee can have one or more specific roles (owner, custodian, or user) to play in protecting information. Employee responsibilities and information classification guidelines are described in broader detail in Chapters 12 and 13 of this guide.

3.2   Corporate Policies — Security

Policy requires managers or plant superintendents to "develop an emergency preparedness plan to address resumption of business operations and security of employees and property." Thus, management is charged with the responsibility not only to protect the information asset's confidentiality, integrity, and availability, but also to ensure that the organization's business function can be maintained (or minimally, quickly recovered) in the event of a disaster.

3.3   Corporate Policies — Standards of Conduct

Policy charges employees with the responsibility to abide by applicable laws, regulations, and standards of professional conduct. This includes a responsibility to avoid conflicts of interest and actions that have the appearance of being unethical. Employees are expected to safeguard information against theft and unauthorized use, and to observe copyright law. This includes not only corporate information, but also the information of employees, customers, and suppliers.

3.4   Corporate Policies — Conflict of Interest

Employees entrusted with confidential or proprietary information shall restrict access and use to authorized individuals inside and outside the company who have a need to know this information for conducting the company business.

No employee who has material nonpublic ("insider") information relating to the company can buy or sell securities (stocks and bonds) of the company, either directly or indirectly. Furthermore, employees cannot engage in other actions to take personal advantage of that information or pass it on to others. Even the appearance of an improper transaction must be avoided to preserve the company's reputation for adhering to the highest standards of conduct.

3.5   Foreign Corrupt Practices Act (FCPA)

The FCPA, which was signed into law in December 1977, made all managers and directors personally liable for the security of corporate assets under their control. The Act requires companies to maintain books, records, and accounts that reflect in reasonable detail the disposition of corporate assets and to implement a system of internal accounting controls. These controls must meet four standards:

1. All transactions affecting corporate information must be authorized by company management.
2. Transactions affecting corporate information must be recorded as necessary to allow preparation of financial statements that conform with generally accepted accounting principles and to maintain a proper accountability of corporate assets.
3. Access to information is permitted only in accordance with management's general or specific authorization.
4. Audit trails must be developed to allow review of and access to corporate information. These reviews are to be undertaken at reasonable intervals. Appropriate action should be taken in the event of any irregularities.

3.6   Federal Copyright Law

It is illegal to make or distribute copies of copyrighted material without authorization from the author or distributor.

3.7   Federal Antitrust Laws

The sharing of one competitor's sensitive information with another competitor can lead to criminal (felony) and civil violations of the federal antitrust laws resulting in fines up to $1 million and triple civil damages. Examples of this type of information are future product plans, marketing strategies, innovative manufacturing processes, and other strategic or sensitive information that is not intended to be shared.

Based on the language of the antitrust law, every company is required to protect competitive information, keep processes secret from competitors, and resist efforts to obtain another company's information.

4   WHAT INFORMATION SHOULD BE PROTECTED?

All information is *not* created equal. Some information may be considered as having higher value if it supports critical business functions, or must be retained due to corporate, legal, or regulatory requirements. To determine which information should be protected and to what degree, each organizational unit should perform an information risk assessment, which includes identifying:

- The business value of the information asset
- Possible threats to the information asset
- Which threats are most likely to occur
- The impact on the business should the threat be realized

With this data, the organizational unit can apply cost-effective security measures to the most important information that is at the greatest risk. An important element to remember is that the cost of protecting information should not exceed the value of the information to the company. The Information Security group can be contacted for assistance in performing risk assessments.

Chapter 11
Fundamentals of Information Security

1 INTRODUCTION

Information security is the prevention of, and recovery from, unauthorized or undesirable destruction, modification, disclosure, or use of information and information resources, whether accidental or intentional. A more positive definition is the preservation of the *availability*, *integrity*, and *confidentiality* of information and information resources. The following sections discuss each element.

2 INFORMATION AVAILABILITY (BUSINESS CONTINUITY)

What is information availability? Information is said to be available when employees who are authorized access, and whose jobs require access, to the information can do so in a cost-effective manner that does not jeopardize the value of the information. Information must be consistently available to conduct business. Business continuity planning includes provisions for assuring the availability of the key resources (information, people, physical assets, tools, etc.) necessary to support the business function.

Corporate
Policy: Information **owners** are responsible to assure the accessibility and availability of information and business functions critical to the effective operation of the company. (From: Company Policy on Security)

Recommended
Standard: Organization management is responsible for:
- Identifying information, applications, processes, and systems required to support critical business processes and functions
- Assessing the cost to the company of a business disruption
- Determining the duration that a business disruption could be tolerated

- Determining resource requirements for recovery and resumption of business
- Determining disruption avoidance procedures and costs
- Defining alternate processing methods to sustain business operations while normal processing is being restored
- Restoring information required by the business process
- Verifying successful recovery

Recommended
Standard:
Organizational unit management shall maintain a business continuity plan that allows critical business functions to continue in the event that primary business facilities or resources are not available. The following are minimum requirements for business continuity planning.

- A business continuity coordinator should be designated for each organization.
- The organizational unit should review and approve the initial business continuity plan and subsequent annual updates.
- The information **owner** should determine what information is to be backed up and the frequency of backup. This activity is to be coordinated with the **custodian.**
- The organizational unit head is responsible for ensuring that information deemed critical is backed up and stored in a secure location away from the primary usage site.
- All critical hardcopy documents should be identified and copies stored off-site.
- The organizational unit head should review the plans of the **custodian** to ensure that the unit's needs are met.
- All continuity plans should be reviewed and updated at least semi-annually.
- All continuity plans should be tested at least annually.

Discussion:
Information, which is considered to be an inherent part of the company's business process and without which operations would be curtailed or otherwise severely impacted, should be identified by the **owner** as *critical.* For critical information and business functions, the information **owner** must consider such key elements as recovery of resources necessary to continue the business function or availability of alternate resources. Consideration should be given to human resources, physical facilities,

equipment, information, finances, and forms necessary to perform critical functions. If the function depends on a computer system, additional consideration should be given to processing hardware, system software, and application programs. For those programs, applications, and systems identified as *critical*, the **owner** must decide how long the organizational unit can function without access to these resources.

Each organizational unit head should conduct a business impact analysis. This process identifies the information created or used within the organization and what the consequences would be to the company's business process if the information were altered or destroyed, or that the method used to process the information was not available.

One of the most important things that can be done to protect the company's business process is to establish a living, working, tested business continuity plan. A business continuity plan is a plan for keeping information and computer systems available in the event of an emergency. Such a plan may make the difference between having just a "problem" or having a business-threatening catastrophe.

3   INFORMATION INTEGRITY

Information integrity is defined as the assurance that the information used in making business decisions is created and maintained with appropriate controls to ensure that the information is correct, auditable, and reproducible.

As each organization develops its own policy on information integrity, it must consider the practical day-to-day operation of the business process, the classification level of the information, and the risk to the company if the information is improperly altered or destroyed.

There are several techniques that can be used to increase confidence that information has integrity. Batch totals and record totals are examples of techniques that help ensure that the information "adds up." Other techniques can be used to help ensure against fraud. There are two basic principles that should be considered: separation of duties and rotation of assignments.

3.1   Separation of Duties

Recommended
Policy: No single individual should have complete control of a business process or transaction from inception to completion.

293

Discussion: This control principle limits error, opportunity, and temptation. Separation of duties can be defined as segregating
incompatible functions (giving these duties to two or
more people). The activities of a process are split among
several people. Mistakes made by one person tend to be
caught by the next person in the chain, thereby increasing information integrity. Unauthorized activities will be
limited because no one person can complete a process
without the knowledge of another.

3.2   Rotation of Assignments

Recommended
Policy: Different individuals should be rotated periodically to
various critical tasks involving the business process or
transaction to ensure business process integrity.

Discussion: There are always some assignments that can cause the
organization to be at risk unless proper controls are in
place. To ensure written task procedures are being followed, as well as provide manpower backup on critical
activities, employees should be assigned to different
tasks at regular intervals.

Some maintain that rotation reduces job efficiency. However, it has been proven that an employee's interest declines over time when doing the same job for an extended
period of time. Additionally, employees sometimes develop shortcuts when they have been in a job too long. By rotating assignments on a regular basis, the organization
can compare how the task was being done and where
changes should be made.

In general, *separation of duties* is designed to ensure that
unauthorized practices require the collusion of several
individuals. The *rotation of assignments* is a complemen-
tary principle that removes one of the colluding parties
from the task, thus exposing the other(s) to detection.

4   INFORMATION CONFIDENTIALITY

For the maximum information value to be realized, the information
owner is obligated to make information accessible to the widest possible
company audience having a demonstrated business need. That is, the
owner is responsible for maximizing the value of information by sharing it
with others while assuring its integrity and confidentiality. Confidentiality

means that the information should only be disclosed to a select group, either because of its *sensitivity* or its *technical nature.*

For example, most would agree that personnel and medical records should not be widely available because this would provide little additional value and represents a serious invasion of employee privacy. To protect employees and the company, this type of information should be highly restricted. Additionally, technical information, or premature, unauthorized information on company stocks (future dividends, splits, etc.) would be difficult for most to interpret correctly. To protect against misuse, misinterpretation, and resultant misinformed business decisions, disclosure of this type of information should also be restricted, either temporarily or permanently.

4.1 Authority to Disclose

Corporate
Policy: Information required to perform company business should not be disclosed to others except with the authorization of the information **owner.** (From: Company Policy on Conflict of Interest)

Recommended
Standard: **User** access to information does not imply or confer authority to act as spokesperson for the company concerning such information or to discuss such information with others.

                User access to information does not imply or confer authority to allow access to others either internally or external to the company.

Discussion: While an open climate of information sharing is desirable to satisfy both the needs of the business and employees, there is a clear need to safeguard corporate information. Access to corporate information should be based on a clear business need. Corporate information is not to be discussed with family or friends, as such discussion can lead to unauthorized third-party disclosure. Discussion of corporate information could result in a significant disclosure that could damage the business interest of the company.

                An official company announcement relieves an employee of his or her responsibility to maintain secrecy to the extent of the information included in the announcement. Speculative press reports provide no excuse for comment on or disclosure of corporate information. Substantial competitive advantage can be sacrificed through untimely disclosures and could result in a loss of customer confidence or business.

4.2   Need-to-Know

Corporate
Policy: Access authority should be granted to those with a business "need-to-know." (From: Company Policy on Information Management)

Discussion: All employees and contractors must be granted sufficient access to perform their assigned duties. For some **Internal Use** information, group or department access may be reasonable. However, at the classification level of **Confidential**, access must be granted on an individual basis. The key to proper control is individual accountability.

Each employee with access to corporate information should be assigned a specific set of functions, privileges, restrictions, and capabilities. The overriding principle of *need-to-know* should govern this process. Under this principle, employees or **users** are assigned only the level of access required to perform their specific job function.

Chapter 12
Employee Responsibilities

1   INTRODUCTION

Although company shareholders are the ultimate **owners** of all information created and utilized in the course of company business, all company and contract personnel are responsible for maintaining the confidentiality, integrity, and availability of corporate information to facilitate its effective and efficient use for company business. (Although not employees of the company, reference below to "employee" is intended to apply to company employees as well as contract personnel performing company business.)

Three responsibility classifications have been defined to assist employees in understanding their roles and responsibilities when using corporate information. Depending on the specific information being accessed, the employee may fall into more than one category. For example, an employee with a desktop workstation becomes the **owner, custodian,** and **user.** This individual is managing a data processing center and is responsible for it.

The definitions and responsibilities described below represent the minimum level of detail necessary for all organizations across the company. Each organization may decide that additional detail is necessary to adequately implement an Information Security Program within their organization.

Corporate
Policy: Individuals and management responsible for creating, administering, or using corporate information are identified as information **owner, custodian,** or **user.** (From: Company Policy on Information Management)

2   OWNER

Definition: The information **owner** is the person who creates the information or is the primary **user** of the information. The information **owner** is assigned the responsibility to exercise the company's ownership rights to manage the corporate information resource.

Recommended
Standard:

Minimally, the information **owner** is responsible for:

- Judging the value of the information and assigning the proper information classification, including a periodic review of this information to determine if the information classification should be changed
- Assessing and defining appropriate controls to ensure that information created is correct, auditable, and reproducible (i.e., integrity)
- Specifying access and control requirements that assure confidentiality, integrity, and availability, and communicating these requirements to the information **custodian** and **users**
- Encouraging access by company personnel who have a business need and could benefit from the information, and preventing access by individuals without a business need-to-know
- Assessing the risk of loss of information confidentiality, integrity, and availability and assuring that adequate controls are in place to mitigate that risk
- Performing periodic reviews of access and control requirements to ensure that information access and control requirements remain appropriate and are functioning adequately
- Ensuring that a disaster recovery plan is available

Discussion:

The information **owner** is usually the creator of the information (or someone assigned by the organizational unit head of the area that created the information) and therefore, on behalf of the company, is assigned the responsibility to maximize its value to the company while maintaining confidentiality, integrity, and availability. The responsibilities of the information **owner** are continuous and, as such, require periodic (possibly annual) review to ensure that information is properly safeguarded.

The information **owner** may delegate these responsibilities to another individual (for example, director to employee), although not normally to someone outside the organizational unit. However, the **owner** may also be a committee of several primary **users** who have agreed to share the ownership responsibility.

3   CUSTODIAN

Definition: The information **custodian** is responsible for protecting the information resource in accordance with the **owner**'s specific directions.

Recommended
Standard: At a minimum, the **custodian** is responsible for:
- Providing physical security for equipment, information storage, backup, and recovery
- Providing a secure processing environment that can adequately protect the integrity, confidentiality, and availability of information
- Administering access to information as authorized by the information **owner**
- Implementing procedural safeguards and cost-effective controls

Discussion: The information **custodian** is responsible for the safe storage and recovery of *information*. The information **custodian** is *not* generally responsible for the recovery of the **owner**'s organization that creates this information. A corporate policy on business continuity planning should charge managers and plant superintendents with the responsibility of developing an appropriate plan to recover their business operations in the event of a business interruption.

4   USER

Definition: The **user** is the individual, or organization, who has been authorized access to the information asset by the **owner**.

Recommended
Standard: At a minimum, **users** are responsible for:
- Using the information only for the purpose intended
- Maintaining the integrity, confidentiality, and availability of information accessed consistent with the **owner**'s expectations while under the **user**'s control

Discussion: Being granted access to information does not imply or confer authority to grant other **users** access to that information. The availability of **confidential** information must be limited. Therefore, if granted access to **confidential** information, **users** should seek the approval of the information **owner** before allowing any other person access. However, for information classified as **public**, the information **owner** is assumed to have granted full disclosure authority to all **users** (unless specifically and explicitly limited).

Chapter 13
Information Classification

1   INTRODUCTION

Information, wherever it is handled or stored (e.g., in computers, file cabinets, desktops, fax machines, voice-mail) needs to be protected from unauthorized access, modification, disclosure, and destruction. All information is **not** created equal. Consequently, segmentation or classification of information into categories is necessary to help identify a framework for evaluating the information's relative value and the appropriate controls required to preserve its value to the company.

Three basic classifications of information have been established. Organizations can define additional subclassifications as necessary to complete their framework for evaluating and preserving information under their control.

When information does require security, the security must be consistent. Often, strict access controls are applied to data stored in the mainframe computers but not applied to office workstations. Whether in a mainframe, client/server, work station, file cabinet, desk drawer, waste basket, or in the mail, information should be subject to appropriate and consistent security.

The definitions and responsibilities described below represent the minimum level of detail necessary for all organizations across the company. Each organization may decide that additional detail is necessary to adequately implement information classification within their organization.

Corporate
Policy: All information must be classified by the **owner** into one of
                     three classifications: **Confidential, Internal Use,** or **Public.** (From: Company Policy on Information Management)

1.1   Confidential

Definition: Information that, if disclosed, could:
- Violate the privacy of individuals,
- Reduce the company's competitive advantage, or
- Cause damage to the company.

Examples: Some examples of **Confidential** information are:
- Personnel records (including name, address, phone number, salary, performance rating, social security number, date of birth, marital status, career path, number of dependents, etc.)
- Customer information (including name, address, phone number, energy consumption, credit history, social security number, etc.)
- Shareholder information (including name, address, phone number, number of shares held, social security number, etc.)
- Vendor information (name, address, product pricing specific to the company, etc.)
- Health insurance records (including medical, prescription, and psychological records)
- Specific operating plans, marketing plans, or strategies
- Consolidated revenue, cost, profit, or other financial results that are not public record
- Descriptions of unique parts or materials, technology intent statements, or new technologies and research that are not public record
- Specific business strategies and directions
- Major changes in the company's management structure
- Information that requires special skill or training to interpret and employ correctly, such as design or specification files

If any of these items can be found freely and openly in public records, the company's obligation to protect from disclosure is waived.

Discussion: Information should be protected according to its sensitivity, criticality, and value. Most often, people think of issues of sensitivity when the word "confidential" is used. However, sensitivity is only one possible element in this classification. Most understand the need to protect the individual's right to privacy and even the need to keep secret (at least for awhile) plans that are being contemplated concerning the future of the company or an organization. Premature disclosure of such plans (especially when they are not firm) could reduce the effectiveness of the plan, removing the element of surprise (necessary in a competitive environment for new product or service offerings) or damaging the company's reputation (in the case of a preliminary "what–if" rate case study, for example).

Some information, while not sensitive, is technical in nature and should not be available even to those with a need to know without expert interpretation by the information **owner.** The nature of the information requires special skill or training for correct interpretation. Access to this information without expert interpretation would likely cause the information to be misinterpreted and decisions that could damage the company's opportunity to operate efficiently and effectively.

Access to this information by individuals not conducting company business is not authorized (except as required by law); access is highly restricted.

It is estimated that approximately 5 to 15 percent of corporate information should be classified as **Confidential.** Due to the nature of their work, some organizations will have more confidential information than others (e.g., those organizations dealing with personnel and legal matters). Information regarded as sensitive should be labeled as **Confidential.**

1.2 Internal Use

Definition: Classify information as **Internal Use** when the information is intended for use by employees when conducting company business.

Examples: Some examples of **Internal Use** information are:
- Operational business information and reports
- Noncompany information that is subject to a nondisclosure agreement with another company
- Company phone book
- Corporate policies, standards, and procedures
- Internal company announcements

Discussion: This classification represents information that is used in the daily operation of the business and generally would not include planning or strategy development activities. Any information that cannot be classified as **Confidential** or **Public** is classified as **Internal Use.** Normally, **Internal Use** information is not labeled as such.

It is estimated that 70 to 90 percent of corporate information can be classified as **Internal Use.** However, organizations such as customer accounting, legal, and personnel departments can be expected to have a larger percentage of **Confidential** information.

Access to this information by individuals not conducting company business is not authorized (except as required by law); access by individuals conducting company business is generally open for inquiry but highly restricted for update.

1.3   Public

Definition: Classify information as **Public** if the information has been made available for public distribution through authorized company channels. **Public** information is not sensitive in context or content, and requires no special security.

Examples: The following are examples of **Public** information.
- Corporate annual report
- Information specifically generated for public consumption, such as public service bulletins, marketing brochures, and advertisements

Discussion: Generally, information that is readily available from the public media or is a matter of public record is classified as **Public.** Information should *not* be classified as **Public** merely because the information is outdated or appears to have no opportunity to damage the company. Information in this classification should be limited to that required by law or regulation and that which is specifically intended for public consumption. To allow other information to be viewed by the public would serve only to provide a potential advantage to competitors and provide the media with the opportunity to shed an unfavorable shadow on the company's reputation. It is estimated that 5 to 15 percent of corporate information can be classified as **Public.** Inquiry access to this information by company and noncompany personnel is authorized. Update access to this information is generally restricted by the information **owner.** Normally, **Public** information is not labeled as such.

2   CLASSIFICATION PROCESS

Recommended
Policy: The **owner** is responsible for classifying information upon creation.

Discussion: Upon creation of the information (whether in a computer, memo in a file cabinet, message in an office automation tool, voice communication, etc.), the creator of that information (generally the information **owner**) is responsible for immediate classification. This immediate classification assists any recipient of the information to appropriately safeguard its value to the company against unauthorized disclosure, loss of availability, and loss of integrity.

Information's value to the company is heavily influenced by the extent to which its integrity is maintained and is available to those with a business need. That is, if the information is not correct or not available to those who need it, it has no value. The information **owner** is responsible to take particular care to assure the integrity of the information for which he or she is responsible and to actively encourage its accessibility by those who can use the information effectively.

The information **owner** must be careful not to over-classify information created. Over-classification might slow down the business process due to the extra precautions required for secure handling and storage. Information that is over-classified will soon cause employees to disregard the classification system, rendering organization Information Security programs ineffective.

3   RECLASSIFICATION

Recommended
Policy: The **owner** should review the classification of information at least annually for possible reclassification.

Discussion: The sensitivity of most classified information decreases over time. **Confidential** information may become **Internal Use,** and **Internal Use** may eventually become **Public.** Because **Confidential** information often has a more restricted audience than **Internal Use** information, it is important that information be properly classified to give the widest and most appropriate audience possible. By maintaining an appropriate classification, the information will provide the maximum value to the company.

If the information **owner** knows the date that information should be reclassified, he or she might label it with

"**Confidential** until (date)." Unless specifically identified otherwise, declassification of **Confidential** information is automatically reclassified as **Internal Use.**

Declassification can also be tied to a public statement, as in the quarterly earnings reports. Prior to the announcement of quarterly earnings, the information is classified as **Confidential.** Once the announcement is made, however, the information can be reclassified as **Public.**

Chapter 14
Information Handling

1 INTRODUCTION

The following chapter sections identify standards and guidelines to help safeguard information during its useful life.

2 INFORMATION LABELING

Recommended
Standard: All **Confidential** information must be clearly labeled with the word "**Confidential.**" Any information not specifically labeled should be treated as **Internal Use**.

Recommended
Procedure: All **Confidential** information is to be marked as follows:
- The name of the **owner** and the date of preparation are to appear on the face of the document.
- The document or any reproduction is to be stamped or marked **Confidential** at the top of the outside cover (if applicable) or on the title page.

Discussion: Proper classification by physical marking, notation, or other means serves to alert the holder the degree of security required for that information. It is *highly* recommended that all organizations employ the standard and procedure listed above. Only through this consistency across organizations can information shared across organizations be protected in accordance with the expectations of the **owner**.

Only **Confidential** information requires labeling. **Public** information should be labeled to identify its intended audience; but, if not labeled, there is little damage to the company beyond lost opportunity to communicate with the public. Information not labeled should be protected as **Internal Use**.

3   INFORMATION USE AND DUPLICATION

Recommended
Standard: Information for which access has been authorized may
                   only be used for purposes identified to and authorized by
                   the information **owner.**

Discussion: When the information **owner** provides access to informa-
                   tion, it is authorized on the basis of the requester's estab-
                   lished business need. Access to information is approved
                   for a stated purpose and does not imply that the request-
                   er has unrestricted use or authority to use for other pur-
                   poses. For example, by virtue of being granted access to
                   information, the requester does not have the automatic
                   authority to duplicate or distribute this information to
                   others.

                   Sometimes the authorization given by the information
                   owner to the **user** needs to be formal and written. In oth-
                   er cases, verbal authorization or a clear understanding
                   between the information **owner** and **user** is sufficient. It is
                   the responsibility of the information **owner** to determine
                   the level of formality required. Often there is the under-
                   standing that the information provided will be analyzed,
                   summarized, and input into some process of the request-
                   er for distribution to others. The essential point is that
                   there be a clear understanding between **owner** and **user.**

4   INFORMATION STORAGE

Corporate
Policy: Organizations shall retain records in the most economical
                   and practical method and location, and shall destroy or
                   relocate them to more economical storage when appropri-
                   ate. (From: Corporate Policy on Information Management)

Recommended
Standard: Information must be stored in a manner consistent with
                   its classification as follows:
                   • When not in use, information is to be appropriately
                     stored.
                   • **Confidential** information is to be stored and main-
                     tained only where it can be verified that access can be
                     adequately controlled.

Discussion: Information, particularly **Confidential** information, must
                   be safeguarded not only while in use, but also when

stored to protect against unauthorized access, modification, or disclosure. This may mean that paper-based information may need to be stored in locked cabinets or desks while not in use. For computer-based information, this may mean physically locking the computer while not attended by an authorized individual or installing an access control software package to protect against unauthorized access.

5 INFORMATION DISPOSAL

Corporate
Policy:
Organizations shall retain records in the most economical and practical method and location, and shall destroy or relocate them to more economical storage when appropriate. (From: Corporate Policy on Information Management)

Recommended
Standard:
Information must be appropriately destroyed in accordance with the organization's records retention schedule.

Information no longer of value to the company should be destroyed.

Confidential information must be destroyed beyond ability to recognize and recover.

Discussion:
When the information no longer has value to the **user**, his or her copy of the information should be destroyed. When the information no longer has value to the company, the information **owner** is responsible for disposal of the information originals. For **Internal Use** information, this might mean simply throwing the report in the trash or deleting the file from the computer.

For **Confidential** information, however, additional care is necessary to ensure that the discarded information cannot be recognized or recovered by anyone. For example, shredding reports and writing over a computer file (just deleting it does not prevent recovery) are effective against recovery. **Owners** and **users** also need to ensure that all data backups of the information are also destroyed beyond recovery.

Chapter 15
Tools of Information Security

1   INTRODUCTION

Information **owners** are assigned the responsibility to manage the confidentiality (disclosure), integrity, and availability of information they create or manage. For information processed in electronic media (such as computers, voice-mail, and fax), the providers of these services should have tools available for **owners** to utilize in fulfilling this function. For nonelectronic media (such as paper-based forms, memos, reports, etc.), the information **owner** is responsible to implement, or arrange to have others implement, appropriate controls to ensure acceptable information security.

There are four key control areas for the information **owner** to consider when safeguarding information: **Access Authorization, Access Control, Backup/Recovery,** and **Information Security Awareness**.

2   ACCESS AUTHORIZATION

Recommended
Policy: The information **owner** is responsible to define access authorization.

Recommended
Standard: It is the responsibility of the information **owner** to identify information assets created or managed, how they are to be protected, who is permitted access, and under what conditions.

Discussion: For information to have value, it needs to be available and have integrity. For information to have maximum value, it needs to be accessible to those who need it and, conversely, inaccessible to those without a business need. Additionally, to maintain its value, this accessibility needs to be tailored to the **user** to provide only the level of access required to perform his or her job. That is, most need only to reference or read the information, while select others, who share in the responsibility to keep the information up-to-date, may need to modify it. Properly tailored access authorization will help preserve the information's value.

3   ACCESS CONTROL

Recommended
Policy: Implementation of **owner**-designated access control authorization is the responsibility of the information **custodian**.

Recommended
Standard: Each **user** should have an identification (userid) within the company's computing system and network environment to authenticate the **user**'s identity; and each identification should be unique, representing one and only one **user**. This identification is normally classified as **Internal Use**.

Recommended
Standard: (The following user identification format standard for computer-based applications and telecommunication systems is maintained by the Information Systems Organization.) The **user** identification (userid) should be in the format X9999 for employees and C9999 for contract employees. For noncomputer-based activities, a similar individual identification scheme may be appropriate.

Recommended
Standard: For computer-based systems, each **user** should have a userid that carries a **confidential** password to authenticate his or her identity. These passwords should:
- Be kept **confidential** and not shared
- Not be displayed or stored in readable text
- Changed at least every 90 days
- Be a minimum of five characters in length

For noncomputer-based systems, appropriate procedures should be implemented that will maintain the integrity of the **user** authentication process.

Discussion: The first way in which a system provides security of corporate assets (whether computer-based or manual) is by permitting access to only those employees with an approved business need. This process is accomplished by identification and authorization.

Identification is the way an employee tells the system (e.g., computer, voice-mail, electronic messaging, etc.)

312

who he or she is. This is accomplished by establishing a unique **user** identification (userid) code.

Authentication is the way a **users** prove to the system that they are who they say they are. This authentication element is known as a password and represents a secure and secret dialogue between the **user** and the system. Coupled with the userid, these two elements allow an authorized **user** access to the various computer systems and information. Because the password opens access to applications and information that a specific individual has been approved for, the password should be:
- Kept secret (do not share passwords with others)
- Difficult for others to associate with you (e.g., no names of spouses, children, hobbies, name variations, home address, etc.)
- Combination of numbers and letters that do not represent a pattern (e.g., ABCD1234 and AAAA1111 are bad passwords)

This process of identification and authentication has been developed to ensure individual accountability. By ensuring that individual userids are assigned to each **user** and by having the **user** assign a unique password known only to them, information **owners** are assured that only authorized **users** have access to the information.

4   BACKUP AND RECOVERY

Recommended
Policy: Information critical to the business function must be backed up (copied) regularly to ensure that the information can be restored should the primary information source be damaged or lost.

Recommended
Standard: The frequency of information backups should be commensurate with its cost of reconstruction and value to the company.

                  Information backups should be stored off-site from the primary information source.

Discussion: Despite all efforts to protect the integrity and availability of information, at some point the information might become lost or corrupted. Regular backup of the primary information is necessary to ensure that it can be recovered when necessary.

The frequency of backup is determined by the information's value to the company (its volatility, criticality, cost of reconstruction, and required availability). For example, customer information changes every second, is critical in providing responsive customer contact, and is expected to be available instantly on request. Real estate holdings information, however, is critical to Plant Accounting, but is much less volatile and **users** could probably tolerate some "downtime" while the information is being restored/rebuilt. The frequency of customer record backup may be nightly with ongoing transaction logging during the day. This would allow recovery up to the minute of failure. Real estate records might be backed up weekly with manual recovery from last week's backup.

5   AWARENESS

Corporate
Policy: Each manager shall develop and administer an Information Security program that makes employees aware of the importance of information and methods for its security. (From: Corporate Policy on Information Management)

Recommended
Standard: Organizational unit coordinators should present awareness materials at least semiannually to organization employees.

Discussion: The single greatest factor in successful information security is the employee. For effective security, employees will need to make the safeguarding of information as natural as answering the phone.

Publishing a set of policies and procedures is no assurance that they will be read and followed. An active awareness program is required, one that will inform employees *why* established policies and procedures make good business sense.

Chapter 16
Information Processing

1   GENERAL

Recommended
Policy: Corporate information will be used only to conduct au-
                       thorized company business, unless specifically autho-
                       rized by the information **owner**.

                       Company-provided resources will be used only to con-
                       duct authorized company business, unless specifically
                       authorized by management.

2   RIGHT TO REVIEW

Corporate
Policy: Auditing has unrestricted access to all records, person-
                       nel, and physical properties relevant to audit assign-
                       ments. (From: Responsibility Statement on Auditing)

Corporate
Policy: Company management has the responsibility to manage,
                       review, and monitor information, personnel, and physical
                       properties relevant to their business operations. (From:
                       Standards of Conduct)

Discussion: With the expanding complexity of the technological and
                       competitive environment in which the company oper-
                       ates, it becomes increasingly necessary for management
                       to efficiently manage its operations. To effectively man-
                       age its operations, management must have the ability to
                       review the details of that operation.

                       Employees often have the expectation that certain areas
                       of their business environment are private/personal. How-
                       ever, management has the responsibility to manage the
                       information of the business wherever it is found. Whether

using a mechanism that is used to transport information (such as electronic-mail, voice-mail, phone/communication lines, or company mail) or store information (such as workstation/computer storage, desk drawers, or file cabinets), these resources have been provided by the company for business use. Although federal law allows management to monitor information, personnel, and properties of the company, recent litigation indicates that a written policy is a key element in avoiding misunderstanding (concerning an individual's expectation of privacy) and potential legal action.

3 DESKTOP PROCESSING

Desktop systems are defined as microcomputers, personal computers, portable computers, laptop or notebook computers, desktop computers, workstations, and small business computers.

Recommended
Policy: The employee's management will provide all necessary desktop hardware, software, and other required information processing resources required by employees to perform their assigned responsibilities.

Recommended
Standard: To ensure proper control and asset security, employees should not bring their own desktop hardware, software, or diskettes into any company facility without prior authorization from the employee's management.

Recommended
Guideline: An organization desktop coordinator should be appointed for each work area with responsibility for coordinating desktop acquisition, use, and security.

4 TRAINING

Recommended
Standard: Organizational unit management is responsible for ensuring that all employees using company-provided resources have adequate training. This training at a minimum should include:
- Proper use of the resources
- Proper use of proprietary software programs
- Precautions to be taken to minimize loss of information
- Compliance with corporate policies and proprietary licensing agreements

5   PHYSICAL SECURITY

Corporate
Policy: Each organizational unit head is responsible for ensuring that there is proper security for all hardware, software, documentation, data, and information. (From: Company Policy on Security)

Recommended
Standard: The following are minimum requirements for physical security:
- Conduct, maintain, and periodically reconcile an inventory of all units, including all hardware and software.
- Ensure that the unit is secured from unauthorized access whenever left unattended.
- Maintain a secure environment for all system control units, file servers, or master units that control or serve shared units and allow only authorized personnel access to these units.
- Back up data and programs on a regular basis.
- Store the backups in a secure off-site location.
- Store removable diskettes containing classified corporate information or programs in a locked storage device when not in use.

6   PROPRIETARY SOFTWARE — CONTROLS AND SECURITY

Corporate
Policy: All employees are required to comply with federal copyright laws, nondisclosure, and vendor licensing agreements governing the installation, use, and distribution of purchased software. (From: Company Policy on Standard of Conduct)

Recommended
Standard: Any employee who learns of any misuse of proprietary or licensed software or related documentation within the company should notify his or her supervisor, local information security coordinator, or Auditing.

Recommended
Standard: Each organizational unit should conduct an annual software audit on its desktop units, comparing the software installed with software proof-of-purchase documentation or the original diskettes.

Discussion: The company is licensed to use the computer software from a variety of vendors. The company does not own this software or its related documentation and, unless specifically authorized in the license for the software, does not have the right to reproduce it.

7   SOFTWARE CODE OF ETHICS

Recommended
Policy:
Unauthorized duplication of copyrighted computer software violates the law and is contrary to corporate standards of conduct. The company prohibits such copying and recognizes the following principles as a basis for preventing its occurrence.

- The company will neither commit nor tolerate the making or use of unauthorized software copies under any circumstances.
- The company will provide legitimately acquired software to meet all legitimate software needs in a timely fashion and in sufficient quantities.
- All employees shall comply with all license or purchase terms regulating the use of any software acquired or used.
- The company will implement and enforce strong internal controls to prevent the making or use of unauthorized software copies, including effective measures to verify compliance with these standards.

8   COMPUTER VIRUS SECURITY

Recommended
Policy:
Information **custodians** are responsible for providing a safe and secure processing environment in which information can be maintained with integrity.

Recommended
Standard:
Custodians of information processing systems must ensure that the system is free from destructive software elements (such as viruses) that would impair the normal and expected operation of the system.

Recommended
Guidelines:
- Where available, a virus prevention, detection, or recovery package should be installed.
- Employees having access to computer systems should attend a training session on the virus threat to understand the damage a virus infection can inflict and understand their personal responsibility for protecting their own systems.
- Viruses often are transmitted through public domain software. Software that is public domain (i.e., nonlicensed software also called "shareware" or "freeware")

or the employee's personal property should not be permitted on company equipment without the explicit authorization of organization management and after
being scanned for viruses.
- Turn off or lock up your desktop system at the end of
the workday to prevent unauthorized access and possible virus contamination.
- Use the "write security" tabs on diskettes whenever
possible.
- Report any type of unauthorized access, theft, or virus
infection to the Information Security group or the Customer Service Center upon discovery.

9 OFFICE AUTOMATION

Office automation is a catch-all phrase that includes such technologies as
desktop publishing, electronic messaging, electronic-mail, voice-mail, cal-
endars, fax, and other such efficiency tools. With the implementation of
such electronic systems, certain steps must be taken that will provide an
adequate level of security. While each of these systems provides the **user**
greater communications possibilities, they also provide additional risks to
the information they carry. Additionally, the company employs resources
such as interoffice mail, filing cabinets and desks, and long-term records
retention facilities to transport and store information.

9.1 Phone/Voice-Mail

Recommended
Policy: **Confidential** information shall be transmitted via
                       phone/voice-mail only when necessary and only with prop-
                       er controls to safeguard it from unauthorized disclosure.

Recommended
Standard: **Confidential** information is not to be retained in voice-
                       mail boxes.

Recommended
Standard: Voice-mail systems are to be secured with a confidential
                       password known only to the mailbox **owner.**

Recommended
Standard: **Confidential** information must be transmitted with re-
                       ceipt confirmation.

Discussion: Several rules are identified in the *Handbook for Employ-
                       ees, The Company & You* concerning the proper usage of
                       company-provided telephones. As the technologies con-
                       tinue to become more sophisticated, one must ensure
                       that information transmitted over phones and stored in
                       voice-mail boxes is properly controlled with appropriate

password security. Because these systems are targets of phone hackers, passwords should be difficult to guess and **Confidential** information should be removed as soon as possible.

9.2   Standards of Conduct for Electronic Communication

Recommended
Policy:

The Company's policies regarding Employee Standards of Conduct, Conflict of Interest, Equal Employment Opportunity and Diversity in the Workplace, Communication, and Information Protection also apply to electronic messages (e-mail), telephone messages (voice-mail), and other internal and external electronic communications, including, but not limited to, computer bulletin boards, news groups, and the Internet.

Transmitted messages are to be created, handled, distributed, and stored with the same care as any other business document. This includes complying with information-access prohibitions, accessing information only for legitimate business purposes, and protecting information from access by unauthorized persons.

Users should be aware that these systems, and the information stored within them, are the property of the company and are to be used only for company-approved activities. The company maintains the right to monitor the operation of these systems.

Because confidentiality is not assured, these systems are to be used only for transmitting information considered "Public" or for "Internal Use." (The definitions for "Public," "Internal Use," and "Confidential" can be found in the Company Policy on Information Protection.) "Confidential" information should not be communicated using these electronic systems. The company's prohibition of derogatory and offensive comments also applies to messages communicated through these systems. Special care should be given to ensure that the style and tone of messages are appropriate.

Every effort should be made to send messages only to those who "need to know." The Company Policy on Communication details the approvals required before distributing information externally or internally through the use of company mailing lists.

Employees are responsible for using these systems appropriately. Inappropriate use could result in disciplinary action.

Recommended
Standard: **Confidential** information is not to be retained in electronic-mail boxes.

Electronic-mail systems are to be secured with a confidential password known only to the mailbox **owner.**

Confidential information should be transmitted with receipt confirmation.

Discussion: As with phone/voice-mail systems, the technologies continue to become more sophisticated. Consequently, one must ensure that information transmitted and stored in electronic-mail boxes is properly controlled with appropriate password security. Because these systems are targets of computer hackers, passwords should be difficult to guess, and **Confidential** information should be removed as soon as possible.

9.3   Cellular Phones

Recommended
Policy: **Confidential** information should not be discussed on cellular phones.

Discussion: Cellular or wireless phones broadcast conversations via radio waves that are subject to interception by inexpensive devices readily available from any electronics store. One of the legal tests for **Confidential** information is the organization's efforts to keep the information secret. By discussing **Confidential** information over a cellular or wireless telephone, the test of secrecy is lost. From a legal point of view, there is no expectation of privacy, because the sender is unable to determine who is actually gaining access to the information. Whenever in custody of **Confidential** information, it is essential that this information not be discussed on these devices.

9.4   Fax Machines

Recommended
Policy: Special precautions are to be taken when faxing **Confidential** information.

Recommended
Standard: Send **Confidential** information by fax only when the authorized recipient is the only person who can access it.

Discussion: Sending information via fax machines can compromise the secrecy of the information. Often, faxed documents are left at the receiving station for hours, thus allowing anyone who wanders by the opportunity to view the information. If sending **Confidential** information by fax cannot be avoided, it is critical that the intended recipient be informed by phone that the information is being sent so he or she can attend the fax station during transmission. This will ensure that only the intended recipient has received the transmission.

9.5 Interoffice Mail

Recommended
Policy: Special precautions are to be taken when sending **Confidential** information by interoffice mail to ensure confidentiality is maintained.

Recommended
Procedure: When transporting **Confidential** information by interoffice mail, the envelope is to carry no labeling to indicate its contents contain **Confidential** information; however, the first page of the document or cover sheet must clearly label the document as **Confidential**.

Recommended
Guideline: When needing to send **Confidential** information, the sender should consider having the information delivered by a trusted courier rather than by interoffice mail.

 The sender of critical information should consider use of a "Valuable Letter Receipt" to request confirmation of receipt by the intended recipient.

Discussion: When employing interoffice mail, the document will pass through several hands and be left unattended many times during the process of delivery. The interoffice couriers, mailroom sorters, and secretaries or office specialists will all have a hand in delivering a document to the recipient. It is important to avoid specifically labeling the envelope during this process. When one identifies the contents of the envelope as containing **Confidential** information, one attracts the attention of the curious. By avoiding external labeling, the envelope looks like any other.

9.6   Office File Cabinets and Desks

Recommended
Policy: Information contained in office file cabinets and desks
                   must be adequately protected against unauthorized ac-
                   cess.

Recommended
Standard: File cabinets and desks containing **Confidential** informa-
                   tion are to be locked when no one is in attendance.

Discussion: File cabinets and desks hold a significant amount of infor-
                   mation that one uses daily in the performance of any busi-
                   ness function. Whether the information is classified as
                   Confidential or **Internal Use**, this information requires
                   the same level of security one might expect is provided to
                   computer-based information. Confidentiality, integrity,
                   and availability considerations are just as critical; but be-
                   cause this information is always so close at hand, one of-
                   ten ignores its value to the operation. It is necessary to
                   consider the disruption that loss of this information
                   could cause and take prudent steps to ensure its security.

9.7   Records Management

Corporate
Policy: Organization management is responsible for the identifi-
                   cation of records required to meet regulatory require-
                   ments and operations needs, and the establishment of
                   retention and destruction guidelines for each type of
                   record. (From: Company Policy on Information Manage-
                   ment)

Recommended
Standard: The official copy of information, regardless of media, is to
                   be promptly destroyed upon expiration of the retention
                   period unless precluded by pending litigation or investi-
                   gation.

                   At least annually, the organizational unit shall verify that
                   records are being retained according to the organization-
                   al unit's established program.

Recommended
Guideline: Organizations should work jointly with Business Services
                   (Records Management) to identify statutory require-
                   ments for records retention.

Chapter 17
Information Security Program Administration

1 INTRODUCTION

Publishing a set of policies and procedures is no assurance that anyone will ever read them. Creating an employee awareness program is necessary to bring the information security message to all employees. Before employees can accept an Information Security (IS) program, they must first understand why the program is necessary and what they will gain from its implementation.

To ensure that all employees have access to Information Security support, representatives from each unit throughout the company have been selected and trained in presenting this program to the employees within their organization. To facilitate this process, a structure has been established to administer the program, its direction and scope.

2 CORPORATE INFORMATION SYSTEMS STEERING COMMITTEE

This committee, consisting of senior management, was established to effectively capitalize on available and emerging information technologies to improve efficiency and effectiveness to meet the competitive challenges that lie ahead. This group has approved and supports the vision and goals of the Information Security program. They provide guidance, ensuring that the program is consistent with company goals, measures, and targets. They ensure the availability of resources necessary for successful implementation and maintenance of the program.

3 CORPORATE INFORMATION SECURITY PROGRAM

3.1 Corporate Information Security Manager

This individual will support and direct the corporate Information Security program. This will be accomplished by ensuring that necessary resources are available.

3.2   Corporate Information Security Coordinator

This individual is responsible for maintenance of the program's vision, goals, and elements, and for proposing necessary changes to the IS Steering Committee for approval. This individual will train and coordinate the organization IS coordinators, supporting them with regular contact, information security awareness tools, consultation, and ideas. To ensure progress throughout the IS program life cycle, this individual will monitor each organizational unit's progress and keep the Corporate IS Manager updated. The Supervisor of the Information Security group has been charged with this responsibility.

4   ORGANIZATION INFORMATION SECURITY PROGRAM

4.1   Organization Management

Organization management has a large impact on the effectiveness of the Corporate IS Program. They will be asked to promote the program by providing appropriate staff and other resources to ensure security of corporate information assets. It is crucial that they also support their organization IS coordinators in the development and maintenance of a local information security program.

4.2   Information Security Coordinators

4.2.1 Organization Coordinators. An Organization Information Security Coordinator is appointed by organization management to develop, implement, and maintain an organization IS program consistent with corporate and organization objectives. These individuals should meet with organization personnel at least semi-annually to build their awareness of information security issues, responsibilities, and solutions. They act as liaison with the Corporate IS Coordinator to report the progress and activities concerning the organization IS program. The Organization IS Coordinator, together with the Corporate IS Coordinator, comprise the Corporate IS Team.

4.2.2 Group Coordinators (Optional). Group Information Security Coordinators assist the Organization IS Coordinator in large organizations. Group IS Coordinators are appointed by the management of groups within an organization to perform group-level duties that support the organization IS program. These individuals should perform group-level information risk assessments and may meet with group personnel to build their awareness of information security issues. They act as liaison with the Organization IS Coordinator to report the progress and activities concerning the group's IS activities. The Group IS Coordinator, together with the Organization IS Coordinator, comprise the Organization IS Team.

4.2.3 Area Coordinators (Optional). Area Information Security Coordinators assist the Group IS Coordinator in large groups within an organization. Area IS Coordinators are appointed by the management of areas within a group to perform area-level duties that support the organization IS program. These individuals should perform area-level information risk assessments and may meet with area personnel to build their awareness of information security issues. They act as liaison with the Group IS Coordinator to report the progress and activities concerning the area's IS activities. The Area IS Coordinator, together with the Group IS Coordinator, comprise the Group IS Team.

Chapter 18
Baseline Organization Information Security Program

1 INTRODUCTION

Information Management Policy states:

> Each manager shall develop and administer an Information Security program that appropriately classifies and protects corporate information under their control and makes employees aware of the importance of information and methods for its security.

Management has appointed Organization Information Security Coordinators (OISCs) to administer the programs for their organizations. Larger organizations have also appointed Group Information Security Coordinators (GISCs) and Area Information Security Coordinators (AISCs) to assist the OISC.

This section of the Information Security Reference Guide is designed to assist IS coordinators with the development, implementation, and maintenance of their Information Security program. Each section below is formatted to supply background information and instruction. *Baseline Program Recommendations* are supplied to serve as possible starting points. Some *how-to* sections are also provided.

Contact the Corporate Information Security Coordinator if you have any questions or require additional guidance.

2 PRE-PROGRAM DEVELOPMENT

2.1 Designing Your Organization's Program

What is an Information Security program? An IS program is a series of actions that:

- Identifies information requiring security
- Develops methods to protect the information
- Documents security methods in a plan that includes specific security goals
- Organizes resources to implement security methods
- Implements and maintains security methods
- Provides security guidance through policy and awareness activities
- Monitors security method and program effectiveness
- Reports plans, progress, and effectiveness to management

The purpose of the IS program is to protect the value of an important business asset — corporate information.

Where should you start? Consider those areas that are going to produce noticeable, short-range results and will make a significant contribution to management's overall objectives. The new program should also promote activities that:

- Have high visibility
- Have a high chance of success
- Can produce high returns on relatively low investments

If there is a near and present danger such as frequent disclosure of confidential information, unavailability of critical information, or proliferation of computer viruses, then the program must address those problems quickly.

The Information Security program is not something apart from the company's business. It is a business activity that supports the business. As with any business activity, the program must make good business sense. Table 1 shows two important business sense requirements that the program must meet.

A program that fails to meet these requirements has no valid reason to exist as part of the business.

An effective and efficient Information Security program is one that provides the highest level of security that is consistent with an organization's requirements for productivity and cost-effectiveness. The program must have a strong organization identification and fit into the organization's environment, culture, and objectives.

Table 1. Business Sense Requirements

1. The *cost* of the program should never exceed the *value* of the information that it protects.
2. The *goals* of the program should be clearly aligned with, and supportive of, the goals of the organization.

Last, the program must *enable* employees by ensuring that the information they need is as accurate and available as required by the organization. The program must not disable them by protecting information to the extent that employees cannot use it. Ultimately, organization management must determine the proper level of security required.

2.1.1 Orienting the Program toward Business Goals. An Information Security program oriented toward business goals should:

- Concentrate mostly on protecting the information that supports the organization's *critical* business functions
- Be structured to avoid the effects that loss of integrity, confidentiality, or availability of information resources will produce on these critical functions
- Offer preventive and reactive measures that are based on a business rationale

Repeating — the program must be business justified. **It must improve your organization's business.**

2.2   A Phased Approach to the Program Process

As the organization's program is developed, take a phased approach. Convince management to allow *adequate time* to develop the program properly. Maintaining a program is a *process*, not an event. Program projects start and end, but the program does not.

Program phasing is a useful method that allows one to take a step-by-step approach toward implementation of the program elements. There are three types of phasing. The one that works best depends on how information is processed in an organization.

Functional Phasing: Functional phasing involves a series of program steps, each of which is carried out throughout the entire target organization before the next step is taken.

Organizational Phasing: With organizational, or group, phasing, one completes the entire process in one group before going on to the next. This may be required by management so that they can see the effect of the program on a test business unit before going on to other groups.

Hybrid Phasing: Hybrid phasing is a combination of the first two types of phasing. It can appear in many variations.

Baseline Program Recommendation. Use Functional Phasing. The guidance supplied in this section of the ISRG takes this approach by breaking the process into three sequential phases:

1. Program Development phase

2. Program Implementation phase
3. Program Maintenance phase

2.3   Getting Assistance

Before getting into program development, always remember — **you are not alone.** There are several employees like yourself who have been given the task of developing a program for their organization. Very few had any experience with Information Security before the responsibility was assigned to them.

Baseline Program Recommendation. Contact the areas below to get help with Information Security or program development.

- Corporate Information Security Coordinator
- Internal Audit
- Fellow Organization Information Security Coordinators

3   PROGRAM DEVELOPMENT PHASE

The development phase of the organization Information Security program includes determination of the program scope, assessment of the information environment, and development of the program elements (policies and procedures, controls, business continuity plan, awareness program, effectiveness monitoring).

3.1   Determining Initial Program Scope and Obtaining Approval

Before assessment can begin, the scope of the program must be identified. Will it include one group, several groups, or the entire organization? If not applied to the entire organization, what is the sequence of implementation? Will some groups or some information types be excluded from the Information Security program? These questions should be answered with input, support, and approval of organization management.

By approving the Information Security Policy and the Corporate Information Security Program, Senior Management has expressed its commitment to the implementation of the security program. What will be important to you is to create a program that meets your organization's business needs and fulfills the requirements of the Corporate Policy on Information Protection.

To meet the expectations of management, it is necessary to understand the business objectives and directions of the organization. Before beginning to develop the organization's program, take a little time and establish where the organization is headed and what the goals and objectives are for the coming year. The program should complement the established business objectives. Once the organization's program is developed, it will be necessary to present the program to management for their review and approval. This approval process should be documented.

Baseline Program Recommendation.

1. Contact the Corporate Information Security Coordinator for help in preparing for meetings with organization and group management.
2. Determine who in organization management must approve initial program activities and the finished program.
3. Establish a draft program scope.
4. Meet with organization (top) management.
   a. Describe the need for them to provide guidance so that the scope of the program can be established.
   b. Request the appointment of Group Information Security Coordinators for large groups, or for groups that may require extensive Information Security activities. (The IS coordinators comprise the organization IS team.)
   c. Describe the assessment process (see below) that will be used with each group.
   d. Have them identify the groups where program implementation will take place. If some will be initially exempt, ask management to identify the date of their inclusion.
   e. Have management identify the *organization* information resources that will be included. If some will be initially exempt, ask management to identify the date of their inclusion.
5. Determine who in group (lower) management must approve the initial program activities and the finished program.
6. Meet with the organization IS team to discuss the information assessment.
7. Meet with group management where information assessment is planned. (Work with Group Information Security Coordinators if they have been appointed.)
   a. Explain the assessment process and request their support and assistance. (This is a good time to describe the advantages of cost-effective security of *this group's* information.)
   b. Have management identify the *group* information resources that will be included. If some will be initially exempt, ask management to identify the date of their inclusion.
   c. Have management identify the **owners, custodians,** and **users** of the information resources. Where none are designated, work with management to establish them.
   d. Have management identify other organizations that may be involved and the nature of their involvement.
8. Provide reports to organization management indicating status of meetings with group management, listing exclusions and dates the

exclusions will be addressed. (Forward a copy to the Corporate Information Security Coordinator.)

9. Provide semiannual progress reports to organization and group management. (Forward a copy to the Corporate Information Security Coordinator.)

3.2 Assessing the Information Environment

The early steps of the program consist of fact gathering and assessment. Before any program can begin, it is important to identify the organization's information and the impact on the business process if the information was modified, destroyed, or disclosed in an unauthorized or undesirable manner. Therefore, it will be necessary to assess the information within the organization. This will require an understanding of how the organization functions.

3.2.1 Identifying Critical Systems Applications and Confidential Information.

What is meant by a *critical system*? A critical system is defined as any system that, if unavailable, would seriously impair the ability of an organization to perform key business functions. The designation *Critical* is **not** one of the official classification categories defined in the Information Clarification Policy. It is an indicator of how important the system is to conducting business. Generally speaking, employees understand the need to protect information classified as **Confidential**, but are sometimes confused over the need to protect critical systems and applications.

The highest information classification level at the company is **Confidential**. Confidential information is defined as any information that, if disclosed, could violate the privacy of individuals, reduce the company's competitive advantage, or cause damage to the company (monetarily, legally, public perception, customer and shareholder confidence, etc.).

Two key questions must be answered when determining if information is confidential. The first questions is — what would be the impact on the company if the information was disclosed? If there is a high risk of loss of privacy, competitive advantage, or damage, then the information should be classified as **Confidential**. The second question to be answered is — how many individuals will need access in order to perform their jobs? A key requirement of confidential information is the ability to keep the information secret both internally and externally. The greater the number of employees requiring access to the information, the less likely that it will be kept secret. If this is the case, then a special subclassification could be established for the organization. This would allow an organization to add a category that meets its needs. The special classification category would fall under an existing classification category and would allow for tighter controls than identified by corporate policy.

Appendix 2A contains a worksheet that could be useful when identifying information, its confidentiality, and its criticality.

3.2.2 Assessing Risk. What is *risk assessment*? Risk assessment is a method for determining the likelihood and impact of loss of information integrity, availability, and confidentiality. The risk assessment method includes information asset valuation and identification of threats to, and vulnerabilities of, the target information.

Why do a risk assessment? The assessment will result in a prioritized list of the information most at risk and which could cause unacceptable losses to the business. The prioritized list provides direction as to where Information Security controls should be applied first and how much to spend on the controls. The assessment results should be reported to management to allow them to make fact-based decisions and provide approval for controls to be implemented. Management will not approve controls for all risks. Where this occurs, management's reasons should be documented for future reference and planning.

The first step in this process is to identify the information assets within the organization. This would not only include information created within the organization, but also any information used by employees. One will want to include such items as databases, spreadsheets, original source documents, bid responses, signature cards, etc. Include all information, regardless of how it is created or the media on which it is stored.

Once the information assets have been identified, consider their impact on the organization. In traditional risk analysis, there are three types of impact:

1. Unauthorized or undesirable modification of information (loss of integrity)
2. Unauthorized or undesirable destruction of, or denial of access to, information (loss of availability)
3. Unauthorized or undesirable disclosure of information (loss of confidentiality)

Each of these impact types can be accidental or intentional. Take a look at threats, vulnerabilities, and loss.

Identifying threats. Threats are any activities or events that, under certain conditions, could jeopardize the integrity, availability, or confidentiality of information. Threats can be natural (storms, floods, lightning, rodents) or manmade (theft, vandalism, electrical fire). The possible threats to each type of information must be identified.
Identifying vulnerabilities. Vulnerabilities are conditions that could allow threats to cause loss of information integrity, availability, or confidentiality. If there is no vulnerability, the existence of a threat is immaterial because the threat cannot cause a loss. Identifying

vulnerabilities is the process of estimating the likelihood that the threats will cause loss of information integrity, availability, or confidentiality. The vulnerability of each type of information must be identified.

Identifying loss impact. Loss impact is the effect on the business when a vulnerability allows information integrity, availability, or confidentiality to be compromised. Loss impact should be identified as a dollar estimate. Loss impacts must be identified.

3.2.3 Identifying Security Controls. Information Security controls are measures that are designed to minimize or eliminate a vulnerability. For each type of information, the risk assessment should identify the likelihood and magnitude of losses that the business could experience. Naturally, the greatest concern should be for information that has high vulnerability and high loss impact. This is where controls should be applied first. The control should be designed to minimize the probability that the vulnerability will occur. The cost of the control should be governed by the loss impact of the vulnerability. It makes good business sense to spend $100 per year to prevent a likely $1000 loss over the same period.

A typical control is to ensure that only employees with a business need are given access to confidential information. Another control would be to establish a systematic backup process for spreadsheets used by the department. When establishing controls, remember that the key element is to ensure that the business process can function while limiting vulnerability and losses to an acceptable level. Controls are discussed in later sections.

Baseline Program Recommendation.

1. Identify the organization's information resources using the Information Identification Worksheet in Appendix 2A. (The worksheet will help document the organization's business functions, and the identification, classification, criticality, and **owner** of the information supporting the business functions.)
2. Identify the risk to the organization's information resources (identified in 1 above) using the Information Risk Assessment Worksheet in Appendix 2A. (The worksheet will help identify and document the threats to, vulnerabilities of, and loss impact of each type of the organization's information.)
3. Identify recommended Information Security controls.
4. Transfer data from the Information Identification Worksheet and the Information Risk Assessment Worksheet to the Summary and Controls Worksheet in Appendix 2A. Prioritize the implementation order of the recommended controls based on the information's

classification, criticality, vulnerability, and loss impact; and on the priority of the business function that the information supports.

5. Additional assessment data can be developed by completing the Self-Assessment Questionnaire in Appendix 2A. (This questionnaire identifies specific controls that should be addressed by the program. Take the document and modify it for your own use. As part of the initial program, the questionnaire is to be completed by each OISC and the results submitted to the CISC. Questionnaire results can be used in the future as a benchmark to monitor how well the organization's program is progressing.)

3.3   Developing the Program Elements

The sections below describe the major elements of the program. These include:

- Program Plan
- Policies and Procedures
- Controls
- Awareness
- Effectiveness Monitoring

The descriptions contained in each section are recommended starting points. Each organization must decide how they should be applied to best protect their business information.

3.3.1 Program Administration. The first organization program element is program administration. This element provides direction for the program and is critical to its success.

3.3.1.1 Organization Management. Organization management is required to appoint an Organization Information Security Coordinator (OISC) to oversee the program. In larger organizations, management may also appoint Group Information Security Coordinators (GISCs) to assist the OISC. Together, they form the **Organization Information Security Team**.

In addition to appointing coordinators, a successful program depends on management to do the following:

- Management should demonstrate and communicate an active interest in having an effective program.
- Management should put the program under the authority of people who have the skills and motivation to make it work.
- Management should provide money and resources.
- Management should support the recommendations of the Organization Information Security Team.

3.3.1.2 Organization Information Security Team. The Organization Information Security Team is a group appointed by management to administer the organization's program. The team may have one or more Organization Information Security Coordinators and several Group Information Security Coordinators. Normally, the OISC will be responsible for most or all of an organization, while the GISC will be responsible for one or more groups within the organization. Organizations with many groups will have several GISCs. Large groups within the organization may have Area Information Security Coordinators (AISCs) supporting the GISC. The qualifications and duties of all coordinators are similar.

IS Coordinator Qualifications — A **Company** employee who:

- Has broad familiarity with the organization or group, which allows him or her to understand its Information Security needs and concerns
- Has easy access to all levels of management in the organization or group
- Is familiar with information technologies
- Has good presentation and speaking skills

IS Coordinator Responsibilities include:

- Attending training conducted by the Corporate Information Security Coordinator
- Working with organization and group management to develop, implement, and maintain an Information Security program consistent with the corporate program
- OISCs meeting with GISCs, and GISCs meeting with AISCs on a regular basis to develop their Information Security responsibilities
- Conducting Information Security awareness sessions on a regular basis in area of responsibility
- OISCs keeping the Corporate Information Security Coordinator informed of progress and activities concerning the development and maintenance of the organization Information Security program. GISCs do the same, but keep the OISC informed. AISCs do the same, but keep the GISC informed.

Typical IS Coordinator Commitment:

- Development Phase (8–12 weeks) — OISC less than half-time, GISC less than quarter-time, AISC less than ten percent of time.
- Implementation Phase (8–12 weeks) — OISC less than half-time, GISC less than quarter-time, AISC less than ten percent of time.
- Maintenance Phase (ongoing) — OISC two to four hours per week, GISC two to four hours per week, AISC one hour per week.

Information on the Corporate Information Security Team and its relation to the Organization Information Security Team can be found in Chapter 17.

3.3.1.3 Organization Information Security Program Plan. The plan documents the purpose and goals of the organization program. The plan should be:

- Initially written by the OISC with the assistance of the organization's IS team
- Reviewed and revised annually, preferably early in the year prior to budget submission, by the OISC and the organization IS team
- Approved by organization management prior to release and implementation
- Compatible with and supportive of the corporate IS plan

A final approved copy of the annual program plan should be forwarded to the Corporate Information Security Coordinator.

The program plan should contain a mission statement, program objectives, and program goals.

Program Mission Statement

The mission statement defines the role of, and the need for, the organization IS program. It also serves to notify management and organization employees as to the overall direction of the program.

Baseline Program Recommendation

Here are two sample IS program mission statements.

- To provide cost-effective security for organization information assets to ensure their availability, integrity, and confidentiality; and to protect management from charges of imprudence in the security of information assets.
- To ensure that organization information resources are protected in a manner that is cost effective and reduces the risk of information loss, modification, or disclosure to a level that is acceptable to management.

Program Objectives

The objectives are general descriptions that define what the program is designed to do for the organization.

Baseline Program Recommendation

Basic program objectives include:

- Protect and ensure the accuracy and integrity of information.
- Protect sensitive, confidential, and competitive information from unauthorized disclosure.

- Provide security from acts that would cause destruction of information.
- Maintain organization Information Security policies and procedures.
- Maintain an organization information security awareness program.
- Maintain organization group business information continuity plans.
- Provide organization groups with direction and technical support to ensure the availability, integrity, and confidentiality of corporate information.
- Ensure the ability of the organization to continue business after disasters.

Additional Program Recommendations

Additional program objectives include:

- Submit an annual information security budget.
- Provide recommendations to organization groups on how to develop and maintain policies and procedures.
- Provide information security awareness sessions and materials to organization groups.
- Provide and recommend cost-effective information security measures.
- Maintain a high-performance Information Security program that achieves the balance of security and productivity desired by management.
- Build a comprehensive Information Security environment capable of meeting the changing needs of internal and external customers.
- Ensure management awareness of the need to protect information, and their support in development of policies.
- Identify and bring to management's attention possible vulnerabilities relating to the security of information assets.
- Protect management from charges of imprudence in the event of a compromise of information security.
- Monitor laws and regulations, utility industry activities, and the Information Security industry for changes that may affect the security of information assets.

Program Goals

The program goals are usually more detailed than the program objectives and should contain measurable targets. It is recommended that both one-year and two-year goals be developed. But remember Business Sense Requirement #2: "The goals of the program should be clearly aligned with, and supportive of, the goals of the organization." Goals are first established when the program is initially implemented and should be reviewed and rewritten at the start of each year.

Baseline Program Recommendation

Some sample one-year goals for a **new program** include:

- Establish an Organization Information Security Team by (*date*).
- Develop and implement organization Information Security policies and procedures and document them in an organization policies and procedures manual by (*date*).
- Develop and implement an organization Information Security awareness program by (*date*).
- Develop and implement organization business information continuity plans by (*date*).
  - Perform an initial assessment of the organization's information environment by (*date*). It should identify:
    - Information that is sensitive or critical to business functions
- Information most at risk to unauthorized access, modification, disclosure, or destruction
- Develop and implement Information Security controls by (*date*).
- Develop methods to monitor for compliance to policy by (*date*).
- Develop methods by (*date*) to encourage compliance (rewards) and discourage noncompliance (enforcement) to policy.

Some sample program goals for an **established program** include:

- Review and maintain the organization Information Security policies and procedures manual.
- Review and maintain the organization Information Security awareness program.
- Review and maintain organization business information continuity plans.
- Perform reassessment of the organization's information environment to identify:
  - Information that has become, or no longer is, sensitive or critical to business functions
  - Information that has become, or no longer is, at risk to unauthorized access, modification, disclosure, or destruction
- Review and maintain Information Security controls.
- Monitor for compliance to policy.
- Encourage compliance (rewards) and discourage noncompliance (enforcement) to policy.
- Evaluate new Information Security technologies.

3.3.1.4 Organization Information Security Program Budget. Organization information assets cannot be protected unless resources are provided by management. The largest cost will be for IS coordinator labor hours required to administer the program and to develop, implement,

Table 2.   Sample Organization 1995 Budget Estimate

Item	OISC (1)	GISC (3)	AISC (6)	Item Total
O & M budget:				
Part-time labor	$2000	$6,000	$6,000	$12,000
Vendor training	$2500	$7,500	$0	$10,000
Professional memberships	$150	$450	$0	$600
Capital budget:				
Awareness materials	(videos, posters, pamphlets, etc.)			$1,000
Physical access controls	(file cabinets, disk storage boxes)			$1,000
PC/Mac access controls	(software for 50 computers)			$2,500
PC/Mac virus security	(software for 50 computers)			$2,500
	Total			$29,600

and maintain Information Security policy, awareness, controls, and compliance monitoring. Some cost, however, will be incurred for educational resources (books, magazines), training, awareness materials (videos, posters, pamphlets), and technical controls such as computer access control and virus-scanning software. As a result, Information Security costs will primarily be Operations and Maintenance (O&M) budget items, along with some Capital budget items.

The IS budget should be prepared and submitted with the organization's other budgets. The budget should include the two-year goals described in the Organization IS Plan prepared earlier in the year.

As one prepares the budget, do not forget Business Sense Requirement #1: "The cost of the program should never exceed the value of the information that it protects." The value, or criticality, of the information being protected should be determined, or at least estimated, as part of the self-assessment (described above) or the business impact analysis (described below).

Baseline Program Recommendation

Table 2 displays a 1995 budget estimate for a sample organization with one OISC, three GISCs, six AISCs, and fifty PC/Mac computers. OISCs and GISCs spend two hours per week, and AISCs spend one hour per week on Information Security.

This sample organization should plan on a *total* IS expense of $30,000 per year. Because 40 percent of the cost is for part-time labor (no additional personnel hired), the actual additional cost to this sample organization is approximately $18,000. It should be easy to show that the value of this organization's information is much greater than the amount spent next year to protect it.

3.3.2 Developing Organization Policies and Procedures. Policies and procedures are the foundation of the IS program. Their purpose is to clearly communicate consistent, effective, and efficient guidance throughout the organization. Organizations should develop their own policies and procedures under the following conditions:

- Where there is a clear business need to provide employees with guidance
- When adequate guidance is not already provided from other sources

In addition to policies and procedures, organizations may find it necessary to develop standards and guidelines as well. Below are some definitions to provide consistency and understanding.

Policy: A general statement that provides direction and establishes the basic philosophy of the organization in areas where controls must be established. Compliance with policy should be mandatory.

Standard: A statement of design or implementation that is a norm for measurement. Use of standards is usually restricted to situations where performance to a specific measurement is required. Compliance with standards should be mandatory.

Procedure: How-to instructions presented in a series of steps that support some part of a policy or standard. Compliance with procedures should be mandatory, with some method for seeking variance.

Guideline: How-to instructions that are an outline of policy and that support some part of a policy or standard. Guidelines should be advisory and allow some level of local option or management interpretation.

The need for policies, procedures, standards, and guidelines can be identified by the IS self-assessment and by reported damage to information assets (incident reports).

Some tips to help with the development effort include:

1. Before you start:
   a. Know organization culture.
   b. Determine the level of control allowed in the organization.
   c. Obtain existing policies, procedures, standards, and guidelines.
   d. Determine who writes them.
   e. Determine if there is a real business need to give employees guidance.
   f. Justify the need by using information assessment results and incident reports.

2. When you start:
   a. Identify the audience.
   b. Make it clear; use simplest appropriate wording.
   c. Avoid absolutes (all, never, always, etc.).
   d. Determine the objective.
   e. Determine the scope.
   f. Determine the purpose.
   g. Provide definitions where necessary.
   h. Identify responsibilities.
   i. Identify who, if any, are exempt from requirements.
   j. Record revision date.
3. Use the checklist in Table 3 after writing the first draft.
4. Finally:
   a. Have organization IS team review the document and provide comments.
   b. Make revisions to include accepted comments.
   c. Obtain management approval.

Table 3. Document Checklist

For a POLICY, STANDARD, GUIDELINE, or PROCEDURE; does the document:

☐ Meet the stated objective?
☐ Clearly describe WHO is responsible to perform desired behavior?
☐ Clearly describe WHEN the behavior is expected?
☐ Clearly describe who is exempt, when, and why? (If required)
☐ Contain simple, unambiguous, and appropriate wording?
☐ Contain proper wording for the intended audience?
☐ Fit the level of control acceptable in the organization?

For a POLICY or STANDARD, does the document also:

☐ Clearly describe WHAT behavior is expected?
☐ Clearly describe WHY the behavior is expected? (Optional, depends on culture)

For a STANDARD, does the document also:

☐ Clearly describe HOW MUCH security is expected?

For a GUIDELINE or PROCEDURE, does the document also:

☐ Clearly describe HOW TO attain the expected behavior?

Baseline Program Recommendation

Refer to Chapters 11 through 16 of this guide to obtain recommended policies, standards, procedures, and guidelines for specific IS subject areas. It is recommended that each organization develop policies in the following areas:

- Business continuity planning (Chapter 11, Section 2)
- Information classification (Chapter 13)
- Information handling, labeling, etc. (Chapters 14, 16, and Appendix 2A)
- Information backup and recovery (Chapter 15)
- Desktop processing (Chapter 16)
- Monitor and control of proprietary software (Chapter 16)

Organizations that develop several IS policies, procedures, standards, and guidelines should consider organizing them into an IS policy manual.

For additional help, contact the Corporate Information Security Coordinator.

3.3.3 Developing the Awareness Program. Many employees will approach the new IS program with concern that it will inhibit their job activities. Some will not understand why it is necessary to implement such a program now — "After all, haven't we been doing fine up until now?" When the program is presented to the employees, be prepared to answer such questions. An awareness program is actually a sales pitch. Remember that the employees already know what is expected in the workplace. The goal is to remind them that information asset security is part of that process.

The awareness program is a management control rather than a technical control. The value of awareness is made clear in the following quote.

> The secret to enforcement is prevention, and the key to prevention is education.
>
> **— R. Wallace Hale**

Employees must be educated, or made aware, that they will be expected to protect information. Education increases their insight and understanding and teaches why they should protect information. Employees must also be told what to protect, when to protect, and how they should protect information assets. One wants to be sure that no one thinks that security is the coordinator's or some other employee's responsibility. All employees, including contract employees, are part of the Information Security process.

The utility business environment is changing. In the past, utilities were able to share information freely. As the business world heads into deregulation, competitiveness will require the **company** to protect some information from disclosure to other utilities. Conducting business as in the past will not allow us to meet the needs of the future. With more and more people having access to company information, it will be necessary to have the proper controls in place to protect the interests of the **company**. The first presentation in the awareness program could be designed to show employees that disclosure of, or unauthorized access to, business-sensitive information could happen in one's own organization.

The Corporate Information Security Coordinator has developed some tools that can be used by one's organization in implementing an employee awareness program. Videotapes, posters, brochures, and other such materials will be available for the program.

Baseline Program Recommendation

1. Refer to the results of your information assessment and identify problem areas in the organization. Target these areas as topics for awareness sessions.
2. Include organization policies as a topic for an awareness session.
3. Ask management for awareness session topics.
4. Include the awareness session schedule in the Organization Information Security Plan.
5. Contact the Corporate Information Security Coordinator for assistance in developing the awareness program.

3.3.4 Developing Information Security Controls. Information Security controls can be separated into two types: management controls and technical controls. Already discussed were management controls in the form of program administration, plans, budgets, awareness, and policies. Other management controls, which are covered below, include business continuity planning, awareness, and compliance monitoring. Technical controls include physical access controls such as locked file cabinets or locked computer keyboards. Technical controls also include software to prevent computer and file access, software to detect and remove computer viruses, software to check that proper passwords are being used, and software to manage computer security.

3.3.4.1 Developing the Business Continuity Plan. The business continuity plan (BCP) is a management-type control to ensure that *critical business functions* can be performed after a disruption of normal business operations. The scope of the BCP includes activities that should be performed before, during, and after such a disruption to business. But what does this have to do with Information Security? Many critical business functions are dependent on the availability of information assets. Each organization IS team should coordinate the development of a BCP that identifies the organization's critical business functions and the information required by those functions. Before writing the plan, a business impact analysis should be done.

346

Performing a Business Impact Analysis

The purpose of a business impact analysis (BIA) is to determine the effect on the organization of loss of critical business functions. The critical business functions directly support the primary goals of the organization and enable the fulfillment of its Value-Added Role.

How-to: (See Information Identification Worksheet, Appendix 2A)

1. Identify the organization's critical business functions.
2. Establish the priority of each critical business function.
3. Determine how long the organization can do without each critical business function.
4. Identify the resources, especially information resources, required to support the critical business functions.
5. Estimate the tangible and intangible impacts on the organization of loss of each critical business function.

One may notice that the business impact analysis is similar to the information risk assessment described earlier. The main difference is that a threat-vulnerability analysis is not performed here.

Writing the Business Continuity Plan

A business continuity plan usually includes four major sections: preventive measures, continuity measures, exercising the plan, and plan maintenance.

How-to:

1. Develop and document the **Preventive Measures**. These include the actions that should be taken *before* a business disruption occurs. Preventive measures are of three types:
   a. Measures that prevent events that could cause loss of critical business functions. Examples include safety measures that prevent injury to personnel and housekeeping measures that prevent fires or damage to equipment.
   b. Measures that minimize negative effects to critical business functions if disruptions occur. Examples include personnel evacuation procedures and fire detection and suppression systems.
   c. Measures that allow restoration of critical business functions if disruptions occur. Examples include having backup personnel trained and copies of documentation, software, and data stored off-site that are periodically updated and available when needed.
2. Develop and document the **Continuity Measures**. These include the actions that should be taken both *during* and *after* a business disruption occurs. Continuity measures are divided into three phases:
   a. Emergency phase measures: procedures that describe actions to be taken during and immediately after disruptions to critical business functions.

    b. Backup phase measures: procedures that allow critical business functions to be performed in a minimal, temporary environment after a disruption occurs.

    c. Recovery phase measures: procedures that provide restoration of the normal business environment and the restarting of business operations in the normal environment.

3. Develop and document procedures to **Exercise the Plan**. To be sure that the procedures in the plan will achieve the desired results, portions of the plan must be exercised (tested) periodically. This requires that procedures and scenarios be devised to exercise the plan.

4. Develop and document procedures to **Maintain the Plan**. The plan must be updated periodically to reflect changes in the business environment and to include required revisions that were identified during plan exercises. The person responsible for review of the plan and the length of time between plan review and revision should be documented.

Additional information on business continuity planning can be found in Chapter 11 or by contacting Information Security and Disaster Recovery Planning.

Baseline Program Recommendation

1. Identify the organization's primary goals or objectives.
2. Perform a business impact analysis. (See Performing a Business Impact Analysis below.)
3. Develop a business continuity plan. (See above: "Organization Information Security Program Plan" and "Writing the Business Continuity Plan.")

3.3.4.2 Common Technical Controls. Technical controls are methods that can be applied to prevent or minimize the loss of information availability, integrity, and confidentiality. Effective technical controls cannot be easily bypassed and are applied when management controls such as policy and awareness either fail to produce desired results or are less cost effective than technical controls.

A detailed discussion of all of the types of technical controls available is beyond the scope of this guide. Even so, some of the technical controls described earlier in this guide are: information handling (Chapters 14, 16, and Appendix 2A), access controls and backing up information (Chapter 15), virus security and licensing agreements (Chapter 16), and encryption (Appendix 2A). More information can be obtained from the Corporate Information Security Coordinator.

Baseline Program Recommendation

1. Refer to the results of your information assessment and identify where technical controls can be useful and cost effective.
2. Provide locks for file cabinets and rooms where information is stored.
3. Provide access control software for computers.
4. Provide easy-to-use backup methods such as making copies of documents, software, and data and storing them in a safe place away from the primary copies.
5. Provide virus-scanning software for desktop computers. This may be available from the Corporate Information Security Coordinator.

3.3.5 Developing Effectiveness Monitoring. It is important that IS coordinators and employees understand that management follows up on approved plans and programs. This follow-up is achieved through effectiveness monitoring. Effectiveness monitoring, or compliance monitoring, is another management-type control. There are two primary things that should be monitored for effectiveness: the *Information Security program* itself and the *controls*, both management and technical, that the program has implemented.

Program effectiveness can be demonstrated by achievement of the program goals. The Organization Information Security Program Plan (described above) contains the objectives and goals of the program. The program's effectiveness in achieving these goals should be monitored.

Baseline Program Recommendation

1. Check that the plan goals are measurable wherever practical.
2. Determine who, how, and when progress toward goal milestones will be monitored.
3. Determine who, how, and when progress will be reported to management.

The second area where effectiveness monitoring should be applied is on the implemented IS controls. Controls such as policy and awareness should deliver the IS message to employees. Delivering the message, however, is not enough. Compliance monitoring and enforcement are necessary to determine the effectiveness of the controls and to let employees know that compliance is being monitored. Also, a method is needed to report incidents where information has not been adequately protected. Last, there should be some method to provide rewards for compliance, additional awareness for initial noncompliance, and reprimands for continued noncompliance.

Baseline Program Recommendation

1. Develop methods to monitor control effectiveness and employee compliance.
2. The awareness program should encourage employees to remind one another of methods to protect information and to comply with policy.
3. IS coordinators who discover employee noncompliance should discuss it with the employee.
4. Where 2 and 3 above fail, develop incident reporting methods for employees and IS coordinators to report noncompliance to local management.
   a. First-time offenders should receive additional awareness from the local IS coordinator.
   b. Continued noncompliance should result in reprimands from local management.
5. Develop incident reporting methods to allow employees to report ineffectiveness of management controls and technical controls.
6. Develop methods to provide rewards and recognition to employees and groups that effectively protect information and comply with controls.

Organizations that desire additional advice on compliance monitoring should contact the Corporate Information Security Coordinator or the General Auditor. The Organization Information Security Coordinator should be notified of any special problems or need for additional support.

4 PROGRAM IMPLEMENTATION PHASE

The implementation phase of the Organization Information Security program follows the development phase and is the introduction, or rollout, of the program to organization employees. Although short in duration, this phase is critical to employee acceptance because "you will never get a second chance to make a good first impression." Employees must be told about the program elements, including corporate and organization program administration, policies and procedures, IS controls, the business continuity plan, the awareness program, and effectiveness monitoring.

4.1 Program Implementation Plan

As with the program development phase, one should work with organization management to plan the program implementation phase. The implementation, or rollout, is similar to an awareness presentation. Normally, awareness activities tell the target audience *what* you want them to do, and *why* they should do it. Before you can do that, however, you need to tell them *what* the program elements are, and *why* they are being implemented. The goal of the implementation plan is to do this in a manner that encourages employees to *want* to support the program's efforts. Here are some recommendations on what to put in the implementation plan.

Communication Methods

- Presentations:
  - Management (1 hour)
  - Employees (1.5 hours)
    - Organization management conducts introduction
- Pamphlets:
  - Corporate and organization policies
- Video
- Handouts:
  - Organization program details

Presentation Contents

- Organization IS program elements:
  - Program administration:
    Organization Information Security teams
    Corporate Information Security team
    IS Plan: mission, objectives, goals
  - IS policies and procedures:
    Corporate policies
    Organization policies
    [*Note:* This will be the first time that an audience may have seen any of these policies. Whenever possible, presentations should *stress the positive* (work can be done more quickly and efficiently if information is available and accurate); however, there are certain elements within that all employees need to be made aware. Keep the policy discussion short and try to provide them with just an *overview* of the policy contents. Inform employees as to where and how they will be informed about organization policies.]
    Information classification
  - IS controls:
    Access controls, information handling, copying/backing up information, licensing agreements, virus security, etc.
  - Business continuity planning
    [Disclosure of information or unauthorized access can happen right in your organization. With the changes in the utility work environment, as we head into deregulation, the need to be competitive will be the making or breaking point for the **company**. Conducting business as in the past will not allow us to meet the needs of the future. With more and more people having access to

351

our information, it will be necessary to have the proper controls in place to protect the interests of the **company**. (At rollout, there may not be many controls to talk about. This will be covered in later awareness presentations.)]

- Awareness program
- Effectiveness monitoring
  Program Effectiveness
  Effectiveness of IS measures

Baseline Program Recommendation

1. Meet with the organization IS team to develop a draft program implementation plan.
   a. Determine how and when you will rollout the program to the organization.
   b. Determine each IS coordinator's rollout responsibilities.
   c. Determine the goal of the implementation plan.
   d. Determine the contents of communications.
2. Meet with organization management and present the implementation plan. Revise as required and obtain approval.

5   PROGRAM MAINTENANCE PHASE

The IS program is not a development event or an implementation event. Information Security is an ongoing process. Due to changes in the business environment and information technology, the Information Security measures implemented today could be less effective or obsolete within a few months. That is why the IS program and its effectiveness must be monitored and reviewed constantly. This allows effective measures to be retained and ineffective ones to be modified or replaced. Here are some suggestions for the maintenance of the organization's programs.

5.1   Conducting Periodic Information Security Team Meetings

Team meetings should be held periodically to:

- Review the IS program and its effectiveness
- Discuss changes in the business environment and their effect on Information Security
- Discuss information technology changes and their effect on Information Security
- Determine if program efforts have retained their business justification
- Review if efforts are following your Information Security plan
- Reinforce team communication
- Review corporate IS program activities